LIFE IN PRISON

Eight Hours at a Time

ROBERT REILLY

Tilbury House, Publishers
12 Starr St.
Thomaston, Maine 04861
800-582-1899 • www.tilburyhouse.com

Life in Prison Eight Hours at a Time

Copyright © Robert J. Reilly
Library of Congress Control Number 2014024901
Hardcover ISBN 978-088448-412-7
eBook ISBN 978-9-88448-413-4

Design by Faith Hague
Jacket photo, author photo, and photos on pages 24 and 211 by David
Lyman; photo on page 25 by Pat Fallon
All other photos by Robert Reilly
All reasonable efforts have been made to identify the copyright holders.

Library of Congress Cataloging-in-Publication Data
Reilly, Robert, 1967-
  Life in prison : eight hours at a time / Robert Reilly.
    pages cm
  ISBN 978-0-88448-412-7
  1. Reilly, Robert, 1967- 2. Inmate guards–United States–Biography. 3. Prisons-
-United States. 4. Prisoners–United States. I. Title.
  HV9468.R445A3 2014
  365'.92–dc23
  [B]
                              2014024901

Printed in the United States of America
14 15 16 17 18 19   MAP   10 9 8 7 6 5 4 3 2 1

For
Sarah, Joshua, Lindsey & Zeke

Acknowledgments

My deepest thanks to the following people for their continued encouragement and support during the writing of this book: My wife Sarah, Doug Croley, Robert von-der-Luft, Nancy J Kennedy, Erik Phelan, Paul Ewing, Tom Laurita, David & Julie Lyman, my friend and mentor Peter Nichols, agent Tris Coburn and editor Celia Johnson.

And to the good men and women of the Pennsylvania county prison system and the Maine State Prison who looked out for me. Thank you. RR

About the Author

Robert Reilly lives and works in midcoast Maine with his wife and three children. In his scant free time he is working on a collection of short stories, and has recently released his seventh studio album with long-time friend and music collaborator Jeff Bishop. The self-titled CD *Bishop-Reilly* is available from iTunes and online retailers, or at www.Eastern-Records.com.

Table of Contents

Prologue

Strangeways Prison, Manchester, England, 1977

STRANGEWAYS PRISON WAS LESS THAN TWO MILES FROM OUR HOUSE. It was the kind of place most kids couldn't stop staring at. And after a century of foul weather and industrial pollution, its grimy fortress walls and sin-soaked battlements oozed agony and a cold, criminal foreboding. At night, I clearly remember staring up at the dim yellow lights glowing behind the tiny barred windows and thinking, *I wonder what happens in there. I wonder what kind of men get locked up in a place like that.* I also never, ever remember anyone telling their friends or parents, "When I grow up, I want to be a prison guard."

"The founders of a new colony, whatever Utopia of human virtue and happiness they might originally project, have invariably recognized it among their earliest practical necessities to allot a portion of the virgin soil as a cemetery, and another portion as the site of a prison."

—Nathaniel Hawthorne
The Scarlet Letter

1

Into the Abyss
Supermax Extraction

FOR THE LAST TWENTY MINUTES, THE INMATE, NAKED AND ON THE edge of hysteria, has been threatening to cut himself if he doesn't get a phone call. He wants to speak to his mother. The sergeant on duty is ignoring the blackmail and instead trying to get the inmate to slide the blade from a "safety razor" under the cell door. The sergeant says that after he has the blade, he'll open the tray slot for the inmate to stick his hands out and get "cuffed up." Only then will the door be opened. After that, the inmate will be brought out into the corridor and the cell searched for anything else that might be used as a weapon.

The dark cell-lined Supermax corridor is strangely quiet. The other prisoners in this Hannibal Lecter Sector, each in their own solitary confinement cells, are listening attentively through the hinges of their heavy steel doors. There is an air of expectation; perhaps there's going to be a show. Beyond the prison walls, a few hundred feet from the unfolding drama, the most amazing Maine fall is in the middle of a full and fantastic golden explosion. People from all over the country have traveled to see it. But this cold con-crete holding tank couldn't be farther away from all of that. There are no seasons in this particular part of New England; there is only despair, an earthly equivalent of Dante's seventh circle of hell—a place where men who've committed the worst crimes imaginable serve out their sentences in a slow, no-contact, twenty-three-hour-a-day lockdown.

The shivering inmate with the razor blade starts to cry and softly say "no" over and over again. It seems like saying no is the only thing he has left; everything else has been taken away.

Then, suddenly, the inmate begins banging his head on the small Plexiglas window in the middle of the cell door. The thump-ing makes a deep tom-tom drumming sound that reverberates through the dark narrow cellblock. A purple contusion appears instantly on his forehead. "I want to use the fucking phone!" The inmate starts to sob loudly. Tears and mucus run from his eyes and nose, over his cheeks and lips, and into his mouth. He pleads for the phone, making no attempt to wipe his face.

"No, you need to pass me the razor. If you're going to act like this, there's nothing we can do." The sergeant's tone is dry and unemotional. He and the inmate are locked in a futile battle of refusals.

Abruptly, the head banging stops. The inmate turns, takes three steps, and then sits down on his empty metal bunk. He opens his clenched fist, grips the thin strip of a blade between his thumb, index, and middle fingers, and then starts slicing. He makes eight or ten short, deep slashing cuts to the soft area inside his elbow between his forearm and bicep. The blood begins to ooze from his arm in the shape of plum-colored leeches. It looks strange, so dark and thick against his milky white skin.

"I told you I would! This is your fault! I'm gonna bleed out and when I die, it's all gonna be your fault."

The inmate's trembling voice echoes from within the cell. It sounds like he's in a meat locker.

From a clip on his belt, the sergeant removes a ring of huge brass keys and slides one quickly into the tray slot lock and turns it a hard quarter-turn to the left. The tray slot falls open like a square metal mouth in the middle of the cell door. The sergeant then removes his mace can from a pouch on his duty belt, points it through the tray slot, and sprays a long sustained blast into the cell. The yellow stream of mace hits the inmate on the knee and then rises to find his neck and face. The sergeant empties the entire can, and the inmate starts to choke, splutter, and claw at his eyes. There's blood everywhere—thick crimson blobs drip from the man's arm onto his stomach, genitals, and legs. The inmate starts choking. After a few seconds, he controls his gag reflex and then begins screaming for his mother.

The show is on. The inmates in the adjacent cells start roaring and howling. Someone makes horribly realistic squealing pig noises; someone else bleats like a distressed lamb. The corridor suddenly sounds like a slaughterhouse. The inmate in the next cell slams the flats of his huge hairy hands against the cell door and rants in a loud hoarse voice, "Kill yourself! Kill yourself, you worthless piece of shit! Kill yourself! Do it now!"

The sergeant looks at me and says, "Reilly, go and suit up."

IN THE LOCKER ROOM, THREE OTHER GUARDS ARE PUTTING ON elbow- and kneepads, rubber gloves, and black-visored helmets.

"Hurry up, Reilly. We don't want to miss all the fun because you're late for the party." I stop and look at Officer B, a huge obnoxious bully of a man, and slowly shake my head. I choose not to respond. I'm thinking about the inmate's blood and wondering what kind of diseases he has. If things get messy and the extraction turns into a five-man wrestling match, which is what usually happens, how am I going to keep all that blood off my skin, or worse, out of my eyes, nose, and mouth? Officer B is getting psyched up and starts telling stupid jokes. "Hey, how many prison guards does it take to throw an inmate down a flight of stairs?"

No one answers: We're all too busy suiting up and trying to find helmets that actually fit.

"C'mon guys! How many prison guards does it take to throw an inmate down a flight of stairs? . . . None, he fell!" Officer B laughs a ridiculous pantomime laugh and slaps his huge thigh. No one responds.

We leave the locker room and walk in loose formation through the facility and back to solitary confinement. The entire prison is on standstill and locked down as the "planned use of force" gets underway. As the extraction team enters the solitary confinement block, the noise becomes absolutely deafening. The window of every cell door is filled with the faces of inmates all fixed with the same maniacal bloodthirsty grin, every one of them pounding, screaming, and whooping with glee.

"Now this is entertainment!" yells a dark-bearded Mansonesque inmate. As I pass his cell, he looks right at me, opens his mouth as wide as he can, curls his lips back, and starts gnashing his teeth and rolling his eyes back in his head. The pungent smell of the cellblock fills my nostrils. Bad body odor, coarse chemical detergent, and the sweet metallic taste of blood wafts through the dark atmosphere and settles on the back of my tongue. I remember a doctor friend once told me, "Smells consist of particles; particles are pieces of the solid or liquid. If you can smell it, guess what, you're ingesting it."

As we reach the cell, the sergeant makes a last-ditch effort to get the inmate to comply with his orders.

"This is your last chance. Come to the door and cuff up."

The inmate is sitting on the bunk, head down, forearms on thighs, bleeding profusely, ignoring the sergeant.

"OK, men, he's not complying. Get ready to go in."

The screaming and pounding from the audience of solitary-confinement, maximum-security inmates continues and intensifies.

As fourth man on the extraction team, I'll be the last to enter the cell. I stand on my tiptoes, peer over the shoulders of the three much larger men in front of me, and try to get a glimpse of the inmate. The inside of my helmet stinks of chewing tobacco and stale coffee. A new, young nurse arrives. I glance at her. We briefly make eye contact. She looks scared and lost. The roaring and bellowing in the dim narrow cellblock become fearsome and brutally loud, even with a helmet on.

"Ready, men!" the sergeant yells. "When the door opens, get in there, restrain him then bring him out!"

The sergeant moves away from the door. The other inmates sense the moment has arrived. They find the beat. In unison, they start thumping and kicking on their cell doors in a barbaric tribal rhythm. The sergeant raises his radio to his mouth, keys the mic, and over the deafening din of the screaming, pounding prisoners, he shouts, "Control, open one sixteen!"

There is a moment's pause. The team tenses up. We all place our left hands on the back of the guy in front of us. The exception is Officer B. He grips the transparent plastic riot shield with both hands and shifts his feet into a boxer's stance. Over the shoulders of the three big men ahead of me, I see the ghoulish-looking inmate get up from the bunk. His pale skin is smeared with blood; it looks like he's getting ready to fight. It's impossible to tell if he's holding the blade. The other inmates all pound, scream, and howl. The door clicks, clanks, and then slides open from right to left. We rush in.

OFFICER B SMASHES INTO THE INMATE SO HARD, HE ACTUALLY GOES flying through the air, bangs against the back wall, and lands in a crumpled heap on the cell floor, a puppet with its strings cut. Dark bloody hand prints and a faint yellow dusting of pepper spray cover the inside of the cell, and the overpowering smell of excrement, urine, and mace fill the air.

The inmate has emptied his bowels and bladder on the floor. The smell is so bad it makes me gag and choke. My eyes water up and my vision blurs. I start coughing uncontrollably inside my helmet; so does the guy in front of me. I suddenly feel sickeningly claustrophobic. Bitter-tasting bile fills the back of my throat. For a split second, I think I'm going to vomit. I want to rip my helmet off. The other inmates continue to chant and scream. The number two man disappears from sight. He's slipped on a puddle of blood. He tries desperately to get back to his feet. The inmate starts screeching like an animal; it sounds like he's being eaten alive. I push into the cell from the back, the inmate's bare and bloody feet appear on the floor between my boots. The number two guy is back on his feet. As quickly as I can, I drop to my knees, retrieve the shackles from a pocket, and slap them on both ankles. I yell out, "Legs secure!" I hold the inmate's ankles together, pushing them down, pinning them to the concrete. I take a good look at his feet. They are covered in horrible scabs and scars. Blood and feces are smeared all over the cell floor, and I am kneeling in it. The inmate is whimpering beneath the pileup. The number two and three guys are trying to get his hands behind his back; they're struggling to get the cuffs on. One of them says quite calmly, "Heads up for the razor."

The inmate's legs and scab-covered feet wriggle and flap for a few seconds. His lower limbs are like a couple of huge exhausted fish on the deck of a boat. I hold on and wait for the brief struggle to end. I raise my head to see what's happening. Officer B glances over his broad left shoulder to see who's looking. He lifts the shield with his right hand, glances over his shoulder once more, and then very quickly punches the inmate in the head four or five times.

"Stop resisting! Stop resisting!" Officer B calls out.

The pig pile continues, and again Officer B pulls back the shield and manages to punch the inmate twice, but this time both punches are brutally hard and hit the inmate square in the face, splitting both lips and causing his nose to crumple and gush blood. I look to see if anyone else is seeing what I'm seeing: a petulant, brutal act of tit-for-tat aggression. No one seems to notice or care about it or even register the presence of more blood.

"Wrists secure!" calls out the number two man.

"Bring him out and take him to the chair," yells the sergeant.

The four of us pick up the handcuffed and shackled prisoner and back out of the cell into the cacophony of the corridor. The other inmates are all going berserk, yelling, pounding, screaming, and laughing. Someone is bellowing at the top of his lungs, "They've fucking killed him! They've fucking killed him!"

Someone else is screaming, "The nurse is a whore! The nurse is a whore!" We carry the inmate down the corridor, through a gauntlet of unimaginable verbal abuse, to an observation cell. He's silent and still and feels like a large wet rolled-up rug.

Inside the observation cell, we position the inmate over the indestructible "restraint chair," which is bolted to the concrete floor. The chair has replaced the straight jacket and its big brother, the padded cell. Its reclined seat, molded to fit legs, buttocks, and back, and the thick nylon belts that fasten diagonally across the subject's feet, knees, thighs, waist, stomach, arms, and chest would stop Houdini on a good day. The inmate gets slammed down with his hands still in cuffs behind his back. A deep gasp of air escapes from his bloody mouth as his back crashes into the black plastic. Officer B is doing most of the heavy lifting and loving it. The inmate appears to be completely broken. His face looks like five pounds of raw meat, and he's covered in blood and feces and so many bruises, cuts, and scars, it's hard to tell what's a wound and what's not.

The sergeant walks into the cell behind us and asks the inmate if he needs to see the nurse. I remember thinking that might be the stupidest question I've ever heard. The inmate nods and mouths the word "yes" but no sound comes out.

"Nurse, are you ready?"

The nurse nods sheepishly and steps forward. The sergeant says, "Good job, guys. Now go get cleaned up and then write your reports."

As I leave the observation cell, something inside me makes me turn and glance at the inmate, one last look at the wreck before I drive off into heavy traffic. As I look at him, he lifts his chin up from his chest, winks at me, and gives me an evil bloodbath grin.

Back in the locker room, I strip and take a long shower. I scrub myself raw in a vain attempt to wash away the filth from the last half hour. As I dry and start getting dressed, Officer B is gleefully retelling the whole extraction and casting himself in the starring role. For some reason, this makes me feel very angry, even furious. I want to walk up to him and smash him in the mouth, as hard as I can. Of course, I don't: He'd cripple me and then I'd be fired for unprofessional behavior.

We write and then rewrite our reports the way we always do, creating perjury on paper and then sealing the lies with our signatures, the same way we did for the four years I worked at the prison in Pennsylvania and for the last eighteen months at the Maine State Prison. We twist the truth until the dialog of lies, poor punctuation, and bad grammar become believable. We have to protect ourselves and make sure we're all singing from the same sad songsheet. By the end of it, the reports all read the same, almost verbatim. I stay almost completely silent throughout the whole thing, ashamed of what I'm doing, unable to alter it.

Shortly afterward, we are told by the shift commander the inmate had been taken to hospital in town, as his self-inflicted injuries and those sustained during the planned use of force are so severe they need to be looked at by a "real doctor." I remember thinking, *if one more inmate dies down here, they're going to lock up the people who run this place.*

The next day, the reports all pass the scrutiny of the warden, whose biggest fear in life is a lawsuit with his name on it.

The sergeant's report reads, "The inmate's injuries are a direct result of noncompliance of orders to stop resisting."

What isn't in the report is that the inmate has a mental age of a ten-year-old and most of the time doesn't understand what's happening around him.

That night I have a terrible dream. I dream I am plunging down a deep, dark shaft into a black, bottomless abyss. I am yelling and screaming as I smash and bounce off the shaft's rocky walls. As I fall deeper and deeper into the darkness, I can see my wife and children peering over the edge of the opening way above me with blank expressions on their faces. I am saved from some terrible unknown end only by my alarm clock going off. I wake up with a start and a splitting headache. I slide out of bed and shuffle naked into the bathroom, turn on the water in the sink, and stare at my stubble-rough face and bleary overtime eyes and say out loud, "You have to get out of this crazy job."

2

Pennsylvania

Spring 2001

I CAN'T BELIEVE I WAS SO WRONG. THE THOUGHT KEPT CYCLING around inside my mind like a stranded rider on a Ferris wheel. The thought was connected to almost everything I did. My dream of making it in the music business seemed like a horribly bad joke and I was the punch-line. I was so confident, so cocky, and so absolutely convinced that I was going to make it, and make it big, nothing and nobody in the world could convince me there might be a chance things wouldn't work out. My mother-in-law once asked me, almost pleadingly, "But what if it doesn't happen? What are you going to do? What's your backup plan?"

At the time, I remember being slightly offended and replied rather indignantly, "I don't need a backup plan. It's going to happen, and it's going to work out."

Now, as I look at my own children and think about their future, I understand exactly what she was trying to say and why. At one point, my in-laws even offered to pay for me to go to the local com-

munity college and get a degree. They said they just wanted to increase my chances of success in case I found myself in a position where I might have to make some sort of a change. Of course, I turned them down. I said thanks but no thanks. I wasn't going to need a college degree. I was just on the verge of making it big and couldn't imagine putting that kind of time and energy into something I wouldn't need.

So, after playing in every toilet between London and Los Angeles, signing a music publishing deal and several small recording deals in the United Kingdom, Australia, and America, getting a few off-the-radar radio plays and a couple of songs in very bad TV shows and low-budget movies, I found myself still married with a three-year-old son, a one-year-old daughter, and a negative bank balance. After a decade and a half of pursuing the specter of success as an immigrant singer/songwriter, I woke up and discovered that I was a thirty-four-year-old failure with no education, no real work experience, and no idea how I was going to provide responsibly for my growing family.

It was time to be completely honest with myself. If I wasn't good enough to make a decent living playing music, I wasn't really a professional. What I was doing was just a hobby. It was a difficult thing to get my head around, but it was the truth.

I became plagued by thoughts that perhaps I'd never been good enough and that I'd made bad decisions with the modest opportunities I'd had. I started to wonder constantly about what I could have done differently. How could I have better spent my time? Was I really just a delusional dreamer? When I thought about all the other ways I could have been productive, I started to feel like a hollowed-out failure and a foolish victim of vanity, ashamed of how I had squandered the last fifteen years. The truth couldn't be denied. I had collided with reality; the dream was over.

*"A voice that sounds as though it's been pickled in nettles
and bourbon for years, reminiscent of Cat Stevens
via Joe Cocker, Robert Reilly is a major talent."*
—Paul Cole, Birmingham Post, Birmingham, UK

*"Superior and engaging, heartfelt songwriting
and performing"*
—Chris Folley, Time Out, London, UK

*"Robert Reilly, soulful, inspired, gutsy, defiant
and emotional"*
—Peter Kinghorn, Newcastle Evening Chronicle, UK

*"For those prepared to look, Robert Reilly's songs and vocals
are excellent and individual; the tracks pour out
of the speakers and grab your attention."*
—S.C. Speakout Magazine, UK

*"Radio ready, passionate and mature with a reputation
for an energetic, inspired live show"*
—David Fenigsohn, The University Reporter, Boston, MA

*"Accompanying himself on acoustic guitar and piano. At the end of
his short set, the quality of his vocals and songwriting transported the
room to another dimension. I don't know if I can accurately describe the
experience, but mesmerizing is a good word. No glitz, just the real deal.
Keep an ear open for this great new talent, you won't be disappointed."*
—Shelly Weiss, Cash Box Magazine, Los Angeles, CA

*"Robert Reilly has established himself as a mature, talented
songwriter who possesses the increasingly rare gift of balancing
meaningful lyrics with refreshing hook laden melodies."*
—Dave Donati, Sound Check Magazine, Harrisburg, PA

"Solid gold, soulful and radio ready."
—Robert Markin, The Aquarian, NJ

"Smart, melodic and meaningful"
—Alan K. Stout, Times Leader, Wilkes-Barre, PA

One afternoon, after cutting the grass, I ran into my neighbor, and he asked me how the band was going.

"Not very well," I replied.

I told him I hated the thought of it, but I was actually thinking of quitting music and looking for a day job. I told him my wife hated her job at the bank and all she wanted to do was to be home with the children. I said I didn't feel like I was doing the right thing anymore, plus, things were getting a little tough on the domestic side and I really felt I had to make some sort of a change for the betterment of the family.

Without hesitating, he told me I should put in an application at the prison. He somehow knew they were hiring and told me, "The Teamsters Union runs the place. They've got great benefits, paid time off, and with a little overtime you can probably make more than forty grand a year."

Forty grand a year! That sounded like a fortune. But working in a prison. . .

"I don't think so. I'm not the tough-guy type. I don't think I could pull it off."

"No, it's not like that," he said. "It's a people job. You're good with people. I see how you are around the neighborhood. I'm telling you, you'd make out just fine."

As I put the lawnmower away, I started to think about it. An hour later I was in my car.

It took about half an hour to get there from the suburbs, along the twisting busy highway that cuts the city in two and then over back roads and through miles of pastoral Pennsylvanian farm land. As I drove slowly up the S-shaped half-mile hill that led to the prison, I felt like I was approaching a fortress. The look of the high chain-link fences, razor wire, and massive gray concrete walls caused a slight fluttering in my chest. I also wondered about being an immigrant on a work visa. Could I even apply for a state or a county job? Don't those jobs have to go to citizens and fully naturalized residents?

After I parked, I just sat and stared up at the prison for a while. I thought about going home. I almost restarted the car and drove away. I was having strong feelings, and a voice inside my head was whispering, "I don't know if this is a good idea." But then I thought, maybe this could create a way for my wife to be at home with the kids. Don't be afraid.

I filled out the application right there in the lobby, a gray, triangular room with numerous doors, a linoleum floor, a desk in one corner, and two sets of steel chairs, bolted to the floor. The room looked like it had been built by a guy who'd flunked out of bus station waiting room design school. The place smelled weird, too, like vomit and disinfectant. As I handed my application back to the grumpy old guard slumped casually behind the desk, several much younger guards walked through the lobby and then disappeared through one of the doors. They looked hard and bored. The people waiting, all women and children, looked hot, tired, and sad.

A COUPLE OF WEEKS LATER MY WIFE, SARAH, TOLD ME I'D RECEIVED a letter from the prison. I opened it and read that I had been invited to try out for employment testing that would take place in a couple of weeks on county-owned farmland adjacent to the prison.

I arrived early on the morning of test day. We were at the county 4-H center in a large field at the bottom of the hill below the prison. It looked like it was going to be an indoor-outdoor affair. Inside the barn/equestrian center were a series of long tables with papers and pencils on them, folding metal chairs beneath them, and a huge empty floor space, clearly opened up for some sort of physical tests. Outside, they had set up a track within a fenced-in riding ring, presumably for a running test.

There were well over a hundred people already there, signing in and being split into groups. I wasn't the only person looking for a Teamsters Union job with good benefits and paid time off.

The crowd was mainly men and a few hard-looking women. It was a mixed bunch—black, white, Latino, and Asian. There were fat guys in their fifties, skinny high-school graduates not old enough to buy beer or tough enough to bounce tennis balls, and a lot of hard cases with crew cuts, big biceps, and tattoos. And then there were a few average-looking guys like myself.

We were all called to attention by a soft-spoken, thin man with bright blue eyes and short curly blonde hair. He told us we would be cycling through a series of tests, and if at any time we failed any of them or went over the allotted time, we would not be allowed to continue with the process.

First, we sat at the tables and did a series of math, English, and logic tests. I was sure I bombed the math portion. Mathematics makes my hands sweat so much; I can hardly hold a pencil. Numbers make me feel very anxious; they always have, ever since I was a little kid.

After the written tests we were put through a series of PT exercises. We did wind sprints, we took turns holding up a hundred-pound dummy pretending to be a suicidal inmate, and then we went outside to run. By now, it was mid-morning and getting good and hot. The temperature must have been in the upper eighties, the humidity, much higher. The run was a timed half-mile inside the horse ring. Most of the older men, a few of the women, and all of the overweight guys failed. Some of the applicants were so out of shape they looked like candidates for the fitness protection program. Apart from the math portion, I felt pretty good about the written tests and had no problem with any of the physical stuff. I've been a regular "jogger" since high school and usually start my runs with sit-ups, push-ups, and a few pull-ups.

A few days later, Sarah told me I had another letter from the prison. I had passed the written and PT sections and was invited to move on to the psychological testing. This test would take place the next week at the prison.

I TURNED UP EARLY AGAIN AND WAITED IN THE GRAY, BAD BUS station lobby. There were about ten of us, all men. After a short while, a cheerful, chubby-looking sergeant appeared from nowhere and told us to follow him. He led us inside the prison administration area, up a flight of stairs and into the "roll-call room" and then told us to sit at the tables.

The test was really funny. It was about eight hundred multiple-choice questions. But it felt as if it was the same twenty questions asked forty different ways. It was a poorly cloaked, overtly masculine quiz. The questions all sounded like they were written by an extreme right-wing homophobe with a profound hatred for the performing arts.

> Example: If you were a newspaper reporter, would you rather write about a Broadway musical or a championship boxing match? *Ooo, I wonder how they want me to answer that one.*

> Example: As a child playing dress-up, given the choice would you rather be a knight in shining armor or a damsel in distress? *Oh my, I wonder what they mean by that.*

> Example: Would you rather be a lumberjack or a florist? *Well, my mother is a florist and it doesn't seem nearly as dangerous or as much work as cutting down hundreds of tons of towering timber.*

The questions were ridiculous but I answered them exactly the way they wanted me to, and then I left. On the way home, I wondered who in the group would be exposed as a bipolar cross-dressing Nazi who enjoyed tofu salads and torturing cats.

A week later Sarah opened the mail and called out, "You have another letter from the prison."

I passed again. If I wanted to continue with the hiring process, I had to attend an interview with a psychologist. Oh dear, I thought, maybe the people at the prison are tricking me. Maybe they had read through my answers from the psych test and were worried about my mental health.

Once again, as a result of years of my father's uncompromising punctuality and planning, I quite naturally turned up a little early, this time at a generic-looking office building in a suburban business development on the edge of town. I entered an office so devoid of character that I had to ask the woman at the front desk if I was at the right place. She assured me I was, so I took a seat and waited.

The psychologist was a well-dressed, pleasant-looking middle-aged man. He introduced himself in a soft calm voice, led me into his office, directed me to a comfy chair, and asked me to sit. I looked out the window and noticed it had started raining. His office suddenly felt quite cozy. If he had started reading something interesting, I would have wanted to stay there all afternoon.

I only remember two things we talked about. First, he told me I did pretty well on all the tests except one.

"Which one was it?" I asked.

"The math portion of the written test; have you always had a problem with math?"

"Yes," I replied. "I'm terrible at math."

Then he said, "I'm not sure, but because you did well on the other parts and in contrast to those sections you did so badly on the math, I have a feeling you may have some kind of numerical dyslexia. Have you ever been tested for that?"

"No," I replied. Funnily enough, this revelation about the chance of having "some kind of numerical dyslexia" didn't hit too hard. I'd always felt smart, but for some unknown reason was a terribly unsuccessful student. Maybe the good doctor was on to something.

He then he asked me what I was most proud of in my life. It was an easy answer. I said, "I'm most proud of Sarah, my wife, and Joshua and Lindsey, my two young children."

He didn't answer. He just smiled and wrote something on his clipboard. It was the truth. After so many years of rejection and disappointment in the music business, I was finally starting to see and realize that having Sarah and the kids in my life meant that I'd actually made it to the big time. I'd won the love lottery and discovered what really was big and important. Little else mattered. My family was the most valuable thing in the world, and I was proud of them and how they made me feel.

THE VERY NEXT WEEK, SARAH CALLED OUT TO ME FROM THE kitchen as she looked through the mail. "Wow, those nice people at the prison have sent you another letter."

"Open it," I said.

"Looks like you passed the psych test, and you have an interview at the prison with the chief deputy warden."

As usual, I got there early and found an empty seat in the lobby. I sat alongside several families waiting to visit incarcerated loved ones. The restless children ran around like wild animals, cried and wriggled on their mothers' laps, and acted just like my own kids. This thought-provoking comparison was interrupted by two heavy metal gates slamming and clanking shut in quick succession. I looked up and saw a thin man with blue eyes and curly blond hair walking toward me. It was the same guy who had led the first selection process I'd attended down below the prison in the fields and the 4-H center.

"Robert?" he asked.

"Yes," I replied as I stood up.

"I'm the chief deputy warden, please come this way."

We shook hands, and then I followed him down a short dark corridor and through the first clanging metal gate. After it closed with a finger-smashing crash, we waited in a small cell-type space for a few seconds before the second gate opened. We then walked down a long gray institutional corridor, turned left, and entered his office. I stood and waited to be asked to take a seat. It was slightly reminiscent of being in high school and having to go to the principal's office, which never happened more than twice a week. I started to wonder: If the interview didn't go well, would I get detention?

The chief was a quiet man who talked and moved easily and without pretense. He seemed almost gentle and worn down by something heavy and invisible. He was not at all what I was expecting. He talked openly and asked me what I expected to get out of the job. I said I wasn't looking for a job; I was looking for a career. He asked me at one point what I thought I would gain from working in a prison. I said, "Apart from providing for my family, I thought I would feel good about serving the community and maybe there was a chance that I could help some of the prisoners in some way."

Without a trace of mockery, he involuntarily laughed out loud.

ANOTHER WEEK PASSED. I WAS HOME ALONE WITH THE CHILDREN when the next letter arrived. Sarah was in Texas at a Mary Kay rally. She had been considering starting her own business and thought cosmetics might be a way for us to get ahead financially. She'd gone down to the Lone Star State to see what it was all about. I was very worried about her. The Mary Kay ladies scared me. There were too many yellow neck scarves, lavender pantsuits, and clouds of noxious perfume that made my eyes water and the children cough. I had a feeling if they managed to convert her, life as we knew it would cease to exist. While she was away I had nightmares about the "New Sarah" cruising around town in a pink Cadillac with members of the Mary Kay mafia conducting drive-by lipstickings.

I didn't open the letter immediately. I let it sit on the counter with the rest of the mail, which mainly consisted of bills and offers to sign up for more credit cards. The children were at the table wearing lunch. I'd wait until I hosed down the kitchen and they were having a nap before I read it. I was sure I was going to be told thanks but no thanks. I had been thinking a lot about whether I was going to get in or not. I was feeling fine about not being a prison guard. I wasn't really suited to service in uniform. If anyone ever asked me if I'd been in the military, I always laughed and told them I was completely unfit for the military and that I'd once failed the physical for the Salvation Army. The truth was, I wasn't crazy about telling people what to do and I absolutely hated being told what to do. I was only interested in the money and the benefits. My motivation was all wrong. The prison administration people knew it, and so did I.

"Congratulations. You have been selected to start training Wednesday, August 15, 2001." There was a lot of other stuff about uniform requirements, morning PT, drug tests, and a six-month probation period. Wow! I couldn't believe it. I had an offer of a job, a real full-time job. Then in the quiet of the kitchen, I was suddenly awash in conflicting emotions. I had pretty much talked myself out of working in a prison, wearing a uniform, dealing with authority, and being a part of a paramilitary establishment. Then, on the other hand, if I could just control my anxiety and get my head on straight, what I wanted for Sarah and the children might just be around the corner.

I STILL HAD SOME GIGS ON THE CALENDAR, BUT THINGS HAD BEEN going so poorly I was more than happy to call the various bar and club managers and tell them that I was going to prison for an indefinite period of time and that I wouldn't be able to make the dates. One agent who had me booked up for a string of college coffeehouse engagements went ballistic and said he was going to sue me. I told him that was fine; he was welcome to sue me for everything I didn't have, so I would see him in court.

The kids were still napping when Sarah called. The Mary Kay

indoctrination mustn't have been going too well. She sounded quite normal. I told her there was something she had to do when she got home. It was something I couldn't deal with myself.

"Oh no, what is it this time?"

She had her exasperated, what-have-you-screwed-up-now voice on.

I said, "You're going to have to tell your boss at the bank you're going to quit. I got the job at the prison."

3

Prison Academy

Wednesday, August 15, 2001

6 A.M. TWELVE OF US—TEN MEN AND TWO WOMEN—ALL WHITE, ALL
wearing black boots and slacks and gray paramilitary shirts gathered in the lobby of the prison. It still smelled of vomit and disinfectant, but this time it had an added hint of body odor. An hour
earlier, while I was getting dressed, I remember thinking I looked
ridiculous. The last time I wore a uniform was in another life as an
English schoolboy.

I didn't see anyone I remembered from any of the selection
groups. Several people talked quietly, but on the whole most sat
silently and waited anxiously for the day to begin. I didn't know
how much sitting around there would be so I took a book with me,
Lady Chatterley's Lover. I thought if things got a little slow, D. H.
Lawrence could keep me entertained. I was wrenched out of the
post–World War I British class struggle by a heavy metal door to my
left swinging open.

A tall, bald, fit guy in his late forties introduced himself as

Sergeant L. He told us he was an ex-Marine Corps sergeant and that he would be our PT instructor throughout the next eight weeks. My initial impression of him was that he seemed laid-back, easygoing, and quite likable. He said that during the next two months, there would be numerous tests we would have to pass to stay in the program. Then, we'd have to take a series of final written, practical, and physical exams, and we needed a passing grade on all three to graduate. He assured us that if we worked hard and applied ourselves, none of us should have a problem.

Crap! I thought. More tests. What if I don't make it, what if I can't handle a certain section of the program, what if I flunk out? A flood of childlike anxiety pulsed through me. Then I thought of Sarah. She was so happy to be at home with the kids. I couldn't let her down; I just couldn't. I had to deal with it; whatever it was, I just had to suck it up, make it work, and get through it.

Sergeant L told us to get up and follow him. He then led us out from the lobby to an annex building at the back of the prison, conveniently called "The Training Center." Once inside, we all took a seat at tables set up classroom style and began introducing ourselves.

The class consisted of an ex-professional boxer, two ex-Marines, an ex-airborne ranger, a couple of people transitioning from juvenile corrections, an older guy in his fifties who had been a victim of industry layoffs, a couple of college graduates, and several others who had made the move from mundane Main Street jobs—ten men and two women. I was anxious about telling people what I'd been doing before the prison. I felt as if the two worlds couldn't possibly have any common ground. I also imagined that I might get mocked for being a musician in such a macho environment. So, I'm ashamed to say I fudged the truth a little. It was what I told the chief deputy in my interview anyway. When my turn came, I told my classmates my wife had a job at a bank and I had been a stay-at-home dad. It was such a boring, uninteresting half-truth; no one even asked any questions.

After introductions, we read through the overview of the training curriculum. During the next eight weeks, we would run and work out for an hour first thing in the morning and then learn about every facet of corrections from a group of senior and experienced staff. We would cover the law pertaining to the relationships between staff and inmates. We would study moral and ethical dilemmas that we would face as new and inexperienced guards. There would be a week of self-defense training, and a week packed with NRA/law enforcement firearms training, first aid, fire and safety, and gang awareness, familiarization with paperwork, count procedure, and key control. All the classroom and practical training would be augmented by short periods of on-the-job training (OJT) with experienced officers. These training officers would size us up, put us through our paces, and report their findings back to the various shift commanders.

My class as a whole was a pretty even-keeled, pedestrian dozen with a few stand-out characters. One of the ex-Marines, contrary to what I might have expected, was one of the kindest, most considerate guys I'd ever met. The former pro boxer was also a great guy. He worked a second job at Dunkin Donuts to make sure his family stayed afloat. He also had a wonderful work ethic and a contagious winning attitude, and just being around him was a real confidence booster. And then there was a mild-mannered good guy who'd been working at a big box hardware store. He was about ten times smarter than everyone else combined. I thought that perhaps he must he must have been dyslexic and mistakenly gotten off at the wrong bus stop. I had the strongest feeling he should have gone to Princeton, but somehow ended up in prison.

AS THE COURSE GOT UNDERWAY, I QUICKLY REALIZED THE PRACTICAL side of the instruction we received—the firearms training, self-defense course, learning how to use the shackles, handcuffs, keys, radios, and understanding the piles of paperwork—all felt valuable. But a huge amount of the training, the lion's share of it, felt like a giant waste of time. There were hours and hours every day spent studying politically correct Bovine-Scatterment from the SOP (Standard Operating Procedure manual).

During the first three weeks of training, I developed a feeling or a suspicion that most of the mock academics were some sort of firewall constructed by the administration to prevent them from being subject to negative legal action. The eight-week training course almost appeared to be one long prosecution escape clause for the warden, whoever he was.

On one memorable day, we had "sensitivity training." Imagine that in a prison. A lawyer from a big firm came to teach us how to talk properly to the inmates and how to interact respectfully and professionally with our co-workers. As our guest instructor removed his paperwork from his briefcase, I leaned over to the guy next to me, a bright, ambitious young family guy who had previously been working at a boot camp for adjudicated teens, and said, "I'd like to teach this class."

"What do you mean?" he replied

"Well, I could teach this class in about ten minutes, and I'd do it for half the price this clown's charging and save the prison a couple of grand."

My classmate looked a little confused.

"Listen," I said. "You know what this whole day boils down to, don't you?"

"No," he said. "What?"

"It boils down to, if you wouldn't say it to your next-door neighbor or your mother; don't say it to a co-worker or an inmate."

My classmate gave me a puzzled look but didn't respond. During the next eight hours, everyone fell asleep at least twice and asked to be excused to go to the bathroom at least five times. After lunch, I kept looking through the folder containing examples of all the institutional paperwork we needed to be familiar with. I sought out the sheet needed to place a prisoner on suicide watch. The lecture was so mind-numbingly boring; I wanted to sign myself up.

At the end of the day, the lifeless, uncharismatic lawyer droned, "I know this has been a long class for some of you, but the best way to stay out of court, keep your job, and remember this material is this: If you wouldn't say it to a family member, don't say it to a co-worker or an inmate."

ON THE TUESDAY OF THE FOURTH WEEK, AFTER RETURNING TO THE training center after PT, running and showers, and about an hour and a half into the first lecture, the phone at the front of the room started to ring. Our instructor stopped talking, walked over to the phone, picked it up, listened intently, and then said, "You gotta be kidding."

He put the phone back down on the receiver, stared into space for a second or two, then told us, "A passenger plane just crashed into one of the World Trade Center towers. I'm going over to the staff room to watch the TV. You're welcome to come if you want."

The staff room was packed. Guards, medical personnel, maintenance men, and administrative staff watched in silence as columns of black smoke billowed out one of the Twin Towers and into a cobalt blue September sky. The news anchors talked the viewers through what little of the accident they could make sense of.

It seemed crazy and impossible to think that such a massive air traffic control screw-up could happen on such a crystal clear day. Then, a minute or two after 9 a.m., the voice of the reporter we were listening to became almost hysterical as we watched in real time as another plane slammed into the second tower.

Someone behind me said, "People are going to be dying in their sleep for years to come because of this."

I suddenly had an overpowering desire to go home and be with Sarah and the kids. After returning to the training center, I asked our instructor if class was going to be cancelled for the day. The instructor said no, the day would go ahead as scheduled.

THAT NIGHT BEFORE BED, I LET THE DOG OUT AS USUAL. I WALKED into the middle of the backyard and looked up. On clear nights, the sky above our neighborhood was dotted with the countless blinking lights of commercial aircraft tracking their way through the atmosphere. We lived close to the Philadelphia, Allentown, and Harrisburg airports and not too far from Newark, JFK,

LaGuardia, and numerous other smaller regional airports. After the day's events, it was a sobering sight to be standing beneath the busiest air space in the country seeing nothing but vast tracts of uninterrupted deep purple space, studded only by the lights of distant stars. The following day, I decided to apply to become a U.S. citizen.

There was lots of paperwork to fill out. There were testimonials and references to send in to the Immigration and Naturalization Service (INS), which was in the process of becoming the Immigration and Customs Enforcement and a part of the Department of Homeland Security. There were my pitiful earning statements to explain about my years of playing music and various immigration interviews to attend. As usual, my wife and in-laws vouched for me, held me up, and again helped me out by being my sponsor and backing my application with their good names.

At one "resident alien" interview, a fat INS man, who had a certain 1970s Elvis look about him, asked me had I been involved in any of the following: prostitution, the selling of illegal guns or ammunition, or drug smuggling. It might have been the most fantastic real question I had ever been asked. Who would say yes? What I really wanted to say was, W*ell, the team of hookers I've been running up on Washington and 10th are part of a nonprofit organization. My AK-47 is legal in the Central Republic of Congo, and the half acre of marijuana I've been growing is for my mother's glaucoma.* But of course I didn't. They granted me "resident alien status" and sent me a green card. When it arrived in the mail, I was amused to discover my green card was pink.

My dad had said something to me when I moved to America. He said he wished his father could see me. My dad told me he thought it was great that his son was seeing something through that his father had started fifty-something years before.

My grandpa, James Reilly, was born in 1916 into abject poverty in the Gorbals, a notorious ghetto in Glasgow, Scotland. As one of eight children, he grew up knowing everything about hunger and hardship. He was a good athlete and a smart student. He played on a prestigious Glasgow boys' soccer team and passed the exams to gain entry into one of the best grammar schools in the city. My great-grandparents were too poor to buy him the books and uniform he needed, so he couldn't go. At fourteen, under the weight of the Great Depression, he went to work. There are some lost years that must have only been filled with desperate toil for next-to-no money in Dickensian conditions. At some point, he decided to leave Scotland and immigrate to America. He wanted something better. He somehow made his way from Glasgow to Manchester. At that time, Manchester was the biggest inland port in Britain. The Manchester ship canal was full of vessels bringing goods in and out of one of Europe's busiest industrial areas.

The factories, mines, and mills of northern England were the crowned kings of steel, cotton, and coal. And throughout the industrial revolution, these mills, sweatshops, and collieries fed and fueled the never-ending needs of the almighty British Empire. The cargo and merchant ships that plowed in and out of the Manchester ship canal also carried passengers. It would be on one of these ships that my grandpa was planning to leave for America.

A day or two before he was to ship out, he went into town to buy a new white shirt to wear when he got to the United States. He was with a friend when he bought the shirt. No one is quite sure if the friend was someone he had come down from Scotland with or someone he had met in Manchester. The two young men were attended at the checkout counter by two young women. A conversation started and ended with a double date for that night. The four went dancing and had a great time. At the end of the evening, my grandpa asked the woman his friend had danced with all night whether she would go out with him tomorrow after she finished work. It would be his last night in England. The young woman said that she thought he was "very cheeky" and wondered why he would dance all night with her friend and then ask her out on a date for the following evening. My grandpa told the young woman, "Your friend is a much better dancer than you, but you're much better-looking than your friend." The good-looking mediocre dancer was my grandma. Grandpa's buddy left for America alone, and my grandpa fell in love and stayed in England.

‖‖‖‖‖‖‖‖‖

AFTER A MONTH AND A HALF OF SITTING IN THE TRAINING CENTER, everyone was itching to actually get to work. The last two weeks of the course would be all on-the-job training. My trainer was Officer S, a tough, single mother who smoked heavily, laughed a lot, and sometimes swore like a pirate. Among the other guards, she was generally well respected and never crossed. A few gossiped about her behind her back, but those who did never had the nerve to repeat what they said to her face.

I liked her instantly. She was warm and straightforward, easy to talk to, and willing to share what she knew. I found her to be firm, fair, and even-handed with the inmates. She was also in control. I think the best way to describe how she conducted business was "very humane." As I followed her around—and that's exactly what I did, follow her around like a puppy—she showed me that you could do the job, act like a human being, have a sense of humor, and not get killed in the process. Occasionally, she did have to play hardball and clearly knew how to make herself understood.

One morning Officer S called out to all ninety-six inmates in the cellblock, "Lock in for eleven o'clock count."

Most of them started moving slowly toward their cells, a few lingered, taking their time talking and laughing. As the minute hand inched closer to the top of the hour, Officer S called out for a second time, "Lock in for count."

Some mouthy wise guy yelled down from the second tier, "Fuck you, lady."

Officer S looked at me, raised her eyebrows, and widened her eyes a little. She turned off the control panel and then casually walked out from behind the desk and into the middle of the cellblock. She put her hands on her hips, straightened her duty belt, adjusted her radio, and got ready to address the ninety-six male inmates.

"Fuck me? No, fuck you! Youse don't lock in *now* and none of youse guys is getting any rec for the rest of the week. I'll keep every one of youse locked in till next weekend, I swear to God I will."

She meant it, and they knew it. The remaining inmates scuttled like scared rats back to their cells, closed their doors, and locked in.

Another day, when Officer S was working in the control center that operated the main gate, a local cop arrived to drop off a new guest at the hotel. The cop had been the recent recipient of a brand-new cruiser, which he quite naturally was extremely proud of. After the drop-off and a good deal of bragging about his new vehicle, he left. While the proud police officer in the shiny new patrol car was leaving the prison, via the twenty-foot-high sliding steel gate, Officer S, for some reason, accidently closed the gate on the exiting officer, crunching the cruiser in the world's biggest rat trap. When the gate was rolled back and the car released, the cop went ballistic. All Officer S had to say was, "I really felt bad, but if you think about it, it's as funny as hell."

She was right; it was.

TRYING TO WORK OUT WHERE EVERYTHING WAS AND WHO DID WHAT seemed like an impossible task. The institution was enormous. I was envious of the military guys and those who'd come up from the "Juvi Hall." It didn't seem to be much of a big deal to them. There was so much to learn that had never been touched on in class. How was I supposed to keep an eye on ninety-six inmates at once? My computer skills were terrible. The computerized control panel on the desk at the front of the block looked like an accident waiting to happen. The phones never stopped ringing. The amount of requests to send inmates off the block was dizzying. Prisoners traveled around the facility in droves to dozens of different appointments, work details, and classes. Everyone had to be signed in and out, their whereabouts accounted for at all times. Other prisoners traveled regularly outside the institution to hospital visits and court hearings. The massive and endless amount of paperwork was categorical proof that the rainforest was on the verge of extinction. Every inmate seemed to have a constant barrage of questions and grievances, none of which I had any way of answering. The incessant radio chatter, orders from supervisors, requests from co-workers, and run-of-the-mill communications were very confusing and difficult to understand. Then, just when everything seemed like it was quieting down, there would be an "assistance" call over the radio and the prison PA as a fight broke out somewhere and every available staff member would go running to lend a hand while the entire facility went into emergency lockdown.

But I was still shadowing my training officer, feeling like a satellite, disconnected and locked in a rookie bubble high above the reality of the job. Officer S did all the work, and all I could do was watch and ask questions. I had no keys, no radio, and no authority. I was pretty much ignored by other staff and viewed with varying degrees of indifference and contempt by the inmates. Although I said nothing to Officer S, a gathering cold front of anxiety filled me with questions about the decision I'd made to enter this line of work. I still hadn't experienced the moment of truth, when I alone would tell a block full of ninety-six professional criminals what to do all day. I constantly wondered if I'd made a huge mistake. I just wasn't sure I could pull it off.

The final written, practical, and physical test was looming, less than a week away. In down time and on coffee breaks, the class as a whole talked about nothing else. One of the women was extremely nervous about flunking the shooting portion. The guy in his fifties was stressed out about the final run. A couple of others and I were worried about various parts of the written exam. Much of it was what to do in which order. I studied, read, and reread, and as the day approached, hoped I could get it all right. The ex-military guys didn't seem to be bothered about any of it. I was envious. On Wednesday, October 3, 2001, all twelve of us took our final physical, practical, and written tests and passed. Most of us were delighted. I was both delighted and extremely relieved. The ex-military guys appeared to be pleased, but in a cool nonchalant way.

ONE EVENING THAT WEEK, AS I WAS BRUSHING MY TEETH IN THE bathroom before bed, Sarah walked in and told me she had some news. She looked a little nervous. She usually never looks nervous.

"What is it?" I asked.

She paused, stared deeply into my eyes, blinked a couple of times, and then said, "I'm pregnant again."

The words hung in the air and became attached to the slight echo that always lives in bathrooms.

"How many weeks?"

"About eight," she said.

"When did this happen?"

"It was that weekend after you got the job and before I quit the bank."

Wow. There was going to be five of us.

As I lay in bed that night, I felt a deep relief that I'd made it through the program. Several weeks ago, I was scraping a living playing in bars, nightclubs, and recording studios. Now, I was about to embark on a career as a prison guard; talk about going from the sublime to the ridiculous. That thought evaporated when I realized, that in a couple of days, I was about to be in charge of ninety-six inmates and still hadn't been tested or been in a cell-block alone. I then realized our family life was about to get a lot more complicated and costly, and my level of responsibility had just gone up, again. I hoped I could hold it all together. There was no going back now; I had to make it work.

.

4

Face Fear or Fail

Wednesday, October 24, 2001

5:45 A.M. SITTING IN THE ROLL-CALL ROOM WITH ABOUT FORTY other guards, I looked around for anyone I might recognize. I saw a few guys I'd met in training and tried to catch their eye in an effort to make a friendly connection, but there was nothing. I felt very uneasy, like I was wandering around in the dark, unsure of what I was about to walk into. I was extremely anxious and quietly questioning myself. I knew in a few minutes, as soon as roll call was over, I'd be alone in a cellblock with more than ninety incarcerated criminals. *Am I ready for this? I hope I can pull this off.* My stomach was in knots, and I had the trace of a headache behind my left eye.

Sergeant V, a tubby, friendly, ex-army guy with twenty years at the prison under his belt, called out names and issued assignments in alphabetical order. It took a long time to get to me, just like in school. Adams, Brown, Charlton, and Dalton knew nothing about the lifelong waiting game that Reilly, Smith, Thomas, and Underwood had to endure.

"Reilly."

"Here," I responded.

"I-Block"

I-Block, medium security. Could be worse. After a few announcements, everyone got up and filed out of the roll-call room, through the staff room, the lobby, and then the sally port gates into the secure inner section of the prison. A wizened old African American man stood by the inside sally port door, waiting to enter the intake-release area, the processing room where inmates enter and leave the prison. The old man was about to gain his freedom. But he was getting impatient. An entire shift of prison guards had to pass through two gates before he could pass through one. He was so close to getting out but still waiting. As I passed him he looked right at me and said, "Dey sho be quick to lock a nigger up, but slow lettinim go."

He hissed his grumblings at me through a set of wrecked teeth that resembled a vandalized graveyard. As I passed him, I glanced down at his prison ID tag. It gave his name, inmate number, and the date he was first incarcerated—1967. The old guy had been coming in and out of this prison since the year I was born.

Once inside the secure interior of the prison, walking down the same long dark corridor I had weeks before with the chief deputy warden, I started to notice things that had somehow escaped my senses while shadowing Officer S. The further down the corridor we went and the closer to the cellblocks we got, the worse the smell became. The air was thick with the stench of bad body odor, poorly masked by thousands of coats of institutional-strength detergent: There was something despairing about it. It was also unnaturally loud, even at 6 a.m. Hard metallic sounds ricocheted around and bounced off glass, steel, and concrete. Handcuffs and shackles rattled. Heavy boots slapped down hard on concrete and linoleum floors. Raucous laughter boomed through corridors and dozens of radios crackled with guard chatter and static. Shift change was the time when the largest numbers of staff were together in one place. As the black- and gray-clad gang of first-shift guards walked toward the thirteen separate cellblocks, someone somewhere keyed their mic and flushed a toilet. There was silence, and then someone else keyed their mic and made a farting sound. Everyone was suddenly ten again and laughed. It was unusually funny. My laughter was definitely relieving some pent up tension, and I was glad for the unexpected opportunity to vent. Then, the shrill voice of an older woman came on the radio and barked, "Stop that immediately. Housing control, what radio numbers were those last two transmissions?"

There was a flurry of clicks and bursts of static. I asked the guy in front of me what was going on.

"Everyone's keying their mic so Sergeant G can't identify who's fooling around. You new guys better watch out for her. That bitch is crazy."

At that moment, we all turned a corner and passed a row of offices, the first one being the chief deputies. Sergeant G, a helmet of bleach-blond hair, tight scowling face, and pantomime evil eyes, poked her head out of one of the doorways and gave everyone in the corridor a theatrical look of absolute contempt. In her mid- to late fifties, and in her day, probably quite good looking, Sergeant G had lots of nicknames, most of them probably not what she signed at the bottom of her Christmas cards. My favorite and the least offensive was "Jane Wayne." She'd earned this jeering moniker on account of being so gung ho about her job and having a seemingly endless desire to please His Royal Highness the Warden. I would soon learn that her hero worship of the warden had an almost fanatical zeal about it. I would also find out later, sadly, according to the staff in the admin office how much the warden talked trash about her and referred to her mockingly as "my own little pit bull."

I walked through the maze of corridors, following the lettered doors passed G- and H-Blocks until I came to I-Block. I pressed the button at the side of the door and waited to be let in. To my left and right, two other guards I didn't know and hadn't met were waiting to enter H- and J-Blocks. The guard to my right, waiting to get into J-Block, a powerfully built African American guy with a shining bald head and a handsome Hollywood smile, called over to me.

"Hey, new guy, have any problems or questions, just give me a call. I'm right next door."

I thanked him as all three doors, H, I, and J, automatically clicked open in quick succession. Then, the three of us disappeared into the dark cellblocks.

The inside of the housing unit was as quiet as the grave. The third-shift guard I was relieving already stood behind the L-shaped desk with his coat on, looking tired and clearly ready to go home.

"First day on the job?"

"Yep," I replied.

"Nervous?"

"Yeah, a little."

"Well, just follow the logbook from the last first shift. That's the best way to stay on point."

He handed me his keys and radio, then walked over to the door, pressed the button, and waited to be let out. After a moment the door clicked open and off he went. Just before the door slammed shut, he poked his head back into the block and said, "Hey, buddy, a word of advice. All that training you just did, forget about it. Most of its horseshit. It's just the warden covering his ass and playing police academy. Like I said, follow the logbook and if you've got any questions, call the guy next door. Whatever you do, don't call Sergeant G."

The heavy metal door slammed shut. Its sound boomed and echoed through the quiet cellblock like a huge steel table being overturned in an empty school gymnasium.

The two-story cellblock was about the size of a small basketball court. Immediately next to the front door stood the guard's desk and a secure restroom with a heavy steel door immediately behind the desk area. Cells lined the walls on both floors. Each floor had a communal shower room and a janitor's closet. The second floor had a laundry room and a visit room, which consisted of a non-contact windowed wall with several booths containing narrow desks, fixed metal stools, and black halitosis telephones attached to the wall. On the other side of the glass, the visitors sat at mirror image booths and talked into their own phones.

The block was dull and gray. The dayroom lights were off. The cells, all forty-eight of them (designed for one inmate, though each held two), were dark except for the dim yellow glow of ever-present nightlights.

The smell of the cellblock was pungent, to say the least. The air was ripe with a sickly combination of farts, foot fungus, body odor, mass-made low-grade institutional food, and a strange oil-on-metal aroma. The "dayroom," the large open space in the center of the cellblock, was set up neatly with a half-empty bookshelf, a few tables, and a dozen large, plastic, riot-proof armchairs in a semi-circle. The chairs were organized around a beat-up TV on a low, heavy-looking wooden table.

A voice, thin and plastic-sounding came over the PA system: "Count time, count time, count time, 6 a.m. count."

The clipboard on the desk listed all the names and cell assignments of each inmate. I started my first solo count. Before leaving the desk I hit the master switch that turned on all the cell lights. Starting on the ground floor at cell one, I knocked hard on each door telling both inmates to sit up or stand up for count. There were lots of unhappy campers not quite ready for tennis and sailing, but I made each one prove they were still alive. I chose to ignore all the special early morning greetings I was being treated to, and then returned to the desk to phone my count into the sergeant's office.

A sharp, officious-sounding voice answered, "Sergeant G speaking."

"This is Reilly in I-Block."

"Officer Reilly, the warden does not want the staff to refer to the accommodations as blocks. Housing Unit is the correct terminology. Do you understand?"

For a second I had to take this in, and then I responded with a passive, "Er, OK, no problem. I-Unit has ninety-six inmates all present and correct."

There was a curt thank you and then the line went dead. After a while, the thin nasal voice came over the PA again, saying, "Count is secure. Count is secure."

Before the echo of the PA faded out, I was startled by the hard knocking sound of knuckles on the inside of several cell doors. Looking up I saw three inmates stood at the windows of their cells gesticulating to be let out. Crap! What do they want and what am I supposed to do? I called the guy next door.

The phone rang a couple of times, then a loud cheerful voice answered. "J-Unit, Officer K speaking."

"Hey, it's Reilly next door."

I explained my problem. He told me not to worry. They were my breakfast trustee workers wanting to get out, to set up for meal. He told me I should check my worker list against the IDs of the guys banging on the doors to make sure the right inmates come out. Then, he gave me some excellent advice.

"Every inmate in the block knows you're a new guy and they're going to screw around with you as much as they can and as much you let them. So, remember, Reilly, it's easier to start hard and soften up later once they know you mean business. Got it?"

"Got it. Thanks, K."

I hung up and did as he said. And despite some objections to having IDs checked, I let out the correct workers and had them set up the breakfast serving tables. Almost immediately after setup was complete, the food arrived, brought onto the block in a huge rolling aluminum cart pushed by a couple of kitchen trustees. The cart contained ninety-six trays half filled with a foul, anemic-looking slop, poorly disguised as food. Eight trays at a time were laid out on the table. Then, using the computerized control panel, I let that many inmates out to get their breakfast. Once the inmates had their trays, one by one, they locked themselves back into their cells. This process was repeated over and over until all ninety-six men were fed.

As soon as the last guys got their trays of wallpaper paste and packing foam, the first set of guys to receive their mush were ready to slop out. Initially, it was chaotic. I felt as if I was barely clinging on to any kind of control. It also quickly became apparent that until I got some respect and became a known quantity, I was going to be challenged by almost every inmate regarding every decision I made.

"We usually have this."

"We usually get that."

"I want to talk to a sergeant."

"I want to talk to a lieutenant."

"I'm gonna write you up."

"I need a new cellie."

"I want to move to another cellblock."

"Do you have a sister?"

"Are you related to Mr. Rogers?"

"Are you gay?"

"I need you to call property for me."

And the most popular by far: "That's not how the other guards do it."

That was something I heard literally dozens of times a day the first couple of weeks.

After breakfast was finished and cleaned up, there was a morning cell inspection. If an inmate did not have his cell clean and his bed made, he would be written up and locked in for the day. Most inmates enjoyed what little liberty they had, so the majority made some effort to square away their cells. From the very get-go, I couldn't bring myself to bust balls about cells being perfect. I wasn't a drill sergeant, and these men were not highly motivated military types. As long as it was tidy and I could see that they had made an effort, I gave them a pass.

Cell inspection was followed by group release and morning recreation. Then, the incessant barrage of phone calls and requests for various inmates to be sent to see medical, dental, or social workers or parole officers; to attend audiovisual court hearings, education classes, or disciplinary hearings; to visit the barber shop; or to participate in outside rec or various institutional work details. All inmates needed to be signed in and out of the block. The inmates who didn't have to go somewhere came up to the desk and asked hundreds of questions, most of which I couldn't answer. The morning went by fast. I called Officer K in J-Block about twenty times. Each time I called him he couldn't have been more helpful. At one point during one of my question-and-answer sessions he told me, "Heads up, Reilly. Sergeant V's on his way through to inspect the block. Make sure you're on point."

Seconds later, Sergeant V wandered casually into the block and was instantly greeted by a throng of needy inmates. He answered some questions, deflected some, and deferred some to me. Sergeant T walked around for a few minutes, checked out the showers and the laundry room, and then came over and sat casually on the edge of the desk. He glanced down at my name tag.

"Everything going OK, Reilly?"

"Yes, thanks," I replied.

"Good. It all looks fine except the laundry room. You had two guys in there who didn't belong. You have to keep checking on that; make sure nothing's going on. There's always trouble in the laundry room."

"OK, thanks, sarge. I'll make sure I do."

On the way out, he turned to me and said, "And by the way, don't let Sergeant G catch that shit. She'll write you up for it."

At some point I got a coffee break. A co-worker took over the block for fifteen minutes while I went to the staff room. At the coffee machine, I asked another guard about the Sergeant G rumors. I mentioned that Sergeant V had told me to watch out for her.

"He would know," my co-worker told me. "She wrote him up recently for not following the SOP and ratted him out to the warden."

Back on the block, I checked the time. It was 10:55. I was only minutes away from the second count of the day—eleven o'clock.

"Lock in for count. Lock in for count," I called out as loud as I could, trying to sound authoritative without yelling. Some of the inmates had already gone into their cells, some were on the way. Others were getting up from watching TV, getting out of the showers, packing up the dominos and playing cards, and wrapping up dozens of conversations. I stood at the desk and called out to an almost quiet cellblock. "Stand by your doors and prepare for count."

One last dripping-wet inmate ran from the showers to his cell with a towel around his waist. His wet feet flapped and slapped in prison-issue flip flops as he scuttled and slid across the cold concrete floor. A few wolf whistles and catcalls were directed at the straggler as he slid comically into his cell and quickly started dressing. The cellblock was almost quiet. I stood at the desk and waited for silence.

The PA blared out, "Count time! Count time! Count time!"

All the inmates stood just inside their cell doors. All of them were wearing their IDs and waiting to get count over with so they could get their lunch. Every inmate was where he should be, all except for inmate M.

Inmate M and I were about to start a personality clash and a battle of wills that would last for the next couple of months and, in many ways, define how I handled difficult inmates and potentially volatile situations.

Standing by the cell door displaying his prison ID card four times a day was not what inmate M considered a good time. He told me on my first day, and almost every day after that, "Standing around and being counted like a child is bullshit!"

Inmate M's voice was smooth and deep and sounded like the bass notes of a clarinet. He was West African, in his late thirties, and stood about six foot six. He must have weighed close to two hundred and fifty pounds. Watching him play soccer or basketball in nothing but shorts and sneakers, it was hard not to be amazed by his perfect physique, coordination, and speed. He looked like the embodiment of the warrior king Shaka Zulu. I remember thinking that if he decided to grab me, he could kill me with his bare hands, and there wouldn't be a damn thing I could do about it. He had recently served several months in "The Hole" for beating three Latino gangsters senseless after they tried to strong-arm him over who was in charge of the block TV.

From the get-go, inmate M harassed me, complained to me, goaded me, and generally tried to rub my rhubarb as much and as often as he could. I didn't write him up or complain. I just tried to roll with it and handle each incident as best I could. I was on a steep learning curve, and I had started to realize that anything but no meant yes. I also started to realize that no matter what I said, it wasn't what inmate M wanted to hear.

Several weeks into my stint as I-Unit's new, rookie, day-shift guard, our differences reached a breaking point. It was right before an 11 a.m. count. During the morning inmate M had asked me umpteen times to be assigned to a work detail in the laundry room. I refused and told him over and over again that there were several guys already working in the laundry and I didn't need any more help. I also told him, for the first time, that if he didn't stop asking me, I would write him up for harassment.

"Harassment, inmate M, is a class two offense, punishable by time in segregation."

Inmate M's response was perfect: "According to the inmate

handbook, harassment, Officer Reilly, is defined as words, gestures, or actions intended to annoy or alarm another person. I am only asking for a different work assignment."

I thanked him for the clear and accurate definition but told him his words and gestures were definitely annoying me. He stared and glared down at me with his massive arms crossed in front of his huge muscular chest.

"That's more of your bullshit, Officer Reilly."

I thanked him again for his opinion, then said, "Now please go to your cell and get ready for count."

The PA bleated, "Count time! Count time! Count time!"

I started on the second floor. Inmate M's cell was third in. I quickly passed by the first two cells, counting the inmates, marking them present on my clipboard, then closing and locking the cell doors. Then, it was inmate M's turn. I walked up to his cell, which he kept Spartan and immaculately clean: perfectly made bed; toothpaste and toothbrush in a cup; a couple of neatly stacked books, a writing pad, and a pen on the metal desk bolted to the wall; clothes and towel folded neatly in a box under the bunk; and a terrified cellmate sitting timidly on the top bunk blinking like a scared mouse.

Inmate M's only luxury was a single Snickers bar that he bought once a week at the commissary. He bought it on a Monday and then placed it on the middle of the one shelf mounted on the wall above the desk. It sat there all week. He never touched it. Then six days later, on the following Sunday, he would slowly eat the Snickers bar while watching TV. Everyone in the cellblock knew about the Snickers bar, when he bought it, and where it was left on display.

Inmate M never closed his door. It was only shut at night and during count, when it was closed and locked by staff. Amazingly, no one ever stole the Snickers bar. I was not sure what kind of mind-control game inmate M was playing, but it was evident the weekly routine held enormous importance. Somehow, it empowered him and at the same time challenged all the other inmates.

Instead of standing up straight and properly displaying his ID, inmate M was doing what he'd been doing every day for the last couple of months: the Chubby Checker twist, with his eyes closed, elbows tucked into his waist, huge hands raised a little and closed into fists at the side of his head, and his knees slightly bent. The second I entered the doorway he would start twisting all the way down into a crouch, then twist all the way back up to tower over me. My reaction was always the same. I completely ignored him. But, on this particular day, for whatever reason, probably because of all the laundry worker requests, I had enough. The time to say something had arrived. As I approached, the giant inmate M started doing the twist. Instead of marking him present and then moving on, I walked into the cell and stood as close as I could without getting hit by the twister. I was now closer to him than I had been at any of the many prior counts.

I waited a few stretched-out seconds to let him feel the change in my routine and then I said, "Ya know, inmate M, for such a big, athletic black man, you really are a terrible dancer."

I then slowly turned around and walked out of the cell, closing the door quietly behind me.

After count was announced secure, I let the trustees out to set up for lunch. Looking up from my desk, I saw inmate M stood at the window of his cell door, his huge frame filling it, blocking out most of the light from the narrow window at the rear of the cell. He was staring down at me. I could feel the weight of his eyes on me, boring into me. I couldn't read his expression, and I started to feel more than a little uncomfortable.

Lunch, in its big, filthy aluminum cart, rumbled onto the block. The trustees set up the serving table and laid out eight or so trays. I pressed the buttons on the control panel to let out the first four cells on the upper right side. Inmate M was among them. Other inmates knew we'd had words but were not sure of the nature of the exchange. Inmate M walked down the metal steps three at a time, passed the food line, and headed straight for me. His hands were behind his back. He was carrying something. As he approached, I stood up and pushed my chair away with the backs of my knees. Inmate M stopped at the desk and loomed over me. I rested my right hand on my radio. The food line halted. Every inmate stared at inmate M and me.

In his rich, deep, velvety voice, he said, "Officer Reilly, you are a funny motherfucker, and I would like you have my Snickers bar."

His hands came around from behind his back. He placed the

treasured candy bar on my desk, smiled knowingly and then sauntered casually over to the food line. It was a Saturday.

A SENSE OF HUMOR AND BRUTAL HONESTY WENT MUCH FURTHER
than any amount of politically correct nonsense, wimping-out,
referring to a supervisor, or the old favorite, "You'll have to ask the
guard on the next shift."

Shortly after the Snickers bar incident, inmate P, a very tough
young African American "gangsta," returned to the block after a
prolonged stay in The Hole—seg, segregation, disciplinary, solitary. Upon his return to general population, he was welcomed
back into the fold like a returning war hero. "His crew" were
delighted to have him back and besieged him with a barrage of
questions about how he was doing, who was down in seg, and what
was happening in The Hole.

As often happened, the inmate arrived on the block without
any of his belongings. When I gave him his cell assignment, he
asked me if I could see about having his things sent over from seg.
I said I would do what I could, but couldn't promise anything. The
truth was that anything could have happened to his property.
There were plenty of guards who didn't care about the inmate's
things, and it often took days for a prisoner's meager possessions
to catch up with him. Also, if a particular guard had an axe to
grind with a particular inmate, often their property never arrived,
or in some cases, it arrived drenched in urine or covered in feces.

After inmate P's arrival and reception party, there was a lull in
activity, so I managed to make a couple of calls, locate the property, match it to the inmate's name and prison number, and have
it brought over to the cellblock. After his possessions arrived, the
inmate was delighted and genuinely pleased to be reunited with
his few paltry belongings. As I handed him his things, he said, at a
decent volume and while surrounded by a dozen or so African
American inmates, "Thank you, Reilly. You're my nigga."

In prison slang, I knew this was actually meant as a backhanded
compliment, but I wasn't about to let the double standard slide.

"Excuse me. What did you say?"

Again, and with a genuinely grateful tone, inmate P repeated, "I said, thank you, Reilly. You're my nigga. I can't believe you got my shit so quickly." We looked at each other for a few seconds.

Then, when I knew I had his full attention, I said, "Just hold on a second, could you imagine if, after you did a good job during a work assignment, I said to you"—in my now ridiculous-sounding English accent—"'Inmate P, thank you for doing such a marvelous job scrubbing the showers. You are my nigger.' That wouldn't be right, would it?"

Silence fell like a nine-pound hammer. The gang of tough young African American prisoners all looked at each other in a state of shock, their wide-eyed expressions all saying, *Did you hear that? Did he just say what I thought he said?*

Before anyone spoke, I said, "Inmate P, I wouldn't dream of addressing you in that manner, so please don't talk to me that way."

Inmate P paused, digesting the thought, and then threw his head back and roared with laughter. The gang, his disciples, surrounded him and followed suit.

"OK, you got a point. No problem. How's this? Thanks for getting me my shit, Mr. Reilly. You da man."

I responded with a cordial, "Inmate P, you're welcome. I'm glad I could help."

After this initial and somewhat tense start to our relationship, inmate P and I developed a mutually respectful rapport. He was clearly an intelligent young man who was well regarded by his peers and blessed with bucketsful of leadership potential. There were days when I actually enjoyed his company. After he was released from prison, it was shocking on several levels to learn that he'd been involved in a gunfight that resulted in the death of a young police officer.

AT WORK AND ON THE HOME FRONT, I WAS FEELING OVERWHELMED. My first few weeks in prison had flown by in a blur. But at home, Sarah had become terribly sick. The first trimester of her pregnancy was brutal. She was admitted to the hospital several times, and after batteries of tests we were told she had viral encephalitis. The integrity of the fetus and Sarah's health were seriously in question. While I was at work, her parents and her older sister, Allison, helped out with the children. This was no easy task for my in-laws. The previous fall, my father-in-law, Zeke, had been diagnosed with lung cancer. It was terrible news. He had only been retired for a couple of years. He had smoked between the ages of twenty-something and fifty-something. He had quit more than ten years previously. One evening he'd slipped coming down the stairs, cracked a rib, and had an X-ray; in the process, the doctors found a dark spot in one of his lungs. In November 2001, after a day of work, I went to the hospital. Sarah was in the isolation unit, barely conscious. I sat silently with her for a couple of hours then went over to my in-laws' place to pick up Joshua and Lindsey, and then I went home. The house was dark and quiet. Being there without Sarah simply didn't feel right. As I put the key in the door, Josh asked me, "Is Mommy home?"

"Not tonight," I answered.

While I was putting Lindsey in her crib, I caught a reflection of myself in the mirror on her wall. I looked terrible—thin, tired, and weak. It was exactly how I felt.

Sarah's paternal grandmother had died in child labor. Zeke was a little older than Joshua at the time. I couldn't stop thinking about it, how something like that would affect a child.

After getting Lindsey sorted out and settled down, I heard Josh moving around in his new "big boy bed." I looked in on him. He was awake and lying on his back. He looked right at me as a shaft of light from the door being opened fell across his face. He smiled then held out his hand. I stepped into the room and we touched our palms together, interlocking our fingers, his tiny digits fitting between mine.

"I love you, Josh," I said.

"Love you, too, Daddy. Is Mommy coming home tomorrow?"

"Soon. Mommy's coming home soon."

Our fingers slipped apart and I walked out of the room, closed the door, and then sat down on the landing at the top of the stairs and wept with worry.

5

Prison Politics

Prisons and the people who work in them protect the community from criminals and the criminals from each other. That's every penal institution's basic mission statement. There were, however, times when I discovered inmates needed to be protected from guards.

In November 2001, I was still new and on probation. I was working second shift overtime as a float. A float is a relief guard who stands in for other guards who are on break. When a float isn't relieving other staff for coffee and dinner breaks, they basically just hang out waiting to be assigned to whatever needs attending to, or for an emergency to occur. I had been called to the sergeant's office and told by one of the second-shift sergeants to escort an inmate to protective custody. The inmate in question came into prison on a sex abuse charge. He managed to keep it quiet until another inmate found his picture and story in a local paper. Word spread like the Ebola virus, and within a day every hardcore con with an image to maintain and a point to prove was out to get their pound of flesh. After the first "lumping up," the battered inmate was wisely sent by the shift commander to PC, protective custody, an act known as "Administrative Segregation."

The Protective Custody block is a world within a world. It houses mainly "skinners and rats" (sex offenders and informants). There are others there, the odd ones who have run up prison debts they can't repay or those who just can't physically defend themselves. Some inmates are basically scared to death of being in prison and can't handle the macho madness of general population. For those prisoners, protective custody is their home.

I collected the inmate and his paperwork from the sergeant's office and headed to the PC unit. PC was at the end of a long corridor, through a sally port, and up on the second floor. After pressing the button on the wall outside the door, the prisoner and I waited for the housing control officer to open the door, I heard a voice.

"Hey, Reilly, wait. We'll help you take that guy up to PC."

Two guards I only knew from reputation walked quickly toward me down the long corridor.

I knew what was coming and pressed the button again repeatedly. The intercom crackled.

"What do you need?" The housing control guard sounded annoyed.

"It's Reilly, taking one up to PC from the sergeant's office."

"OK, stand by."

The two guards had now covered half the distance from the end of the long corridor toward me and my assigned inmate.

"Hey, Reilly, hold that door when it opens."

They were getting closer. The inmate instantly felt some weirdness and asked me what they wanted. The sally port clicked open. The two guards picked up the pace and broke into a jog. I pushed the door open with my right foot, shoved the inmate through the opening, and quickly closed the door behind me. I was now locked in the stairwell with the inmate. The door I had just come through would not unlock until I went through the second door at the top of the stairs. The two guards stood angrily on the other side of the door. One of them rapped hard on the glass with his fist and glared through the window.

"What the fuck are you doing? We were going to help you with that guy."

I played dumb, shrugged, turned my back on them, and then led the inmate up the stairs to be handed over to the guard on duty in the PC Block. Inside the stairwell, there were no cameras. It was a complete blind spot.

Minutes later, I descended the steps, only to find my two happy helpers waiting for me in the hallway outside the door.

"Reilly, what did you do that for?"

"Do what?"

"Lock us out the sally port. We were gonna, you know, get some. You know what that guy's in here for right?"

The two goons grinned at one another menacingly, and then turned to me, pointing. One said, "Next time we tell you to wait, you better wait. Understand?"

My heart started to race. The palms of my hands got sweaty. My cheeks felt flushed. I could feel myself breathing lightly through my nose. I was at a major intersection, and I knew it. I was either going to kowtow to their bully-boy tactics or make a stand. The bozo twins hovered over me and waited for an answer. I felt the pressure of their combined four hundred pounds pressing down on me. I had a flash thought about being a new guy still on probation. If I screwed up, I'd get canned. It happened all the time. The two thugs shuffled from one foot to another, anticipating a response. Then, I suddenly thought about my dad. I imagined he was standing right beside me. I thought what would my old man do? I thought about how he never took an ounce of crap from anyone his whole life. I thought about how he never ran away from any tough situation he had ever faced. I thought about a few of the battles I knew he'd lost, but how he'd always won the war in the end. I thought I can't let myself, my family, or my dad down. These two guys weren't planning to give the inmate a bubble bath and a couple of Bible readings. They were going to beat the crap out of him while he was under my supervision.

With my family and my father in mind, I pointed at both of them and said, "I won't have any part of this. It's not our job to beat up inmates. If that guy took a pounding and it was found out he was under my supervision, I'd get fired, and getting fired wouldn't be good for my family. Don't ever ask me to be a part of anything like this again."

Then I walked off.

Things were difficult for me for a while after that. I was anxious about being at work and often felt like quitting. Some guards ignored me, others called me an inmate lover behind my back, and some called me it to my face. The good guys told me to keep doing the right thing, get through probation without attracting any attention, and not worry about the bullshit.

DURING ANOTHER SECOND SHIFT OVERTIME, WHILE WORKING ON the protective custody unit, I struck up a conversation with a young trustee. He stood about five foot six and probably didn't weigh much more than about a hundred and twenty pounds. His hair was long, dark, and greasy. His complexion was that of a spotty teenager who had just had his first shave and was a little embarrassed about the results. The kid was only nineteen years old and scared of everything, particularly his cellie, inmate N, a large, volatile inmate who hated the world and me. I know he hated me because he told me regularly. During one count, inmate N refused to close his door by standing in the thick steel doorframe. I told him twice to move and then pushed the door closed. He reacted quicker and with more strength than I thought he could. He threw himself against the door and started pushing back, screaming that he was going to kill me. I believed him. After about thirty seconds of struggling, with his long arms flailing out the door, trying desperately to grab me, I managed to lock him in. Inmate N was released from prison not long after that. It didn't take him long to get back inside, forever. He was handed a life sentence for raping four prostitutes and murdering one.

As the young fear-filled inmate mopped around my desk and emptied the trashcan at my feet, we started to talk. All other inmates were on lockdown and secured in their cells. The only other person present was a fifty-something, exhausted prison psychologist sitting at a table in the middle of the dayroom, process-ing paperwork. Every now and then, he asked me to let an inmate out so he could get him to sign something, and after he had the signature, I'd lock the inmate back in. I quietly asked the young trustee to stop work and if he wouldn't mind sitting down and talk-ing with me for a moment.

"Why, what do you want to know?" he asked rather suspiciously and defensively.

I turned my chair around to face him and told him to sit in one of the plastic riot-proof armchairs he was mopping around. I told him I thought he didn't fit in, and something about that both-ered me.

"Why don't you think I fit?"

He looked down at his feet when he talked and picked con-stantly at a large cold sore at the corner of his mouth. When he did look up, he glanced at me nervously, his eyes hardly ever meet-ing mine.

"This unit is full of sex offenders and prison informants, and I don't know why, but for some reason I don't think you're in the right place."

The young inmate put the mop in the bucket, leaned the han-dle against the wall, and tentatively sat down opposite me.

The old psychologist looked up to see what was going on. He recognized a break in the regular routine, an unusual interaction between guard and prisoner. I glanced up at the psychologist. He immediately looked back down at the paperwork in front of him.

Out of the blue, the inmate asked me, "Do you have kids, Mr. Reilly?"

Normally, I would say I'd rather not talk about my family, but that night I answered, "Yes, I do. I have two young children and my wife is pregnant."

Then, the inmate said something that completely took me by sur-prise. He said, "I bet you're a really good dad. You wanna know some-thing?" He paused and made eye contact. "I've never met my dad."

The following is my best recollection of what the young pris-oner said next:

"Once, when I was about eight or nine, my mom told me my

dad was going to take me to the Philadelphia Zoo the next day. She took me shopping and bought me new sneakers, jeans, and a sweatshirt. It was really exciting, I had new clothes, was going to meet my dad, and go to the zoo, all on the same day. The next morning I got up really early. My mom was already up and had made me a big lunch and put it in a brown paper grocery bag. She told me my dad was going to come by and pick me up after breakfast. Each time the phone rang or a car passed our trailer, I asked my mom, 'Is it my dad, is it my dad?'

"The morning lasted forever and slowly turned into lunchtime. I got hungry and ate some of my sandwich and snacks. I saved the rest for later, to eat with my dad. Sometime in the middle of the afternoon it started to rain. I remember my mom started to clean like crazy. I was pretty positive she was getting everything to look really nice because if the trailer looked great, maybe my dad would want to come and live with us. All afternoon, the rain poured down and the cars kept flying by. None of them stopped.

"At dinnertime mom ordered pizza and one of those big bottles of soda. As it got dark, the rain kept coming down really hard, but I didn't care. For some reason, I was convinced the zoo would be open at night because that was where the animals lived. My mom let me eat as much pizza and drink as much soda as I wanted. My belly swelled up like a balloon and I watched cartoons until really, really late. I also remember my Mom's face being all red and swollen. I kept asking her over and over again, 'When's my dad going to get here? When's my dad going to get here?' That's when she started to cry, and said she was so sorry but she didn't think he was coming."

After the young inmate finished talking, a deep silence seemed to separate us for a long time. I kept looking at him until he finally raised his eyes to meet mine.

"Did you ever meet your dad?"

The young inmate shook his head and stared blankly down at the floor again. I sensed a movement and looked up. The old psychologist was watching and listening. Again, I looked at him and again he quickly looked down, returning to his paperwork.

"So," I said, "tell me, how did you end up in prison?"

The inmate raised his head and looked right at me. "I got my girlfriend pregnant. Her mother went crazy and called the cops. I'm nineteen, she's fifteen. I got a year for statutory rape." Looking at the inmate, I thought he looked a lot more like a fifteen-year-old than a nineteen-year-old.

I said, "You were worried about general population, weren't you?"

There was another long pause: "Yeah, I can't fight and I'm not even a good talker. If those guys found out about my charges, I wouldn't be able to handle it. I'm not a rapist, Mr. Reilly, honestly, I'm not."

"So you took protective custody right?"

"Yeah, I just felt like it would be safer up here, but now I'm not sure. My cellie, inmate N, he's crazy."

"So, what are you going to do when you get out?"

"I'm going to try and get a job and be with my girlfriend and the baby. We love each other."

There was nothing to say. It was impossible to know how much of the story was true. I had a feeling that most or all of it was. So, I clumsily fumbled around for the right words. "I hope it works out for you. Thanks for talking with me. You can put the mop away and then lock in."

The inmate stood up, said, "Thank you, Mr. Reilly," and then returned to his cell.

The tired-looking psychologist collected his papers. After he stuffed them in his old brown leather case, he stood up and walked toward me and the cellblock door. As he approached, I picked up the radio, keyed the mic, and asked the housing control officer, "Open Charlie Two." The door clicked open. But instead of leaving, the psychologist put his bag on my desk and said to me, "I've been doing this job for over twenty years and in all that time I've never heard a guard talk to an inmate the way you talked to that young man tonight."

Before I could answer, the psychologist sighed through a tired, defeated smile, shook his head slowly, and left. The door slammed heavily behind him.

A few months later I was in the grocery store and a thin boyish voice behind me said, "Hello, Mr. Reilly."

It was the young inmate from protective custody. He looked exactly the same: malnourished, skinny, and scared. A very young girl with a baby stood next to him; she looked about sixteen and not old enough to drive.

EARLY DECEMBER 2001. AFTER SPENDING EIGHT HOURS WITH misfits, murderers, and sex offenders, it felt great to be unlocking one last door and hear Sarah and the children laughing and playing as I entered the house. Sarah had pulled through. It was such a relief to have her back. No words could convey how wonderful it felt. The baby was going to be fine. Josh and Lindsey were delighted their mommy was home. We were out of the woods.

Things with her dad, however, were pretty tough. He'd just been through one round of chemotherapy and had two-thirds of one of his lungs removed. He was home but looked thin and frightened all the time. I wanted to hug him each time I saw him . . . so I did. My in-laws lived close by and I stopped in daily. Despite his illness and the uncertainty that surrounded it, Zeke was always interested in how I was getting on at the prison. I told him stories about what I was doing and who I was watching over, and he asked question after question and showed great interest in my progress. He mentioned family a lot and always circled back to the fact that we were all so lucky to have each other. He also never once talked about himself or complained. He never once told me how tired he was or that he wished he was feeling better. He never mentioned the terrible fight he was engaged in. He coughed all the time and even apologized for doing so.

Back at work, at roll call one morning, Sergeant G gave us all a long lecture about professionalism and the use of appropriate terminology. She told us all the words "prison guard" were no longer the correct term to describe our very important work. She let us know that this change in our professional title and vocabulary had come down directly from the warden himself. The proper way to now describe ourselves was as "corrections officers."

A juvenile smirk ran around the inside of the roll-call room.

Sergeant G looked up furiously from her clipboard and scanned the gang of grinning guards with a look of absolute contempt. No one moved: We all became silent and still and collectively denied her the opportunity she so desperately wanted—to give someone, anyone a write-up.

This politically correct term—"corrections officer"—suddenly sounded like a joke, especially the way Sergeant G was over enunciating it, rolling her Rs, as if she imagined the warden was watching, listening to her, hanging on her every word. The truth was, up to this point, I hadn't seen any correcting or officiating going on, only a whole lot of guarding. I thought back to the incident a few weeks prior, when two of my co-workers wanted to beat up an inmate. Where would that go on the professionalism scale? Then, I thought about the warden; I wondered if he thought the word "Officer" made him feel better about himself and his position. Although I'd not met him yet, I'd started to hear plenty from inmates, other guards, and of course the union reps. I imagined him sitting at his desk in a large, wood-paneled office, surrounded by hunting trophies and framed photographs of himself waterskiing, motorcycle riding, and trap shooting. I wondered, did saying the words, "I oversee two hundred corrections officers" make him feel more like a gentleman? I bet some middle-management minion in human resources down at DOC headquarters must have come up with the term. I bet he got a big promotion to upper-middle management because it sounded so nice and friendly, not at all punitive or in the least bit draconian.

Midway through the month, I was still on a steep learning curve. There was a lot to take in. It was becoming apparent that the way I was going to get the job done was to have a sense of humor and to try to treat people the way I wanted to be treated. I had recognized a couple of things right away. One, I could talk to staff and inmates in an honest straightforward way and get a fair or even a good result. The second, despite being fairly fit and physically confident, was that I was not a tough guy, not that I ever thought I was. In the short time I'd spent working at the prison, I had been exposed to some real-deal hard cases, on both sides of the bars: brutal, uncaring men who knew everything about cruelty and violence and who were never too far from admitting that they liked it. It was the most basic form of power. This knowledge was just an affirmation that the only way I was going to have success was to understand my surroundings and be smart with the words I chose to use. However, I was about to find out that straight talk, humor, and diplomacy would only get me so far. I was about to have my first real run-in, and it would be all about nerve and raw machismo. It was the kind of examination that ran contrary to every form of conventional schooling I can think of. I would have the test first and then the lesson later.

I was finally finding a rhythm and getting the routine down: 5:45 a.m. roll call, 6 a.m. count, breakfast, breakfast cleanup, cell inspection, morning recreation, send inmates out to a million different meetings, sign them in, sign them out, avoid Sergeant G like the plague, lock the inmates in for the 11 a.m. count, lunch, lunch cleanup, afternoon recreation, 1:55 p.m. shift change, and then go home at 2 p.m.

Despite the boredom this routine sometimes created, there were always surprises. When you have ninety-six men locked up in one big room designed for half that number and only one guy overseeing their activities, there are a lot of variables.

During my scheduled days off, a new inmate had arrived on the block. Although I was the regular day-shift guard and by this point, treated fairly respectfully, the new inmate, inmate H, a mid-twenties Italian guy posturing as a hard man, was acting as though I was an interloper. He gave me the evil eye every time I made an announcement or went on a round. I could feel him staring at me. His looks and body language were aggressive and overtly challenging.

As the morning came to an end, shortly before 11 a.m., I called out for everyone to lock in for count. The inmates put down their dominos, turned off the TV, closed magazines and books, and slowly headed to their cells. Inmate H, the new arrival, stayed sitting down at a table shuffling playing cards in his lap with his legs stretched out in front of him. His cellmate and card partner said, "C'mon, man, it's time to lock in."

Inmate H ignored him and kept shuffling. I called out a second time, "Lock in. Lock in for count."

I walked over to the table and said to inmate H, "You have to lock in for count. I don't want to ask you again."

The inmate sneered and said, loud enough to be heard by everyone, "I'm not locking in. What are you gonna do about it?"

This was the first time since I started that I had been directly challenged and openly disobeyed in this way; it was very much a physical challenge. The other inmates stopped what they were doing to watch and listen. Maybe there was going to be a bit of a show. Was I going to press the panic button? Was I going to call for assistance? Was the goon squad going to rush in and kick some ass?

I said to inmate H, "I'll tell you what I'll do about it. If you don't lock in, I'm going to make you lock in."

The inmate turned in his chair and said, "You touch me and I'll fuck you up."

We looked at each other for a moment. Every inmate in the block watched in silence. Then I said, "OK, I'll be back for you."

This response was absolutely not the right thing to do. But I felt that if I backed down and called for help, I would lose the ground I had gained with the rest of the inmates over the last couple of months. The other major factor was that inmate H and I were evenly matched physically. I felt quite confident making a stand. It has to be said, if he had been a three hundred pound inmate glad-iator, I would never have put myself out in the same way.

Slowly and methodically I went to every cell, made sure both inmates were there, quietly closed each door, and pulled on the handle, checking it was locked. Inmate H watched my every move. A couple of minutes later, the only door still open was the one belonging to inmate H. I walked over to the cell and looked in. Inmate H's cellie was sitting on his bunk looking anxious. I put my head in the door and said, "Are you all right?"

"Yes," he replied.

"Good, I'm glad to hear that. No matter what happens here, don't get off your bunk, OK?"

The cellmate nodded nervously. Every window of every cell door was filled with two faces fogging up the glass, waiting to see the show. I walked over to the table and stood a few feet in front of inmate H. He glanced around the dayroom. Now it was just the two of us. I knew his cellmate had no intention of coming out. Inmate H moved around uncomfortably in his chair. He repeated the threat.

"I told you, if you touch me, I'm gonna fuck you up."

What I did next was unprofessional and probably rather foolish, but for some unexplainable reason, I took my radio out of its pouch and my pen out of my shirt pocket. I clipped the pen to the clipboard then placed both the radio and the clipboard on the table next to inmate H.

I moved around and stood in front of him and said, "OK, get up."

He looked at me, opened his mouth a little as if he was about to speak, but nothing came out.

"Right. Let's have a go, inmate H. If you want to fight, that's fine. Go ahead. Let's get it over with."

Inmate H stood up. I took a step back and raised both my hands. We stared at each other for what felt like a long time. I wasn't going to hit first. I had to be able to say, "I was defending myself; he attacked me."

He didn't raise his hands. They hung open and limp at his sides. He wasn't holding anything.

"Now go and lock in," I shouted, pointing to his cell.

He turned and walked away from me. I walked behind him as he crossed the dayroom floor and entered his cell. I closed the door slowly behind him until it locked with a quiet click.

He turned around and looked at me. We were now only inches apart, only the Plexiglas separated us. We stared at each other, and then through the door, he asked me, "Are you going to write me up for this?"

"No," I said.

"Why not?"

"Because you're going to do something for me."

"What is it?"

"You're going to ask around about me and find out what kind of guy I am. Then come and talk to me."

"OK," he said and went and lay down on his bunk.

The next day inmate H came over to my desk and asked for the

Scrabble board. I took the game out from a drawer, asked inmate H for "a deposit" (his ID card), and then we made the exchange.

"Mr. Reilly, about yesterday, I did like you said, I asked around like you told me to. I'm real sorry I acted like that. Thanks for not writing me up."

After this unprofessional and foolhardy performance on my part, I learned a couple of very important lessons. Sometimes, making a stand makes a huge statement. And sometimes, violence or just the threat of it has more effect than volumes of well-chosen words. I also learned that half of making someone believe they might get hurt was what I was capable of, and the other half was what they thought I was capable of.

After the big inmate H scene, my stock amongst the inmates seemed to rise dramatically and my workload seemed to lighten considerably. About twelve months later, inmate H would be shot to death in a gang-related gun fight in New York City.

6

"On the First Day of Christmas . . ."

Tuesday, December 25, 2001

I LEFT FOR WORK AT 5:15 A.M. WITH TWO POUNDS OF PORK SAUSAGES. Everyone on first shift had signed up to bring something in for a big holiday breakfast. A couple of the older guards were going to spend the morning making, or should I say frying, the food. When we were relieved for our first break, we went down to the staff kitchen and enjoyed the all-you-can-eat prison guard buffet. Everything was loaded with so much fat and cholesterol; during moments of quiet, you could actually hear people's arteries hardening.

In the cellblock, everything was very subdued. I only turned half the overhead lights on. It softened the harshness of all that gray concrete and steel. There were no programs or activities, and I cancelled cell inspection for the day.

After a very quiet inmate breakfast, the few who came out of their cells and ate went straight back to bed. Some stayed out in the dayroom. It was mostly the guys who lived in the back corner cells. The corner cells were always cold and damp. Some kind of construction screw-up caused that part of the block to leak constantly. These few inmates shuffled around the dayroom in their baggy prison-issue clothes like mentally ill homeless men lost in a big bus station.

I looked at the phone on the desk. It hadn't rung once since I started my shift two hours earlier. I got up, turned off the control panel, and started to make a round. As I walked up to the second floor, my feet on the metal steps and the jangle of the keys attached to my belt sounded too loud, so I put my hand over them. I looked into each cell. Most beds were occupied by inmates in the fetal position, covered up by their scratchy, gray woolen blankets. I thought about my kids in their beds in our nice, comfy, little house. At some point in time, every inmate in this entire prison had been an innocent child, no matter how fleeting and brief his childhood may have been. How many great Christmas mornings had these men had as kids? Had they any? When did the magic evaporate, and when did the real world crush the fantasy? I thought about my own childhood, how my parents were always there, how they worked so hard to protect us and give us everything we needed. How does an innocent, fun-filled kid turn into society's trash? Could that have somehow happened to me? The answer was starting to become all too apparent: Without loving, caring parents, yes, it could easily have happened to me.

Back down in the dayroom, three men sat silently in front of the TV, watching a Christmas morning re-run of the Maury Povich show. Saint Maury was trying to establish the paternity of a six-year-old child who was sitting backstage looking bewildered. The child's mother, a tearful, overweight, white woman in her early twenties, swore the child's father was the aspiring African American rapper sitting opposite her on the stage. The cameras switched between the three media victims and the vampire Povich. The child looked increasingly nervous and lost. The young man on stage called the mother a slut and a whore. The audience booed and jeered. The inmates reached a quiet Christmas morning consensus and agreed the rapper probably is the father.

The mother dissolved into tears. Povich the Benevolent flashed his fangs and put on a mock display of concern, placing a parasitical arm around the young woman. The audience let out a cheer of approval for the fake show of paternal affection. Povich withdrew his leech-like limb and made a dramatic presentation of the envelope containing the results of the child's blood test. The audience became quiet, collectively holding their breath. The mother moved around uncomfortably in her chair and bit her bottom lip. The potential father shifted the brim of his ball cap to one side, crossed his arms in front of his chest, and put on a ridiculous wannabe gangster look, snarling and bobbing his head up and down.

"He. . ." Povich the Merciful made a dramatic pause and the audience clung to his every word, ". . . is not the father."

The young man jumped up out of his chair pumping his fists and gave Maury a high-five. He yelled and pointed menacingly at the young mother. Most of what he yelled was bleeped out. Then he ran off-stage, completing his fifteen minutes of fame. The young mother slumped over and sobbed bitterly. The audience went wild. The camera flicked over to the child backstage, who heard the noise and smiled nervously. The inmates all agreed they were wrong. They all thought the rapper was the father. They switched the channel and started watching *Cops*.

At another table, two old African American men sat quietly playing Scrabble. The board was in near tatters but there were hundreds of both wooden and plastic letters. Over time the boards wear out, but the letters don't. It looked like there were enough letters on the table to rewrite the Old Testament. I wondered if the letters were reproducing at night when they were locked in the desk drawer. The two old men couldn't have been more different. One was big and fat with a bushy beard and a huge white afro. The other was small, pencil thin, and as bald as brass. The big man had no teeth and the small man had a glass eye. Both men looked up and saw me approach.

"Mornin', Mr. Reilly," they said in unison.

"Good morning and Merry Christmas to you," I responded.

They ignored the holiday greeting. I asked the small man with the glass eye if it was true that he had been fired from his job in the kitchen. He abruptly pushed his chair back from the table and glared at me with his good eye.

"What you talkin' 'bout? I ain't been fired from no job in the kitchen. Shit, that place couldn't run widout me!"

But behind the indignation was a look of confusion. After a moment he calmed down and said, "Tell me what you heard, Mr. Reilly."

"Well, I heard that you had been caught sneaking food out of the kitchen and bringing it back to the block."

Once again, the old man became agitated and vocal. "I don't know what you talkin' about. That job's too important to me to do a fool thing like that."

"Well, I heard that you have been stealing hardboiled eggs and smuggling them back to the block in your eye socket."

It took a couple of seconds for it to sink in. Then, the two men fell about laughing, slapping their own knees, and each other's shoulders.

"Now that's funny as shit," said the big man to his skinny friend.

Both men laughed raucously for a good long time. I joined in and the three of us were transported out of the prison and into Christmas for a minute. The laughter was infectious. The three guys watching TV turned to see what was so funny and also broke out into grins.

When the laughing stopped, the big man said, "Mr. Reilly, I'm glad you come over 'cause I got a question for you. My partner here says this ain't a real word."

I looked down and saw a few monosyllabic words dotting the tattered board—COPS, ASS, TITS—and the word he was pointing to, BEEF.

"Of course it's a real word," I said, "Beef. You know, it's the meat that comes from a cow."

"No, no, I know that. I'm gonna add to it, look."

After the word BEEF, I watched the big man add the letters UCKEDUP.

I looked at the word and didn't understand. "No, that's not a word. It doesn't even make sense."

The thin man with the glass eye grinned. "See, I told you so, dat ain't no real word."

The big man became defensive. I suddenly wondered if I had unknowingly been condescending.

"No look, Mr. Reilly. 'Beefuckedup.' That's a real word. Let me tell you, getting up at six o'clock in the mornin' to be counted like an animal beefuckedup. Having cell inspection every day beefuckedup. Oh, and thank you, by the way, for not doing it today."

"You're welcome," I responded.

"And being locked up in this shithole for nonpayment of child support, and not bein' able to have a cigarette on Christmas day, now that really beefuckedup. If beefuckedup ain't a real word," he said, stabbing a thick stubby finger on the board and making the pieces jump around, "I don't know what is."

7

Sergeant G

THE TWIN BROTHER OF PRISON DRAMA IS BOREDOM. AT TIMES THE
dull monotony of institutional life and the apathy-infused malaise
it created felt like it might engulf the whole facility. Some days the
entire place seemed to be cloaked by one enormous sinful cloud of
depression. During most shifts there were periods of "lock down,"
when all inmates were confined to their cells. Sometimes, these
periods lasted for hours. The staff enjoyed the break and used the
time in lots of different ways. Many slept. They called the housing
control center, let the guard on duty know they were going to have
a little nap, and asked if a supervisor approached the block to
please give them a wakeup call on the phone. Some spent the
entire time on the phone talking and gossiping with co-workers.
Some polished their boots and reflected on how good they thought
they looked in uniform, and others put on the cellblock TV and
caught up on their favorite daytime soaps and infomercials.

A few, including myself, read. This downtime created a great
game of cat-and-mouse with the princess of darkness herself, Sergeant G. The good and well-respected supervisors knew exactly
what was going on and played by the rules of, if you got caught, it

was on you, and if you got away with it, good for you. That, however, was not the case for Sergeant G. She considered the policing of staff shenanigans to be her own private crusade and made it a top priority to catch anyone slacking off. It often appeared to be more important to her than the monitoring of difficult and dangerous inmates.

Usually, the housing control guard was great about keeping lookout. Everyone rotated through housing control and it was expected of you to keep watch over your workmates, especially when it came to Sergeant G. But there were times when housing control became very busy. The enormous electronic control pads that governed every door inside the prison could become a dizzying and intimidating light show that needed your absolute attention. Inmates and staff could be entering and leaving numerous parts of the prison all at the same time. Doors had to be opened and then secured via electronic keypads. Radio requests and phone calls had to be attended to. Keys, shackles, handcuffs, and paperwork had to be handed out and logged back in, and all manner of institutional announcements had to be made over the PA. While doing all that, hallway cameras had to be monitored, intercoms had to be answered, and verbal and visual identifications had to be made. When it got busy in housing control, it was stressful. It was the prison version of air traffic control. It was during these very busy times, when the HC guard was snowed under, Sergeant G liked to strike.

January 2002. THE BRAND NEW YEAR HAD BROUGHT WITH IT A BRAND new assignment. I had been moved next door to J-Block. It was a big jump up. J-Block held prisoners with a much higher security classification. They were generally older than the inmates on I-Block and were all being locked up for much more serious crimes. In some ways, it felt like I had to start all over again. I had to get to know the inmates, let them get to know me, set a tone, create expectations, be consistent, and not get taken advantage of. Inmate TQ was the celebrity when I arrived. He was the classic nightmare prisoner, huge, hairy, surly, and antisocial. He was locked up for dismembering his mother's boyfriend with an axe. Inmate TQ was in good company. He was housed alongside other murderers, bank robbers, drug dealers, and members of the KKK. The best part about working on J-Block was that the inmates had a lot less free time. The block was kept locked down a lot more than their I-Block neighbors.

During one of these all-afternoon lockdowns, while the radio chattered away with the humdrum activity of everyday prison life. I leaned back in the chair with my feet on the desk reading *Tess of the d'Urbervilles*, and in the muted silence of the cellblock, I found myself thoroughly enjoying every page of it. I'm not sure why, perhaps I felt an evil presence, but I looked over my shoulder and there standing in the sally port, staring at me through the window was the bride of Nosferatu herself. The grimacing face of Sergeant G was glaring at me through the bulletproof glass. How she managed to get from the hallway and into the sally port without me hearing was a supernatural act beyond human understanding. I pulled my legs down from the desk, jerked into a sitting position, and stuffed my book into a thin space between the underside of the desk and the top of the block's filling cabinet. Sergeant G keyed the door and strode into the dayroom with a certain Hermann Göring strut to her step. She looked delighted with herself, like a cat that'd just caught its abusive owner's favorite pet canary.

"Have you been reading, Reilly?"

Do I lie, did she see me, and how long had she been there?

"Yes, Sergeant G, I have been reading. Thomas Hardy's *Tess of the d'Urbervilles*, actually. Have you read it? It's fantastic!"

She gave me a withering look, but didn't respond. She walked around the desk and said, "Excuse me?"

I stood up from the chair. She walked in front of me, kneeled down, and thrust her right arm up into the hiding place between the filing cabinet and the desk and pulled out poor old Thomas Hardy. Then, she went in for another try. While she was down on her knees, rooting around in the dusty recesses of the cellblock, I glanced up and saw one of the inmates standing at his door looking through the window. He pointed down to the floor and mouthed, "Sergeant G?"

I nodded and mouthed back, "Yes."

He rolled his eyes, put a finger pistol to his head, and pulled the trigger. Yes, I nodded back in agreement.

"Oh, look, what we have here?" Sergeant G said with a gloating tone in her voice.

Oh no. . . . Out came a *Hustler* magazine.

"Now wait a minute, the novel is mine but I'm not responsible for the *Hustler* magazine."

She refused to respond, stood up, dusted off her knees, turned, and then walked away. As she went through the door and back into the sally port she said, "Come to my office on your break."

On my coffee break, I went down to her office and received my write-up. Sergeant G took great pleasure in telling me reading was absolutely forbidden, and that this write-up was going to be a permanent part of my personnel file. She asked me if I had anything to say.

I responded, "Yes, I was reading the Thomas Hardy novel, but the porno magazine was not mine."

She smiled like she'd just been caught farting in church, which meant she didn't believe me. Then, I asked, "If the block is on a multi-hour lock down and I'm on duty why can't I read?"

She seemed a little surprised by the question, and replied, "Because that's what the SOP says."

I left her office with a copy of the write up in my hand, returned to the block, promptly tore it to pieces, dropped it down the staff toilet, urinated on it, and then ceremoniously flushed the shredded written reprimand down the pipe.

8

Cars in the Distance

February 2002

"WHAT ARE YOU LISTENING TO?" I ASKED INMATE B, A TALL, SKINNY, scruffy looking white prisoner with long matted blond hair and a matching bird's nest beard. I'd been told inmate B was a member of a motorcycle gang and was in prison for cooking and selling crystal meth, but I didn't know if that was the truth.

"All those cars in the distance, and I ain't in any of 'em."

The inmate was staring through the fence, past me and down across the brown lifeless fields toward the road. The icy wind passing through the high chain-link fence let out a long-suffering sigh. During strong gusts, its plaintive unbinding voice whistled eerily as it rushed over a million coils of razor ribbon. The shotgun slung over my shoulder was so cold I didn't want to touch it. It hung passively across my back, like I used to carry my guitar. It was so cold. I highly doubted anyone would be making any attempts to escape.

Some guards loved to talk about being out on perimeter duty during an escape attempt.

"Shooting an escapee would be awesome," one guy told me.

A couple of years earlier, the warden, in a shortsighted attempt to save money, had one guard overseeing two yards at once. While the guard was busy getting distracted in yard #1, an inmate in yard #2 climbed the rec-yard fence, crossed the inner perimeter, scaled the second, much higher fence, and then evaporated.

I told the co-worker who was living for the day he could shoot another human being, "It's a good job you like the prison food, because if you shoot an unarmed inmate you'll be thrown into prison yourself."

My associate did like the food but didn't like the joke. He said, "Why have guns if they don't want us to shoot escapees?"

I told him, "In my opinion, the guns are only deterrents. There are certainly high-security prisoners here, but there are also people in for the weekend that didn't pay their parking tickets. If you shoot the wrong, unarmed inmate, during the legal maelstrom that follows, the warden will pull a full Pontius Pilate, wash his hands of you, embrace all the more endearing elements of human sacrifice, and feed you to the lawyers. Even lousy lawyers are smarter than the warden, everyone knows that."

It was too cold to shoot anyone anyway, and my gloves were so thick I couldn't have put my finger through the trigger guard even if I wanted to. I hoped Sergeant G wasn't watching me through binoculars and taking notes about my overly insulated, unprofessional gloves.

A red-tail hawk cut across the blank blue sky above me and hovered over the yard. It saw me, of course, but I was not what its sharp eyes were looking for. This giant human holding tank was hell on Earth to some men but a sanctuary for birds. They lived and nested by the hundreds in its countless undisturbed nooks and crannies. While I was watching the hawk, I had an idea. It was such a good idea, I thought perhaps I should go and talk to the warden about it. Maybe even the prison board. In my mind's eye, I saw a sign. The Audubon Society and an extreme right-wing political group could go in on it together. They could erect a billboard at the side of the road, right below the prison. It would read: PENN-SYLVANIA'S BIGGEST OPEN AIR AVIARY, BOUGHT AND PAID FOR BY

THE WAGES OF SIN. If they gave tours to neo-conservative ornitholo-gists, it might be a nice little moneymaker. Yes, I thought, I'll go and talk to the warden about it on my lunch break. It might be a nice way to finally meet him.

Meanwhile, the few brave souls who had come out to the yard were playing some kind of free throw/winner-stays-on basketball game. The half court was being dominated by one player.

There were less than five minutes to go before the end of rec. I was frozen and dying for a pee and a hot cup of coffee. The ath-letic inmate L, the undisputed three-point king of the hill, bounced the ball rhythmically from his left hand to his right. He never once looked down. He stared out into the distance, hypno-tized by the hoop, his face passive, almost sad-looking. His side-kick, a worn-down strip of an African American man in his indiscernible sixties, gaunt and grim-looking, toothless and yel-lowy eyed, stood by the cellblock door, talking loudly and carrying on comically. The sidekick could say almost anything he wanted on account of being inmate L's cellie and being an "old head."

The clock was ticking. Any moment now the two ass-freezing hours of rec would be up, and the door to the warm cellblock would click open. Inmate L pulled the white towel he was wearing as a hat from his head. Steam rose from his neck, face, and shin-ing, bald black head.

The sidekick yelled down from the steps. "C'mon, brother, you can do it. Do it for Sidney Poitier. C'mon, Sidney, you got it."

The ball stopped bouncing. Inmate L lifted it up and flicked it off the end of his fingers. It traveled smoothly through the air and dropped through the hoop.

"Sidney Poitier. Oh, yeah, Sidney Poitier, you are the man," the sidekick yelled out.

A young runner returned the ball to inmate L.

The shot was a great one and not unnoticed by all, but L always made great shots. Again inmate L stood with his broad shoulders two feet from the back fence, eyeing up the hoop, unemotionally.

"This time do it for Muhammad Ali," called out the sidekick. "Knock 'em out. You can do it, Ali. Float like a butterfly, sting like a bee."

Again the ball was hoisted aloft. It moved through the cold air and dropped through the hoop. Nothing but net.

"Oh, you the greatest, Ali. You the greatest. Oh, how the mighty have fallen. You got 'em on the ropes now."

The sidekick put up his fists and hopped hilariously from one foot to another in absolute delight. Now, everyone was looking. Inmate L was center stage.

"That's why we call him the 'king of the hill,'" the sidekick cackled.

Except for the wind and the hard, rubberized, echoing sound of the ball bouncing on the rock-hard blacktop, the yard was silent.

"The brother got game for real," whispered an admirer.

"Hush the hell up," hissed the sidekick.

Some eyes glance nervously toward the cellblock door, hoping it won't pop open and break the spell. Inmate L didn't move. He bounced the ball hard and fast between his feet, his head steaming like a race horse. The sidekick stepped forward, sensing something great.

"Now, c'mon, do it for Dr. J. I got your back, my brother; it's going in. C'mon, Dr. J."

The yard went completely still, all movement stopped, even the wind lightened up. I stepped up to the fence and poked my gloved fingers through the chain links. Inmate L seemed unaware of the audience and the silence.

"C'mon, Dr. J, you got it," whispered the sidekick.

L went for it again. For the umpteenth time, the ball became airborne. It floated off the end of inmate L's fingers. His chin rose, his knees bent a little as his sharp eyes followed the orange orb through the air. Whoosh, the ball dropped through the ring as if guided by God.

"Who's the king? Who's the king? You da man, Dr. J. Oh yeah, you da man. The doctor is in the house."

A loud cheer erupted from the audience. Clapping and whistling filled the air. Inmate L had the ball, oblivious to the surrounding racket. He was going for it again. The cellblock door was going to open any second. Why was it taking so long? Everyone became quiet.

Inmate L never turned to acknowledge his companions. His

facial expression never changed. He seemed immune to the cold and the pressure and the collective desire surrounding him to make one more great shot before the end of rec.

"OK, now, do it for Jesse Jackson. C'mon man, do it for Reverend Jesse. C'mon, baby, you got it."

The ball bounced twice, sailed through the air in a perfect arc, hit the backboard, and dropped through the hoop.

"Thy will be done on Earth as it is in heaven. Reverend Jesse Jackson, you are a great black American!"

The sidekick exploded. Everyone cheered wildly, including me. I was no longer a guard. The gun and the uniform had gone. The fence had come down. We were all clapping and cheering for the same hero, someone who was doing something we all wished we could do. During the clapping and cheering, the ball had rolled into no-man's land. A thick yellow line ran around the inside of the yard. The line was about two feet from the fence. Inmates were not allowed over the line. Inmates were not allowed to touch the fence. Inmate L looked at the ball and then looked at me. We stared at each other. The ball was no more than two feet from my boots. Inmate L crossed the line, picked up the ball, and casually walked back to the far end of the yard, coolly bouncing the "pill" in a slow dribble. My radio crackled. The rec yard door was going to open any second. The sidekick held up both his hands to signal for quiet. The gesture was pure drama: Silence reigned.

"Here we go now. I can hear Colin Powell knocking on the door of the White House. You can do it, General Powell. You can be the first black president if you want to. There ain't gonna be no more White House when you get up in there. It gonna be the Black House."

The sidekick was working himself into a Pentecostal frenzy. Inmate L moved from one foot to another. The ball drummed up and down. We all held our breath. Inmate Paula, an overtly feminine, openly gay inmate, covered her eyes. And speaking in an affected false Southern accent, she said, "Tell me when it's over. I just can't bear to watch it anymore."

Someone handed her a sweatshirt and she buried her face in it. Inmate L made his move. The ball bounced one last time and then was propelled through the air. It hung in the sky for an age against an infinite backdrop of blue. The wind seemed to stop completely.

The still air stole our collective breath and all but inmate Paula, who had her face buried in the sweatshirt, watched the bomb drop.

In those two seconds, the sidekick became a statue. Pre-execution tension stopped time and tormented the crowd. The ball hit the backboard, rolled all the way around the right side of the rim, and dropped to the ground in the negative.

The silence deepened into a gulf. I found myself holding my gloved hands against my face. The sidekick stepped forward, pointing a pious, accusatory finger at inmate L, and yelled out angrily, "Nigger, get your black ass back to the plantation."

Hysterical laughter erupted from the mainly African American inmate audience. The heavy steel door buzzed loudly and popped open.

Most of the men, laughing and talking, surged into the warm cellblock. Waves of heat wafted out of the building and into the freezing air, distorting the gray wall next to the door, making it ripple and shimmer. Inmate Paula was crying. The sidekick placed an arm around inmate L's shoulders and slowly shook his head. Before the door slammed shut, inmate L looked back at me and silently mouthed, "Thank you." I held up my right arm with my open palm facing inmate L and clenched my hand into a fist.

"That was great," I called through the fence.

Inmate L nodded, looking sad and lost. He turned his back and disappeared into the dark cellblock as the steel door slammed heavily behind him.

9

The Warden
Vs. The Union

INMATES AND CO-WORKERS WERE NOT THE ONLY THINGS I HAD TO
learn about. There was the ever-present Machiavellian power struggle between the warden and the Teamsters Union. At first, I was
very wary of the union. All of its militant chest-pounding and angry
rhetoric turned me right off, so I didn't become a full member. I sat
on the fence, made the minimum compulsory commitment, and
became a "fair share" member. This meant I had all my union benefits, but could not vote or get union representation if I got in trouble. I received a lot of flak from some of my co-workers for this. I
was, however, adamant that I wasn't going to do anything to get
myself in the kind of trouble that needed union representation.

It seemed to me that the staff who continually needing to be
bailed out didn't deserve to have a job anyway. Some people called
in sick at least once or twice a week, *every* week. Others were
arrested for drunk driving. One guard was being "investigated"
because a female prisoner under his supervision somehow became
pregnant, and it definitely wasn't an immaculate conception. A

very strange bird on third shift was "allegedly" having sex with a mentally ill inmate while the rest of the prison slept. According to gossip, other guards let inmates out at night to fight each other. Some of the staff were so out of shape they were basically incapable of performing the job safely. On one hilarious occasion, three guards went golfing instead of attending mandatory staff training. The peanut butter hit the pantry fan, the union and the administration locked horns, got their handcuffs in a helix and "golfergate" became a big deal that dragged on and on month after month. It appeared to me as though the union spent most of its time keeping useless people employed instead of holding them accountable. However, I quickly started to understand that if it wasn't for the union's overly sensitive watchdog attitude, the warden would without a doubt go unchecked.

Without the constant threat of Teamsters' legal action, the warden would whittle down wages and benefits, fire at will anyone who didn't suck up to him, and quickly transform himself from a local bottom-feeder bureaucrat into a full-blown tin-pot dictator. A very well-liked and respected shift commander had seen the warden in a department store in town one day and said hello Mr. ----, using the warden's last name. On his next day back at work, the supervisor was called into the chief deputy's office and told by a rather embarrassed chief that he had been informed by his highness the warden that if he was seen in public by any of "his staff," he was to be addressed as either warden or sir. On another similar occasion, a rather combative union rep, who was also a guard, addressed the warden by his first name during a contract negotiation. That didn't go down well; he was disciplined for insubordination.

The first time I actually met the warden was in the staffroom. It was February 2002. He walked into a conversation regarding the earth-shattering subject of outdoor decking. The warden joined the discussion and interjected just how much he liked the plastic imitation-wood decking that was new to the market. He started raving about how weather-resistant it was and how he loved its non-slip textured finish. I innocently offered up that my next-door neighbor had that type of decking. He'd told me that, after a couple of years, it started to fade and warp and didn't actually wear nearly as well as good old-fashioned wood. It was something to do with the way the heat and humidity affected the plastic. The warden reddened slightly and then turned on me angrily, his tone of voice aggressive, and in no uncertain terms, I was told that my neighbor and I were absolutely wrong. Plastic imitation-wood decking was the only way to go, and that was all there was to it. In that moment, with the warden's look and language over a subject as all-important as decking material, I knew all I needed to know about what kind of man he was. The funny thing is, I don't think he believed what he was saying. My sense was that it was more about sounding off and being right in front of the other staff, having the last word, and being seen as the big boss man.

There were other signs of his petulant power-tripping attitude. In fact, it was boldly on display in a Pennsylvania city newspaper article. The union had said no to what was on offer in some contract negotiation. The warden was quoted as saying, "I think they should grow up and sign the damn thing."

Another hilarious incident involving a female guard getting fired for appearing in *Playboy Magazine* had the warden and the union exchanging blows. This made-for-TV story had the warden under siege from numerous media outlets, who all wanted to discover the true identity of the young woman in the photos and find out if she was she going to get her job back. The warden refused to comment. Probably because he was embarrassed, not because of the female guard's photographs, but because he didn't want it to come out that he allowed inmates to receive *Playboy* in the mail, something leading prison administrators and best practice proponents were against. In the end, the union rolled over the warden, and the guard got her job reinstated, less back pay.

10

From Robber
to Murderer

THE LONGER I SPENT INSIDE THE PRISON, THE MORE I KEPT ASKING myself, am I really that different from some of these guys? Most of the time, what was happening around me was so fascinating, I didn't even feel like I was at work. It felt more like I was a paid participant in some sort of insane science project. I thought about being young and unsupervised, and how poor decisions and bad situations can go from dangerous to disastrous in the blink of an eye.

In March 2002, I was talking to an inmate who was waiting to go to trial on a murder charge. He wasn't the kind of guy you'd have housesit, but he also didn't fit the homicidal-maniac profile either. He told me, with great and genuine regret, how he'd been doing robberies to pay for his drug habit and carrying a handgun for protection.

"Some girls really get turned on if they know you carry a gun, and most dudes are afraid of you."

He told me how a robbery had gone terribly wrong when the victim refused to hand over his wallet.

"I pulled the gun out and was pointing it at him, we were screaming at each other, then next thing you know, the gun went off and the dude's dead. All I was doing was waving it around."

What the inmate told me made my mind spin. Could that have been me? Could I have done something so stupid and life-changing? I tried to think of something in my own safe, little middle-class experience where the result could have been twenty years to life.

It was easy enough to find something that would fit the bill. Once on a camping trip, I got into a big argument with a guy about something so stupid I can't even remember what it was. The stupidity was compounded by beer drinking and the guy insulting and threatening me. I didn't think; I lost it and lashed out. I punched him in the face. He fell backward and hit his head on a rock. He lay still, out cold and unconscious, not from the punch but from the rock he'd hit. A group of his friends came toward me, and I took off running. It wasn't a gun and I wasn't a tough street kid, but I was an eighteen-year-old adult, and I was guilty of assault. What if that guy had fallen and hit his head so hard he died? Accidents like that happen all the time. My father often told a story about a man he knew who locked himself out his house. While climbing in through his first-floor window, he slipped, fell backward three or four feet, banged his head, and died. If the guy I'd punched had died, in the eyes of the law, I'd be guilty of manslaughter at best, or murder at worst. That can get you twenty years in prison. Wow, because of one act of sheer stupidity, it really could be me in here.

So, THE MORE I THOUGHT ABOUT HOW VERY LUCKY I WAS, AND THE more Sarah and I waited anxiously for the arrival of baby number three, the more I started to think about where we lived, what surrounded us, and what as parents we were going to offer our children as they grew up. As these thoughts sped through my mind with alarming regularity, at work, I often found myself thinking about the inmates as kids and wondered about their own dark journeys and what sad series of events had led them into the same place as myself, albeit on a different side of the bars.

Not long after I started working on J-Block, I started having the same terrible dream over and over again. I dreamed that I had fallen asleep on the job, a firing offense. I awoke with a start, heart pounding, sweaty and unsure of how long my eyes had been shut. It was the same pre-panic jolt you have when you realize you've involuntarily nodded off while driving. As my vision quickly cleared, I realized something dreadful had happened. While I was asleep, all the inmates had turned into children. The kids looked like any multiracial group of six- to ten-year-olds. They were all running around the place, screaming and laughing, all dressed in their child-size baggy prison blues. Some were watching TV. Some were playing board games. Some waited impatiently in line for the rec yard door to open, and others stood around laughing and talking.

In a shadowy corner at the back of the block, I saw two adults in armchairs. They were having a heated discussion. In the dream I was always startled and would think, *What are they doing? They don't belong here.* So I would get up from the desk and walk across the dayroom to see what was going on. But something was wrong. The cellblock floor was not flat, but somehow on a steep slope. As I walked toward the two adults, I felt like I was heading down a hill, almost sliding out of control. The kids were completely unaware of me moving amongst them. As I got closer to the two adults, I noticed that they were both tall and athletic-looking. They wore almost identical gray suits. The only thing different about them was their faces. One of the men looked positively pompous. His thick, oily hair was swept back, and there was a greedy arrogance in the way his eyes fluttered and his jowly mouth moved when he talked. The other was handsome in an unpretentious way, kind and approachable-looking, and had a soft, unassuming smile. His hair was thick, brown, and uncombed, very casual.

To my absolute horror, I suddenly realized it was the devil and an archangel. The devil gave me a condescending look as I approached. He sneered and then turned back to the angel, dismissing my presence. The angel was now facing me. He looked up at me and smiled briefly without getting distracted from the conversation. I couldn't get any closer. I was suddenly too busy holding on to nothing, desperately trying not to slip into the unknown. I could only hear fractured pieces of their conversation. The two visitors were talking about the children, pointing to this one and that one. A child ran past them. The devil smiled and patted him on the head.

The angel said, "No, you can't have him."

I would always wake up sweating and gasping for air. Sometimes, I woke up yelling. I would look at the clock on my night stand. Most of the time, I'd only been asleep for an hour or so.

11

F-Block

F-BLOCK WAS THE ONLY FEMALE HOUSING BLOCK IN THE PRISON. During the training course, there was no extra time allotted to prepare us for the things we might encounter there. The block contained well over a hundred women, many of whom where serving sentences for terrible crimes.

In April 2002, after working at the prison for eight months, I did my first full shift on F-Block. It was quite an eye opener. It smelled a lot better than the men's blocks. There was a lot of institutional soap and shampoo scent in the air. It was a lot cleaner, too. The laundry room was a lot tidier, and the block felt warmer somehow. There was also an air of organization, especially in the janitor's closets and the laundry room, as if the work was being done by people who cared or knew how to do it properly. There were a lot more books and magazines on the cellblock bookshelf. The floor was clean, and the block looked brighter, like they had higher-wattage bulbs in the lights. It was also much louder and had a much busier feeling than the men's blocks. Apart from having three guards working there instead of just one, there was something else, too; it took me a while before I got it. There was much more physical interaction on F-Block. Some women walked around holding hands, some arm in arm. As I looked around, half a dozen pairs were brushing, combing, braiding, and weaving each other's hair. Backs and necks were being rubbed. Fingernails were being clipped and manicured. Those watching TV were leaning affectionately on each other. There was none of this openly tactile behavior on any of the men's blocks. It was a magnified version of what happens on the outside. Broadly speaking, I think it was a warped way of proving that Western women are much more comfortable being openly affectionate with each other than Western men. And because of this, the female inmates seemed to be socially miles ahead of their male counterparts. The first female inmate I got to talk to made me laugh out loud. After exchanging a few ice-breaking pleasantries, I asked her what she was in prison for. She said, "I got propositioned for sex, handed forty bucks, then cuffed up. I said honey, that's gonna cost you extra."

But right below the seemingly civilized veneer, F-Block had plenty of horror. The lack of almost any kind of female dysfunction in my family made the inmates of F-Block far worse for me than they might be for others. Sure, my family had a few modest moments of female madness, almost exclusively from my maternal grandmother, like the time she burst in on my sister, Kathryn, and cousin, Ros, stark naked and shouted, "This is what it all comes to!" Or the time, right after she'd had a stroke, my parents, my sister, and I all went to the hospital to see her. We arrived just as they were serving dinner. The meal was a culinary masterpiece and the perfect thing for a stroke patient with false teeth, bangers and mash, two huge pork sausages and a pile of potatoes, big and lumpy enough to intimidate a crowd of energetic Sherpas. Anyway, the nurse placed the meal on the bedside table and then rolled it into position. My mother fluffed up a couple of pillows and tried to get Gran prepared to make a tactical assault on the sausages. We all watched in uncomfortable silence as Gran picked up a fork with her one good hand, stabbed one of the sausages, hoisted it with some difficulty above her head and yelled at the nurse, "You call that a penis? My husband had one twice the size of that." My extremely conservative father left the room abruptly. My mom went beetroot red and said, "Oh, Mother!" It was a good job we were at the hospital because my sister and I nearly died laughing. The nurse must have been thinking, *Well, now I've heard everything.* But then Gran knocked over the cup of tea on her tray and yelled out after my father, "Oh, and by the way, the tea in here tastes like piss."

But, generally speaking, the women in my family were and are wonderfully kind, caring, loving people. Because I'd grown up surrounded by women who were all pretty normal, I had no frame of reference when it came to dealing with women who were murderers, prostitutes, and drug addicts, not to mention child abusers, bank robbers, and arsonists. I couldn't start to comprehend what would possess a woman to kill her baby by packing its mouth full of salt or how a person could be so far gone on drugs she'd end up giving birth alone in a cheap motel, call 911, and be shooting up with the newborn laying on the bed, still attached by the umbilical cord when the cops arrived.

What do you say to the woman you have to escort to a medical appointment when you know she paid her adult son to chop up her boyfriend with an axe? The very same son I had been watching over on J-Block. And then if that wasn't bad enough, you and the mother pass the son in the hallway, cuffed and shackled on his way to his court hearing.

It was difficult to see a fight between two women that was as vicious and violent as any fight I'd ever seen between two men. But, at times, there were also flashes of humor, tenderness, and uncommon caring.

Once, while I was doing a round at count time, making sure everyone was present, I stopped at one cell to check a face against an ID. The prisoner was an older black lady. She could have been fifty or sixty-five—it was impossible to tell. She was big, heavy-set, and she smiled broadly and warmly at me as I stopped in front of her. Something didn't look quite right. I quickly realized it was her ID. The woman's hair had gone completely white since she'd been in prison. On her ID she had black hair and an exhausted, deeply sorrowful expression on her drug-ravaged face. The photograph and the woman I stood in front of looked like two completely different people. She looked at me and knew exactly what I was thinking. Going to prison had saved her life. Apart from the white hair, she now looked twenty years younger and forty pounds healthier. As I reach for the door handle, silently letting her know it was time to lock in. Slowly, she raised her hands toward my neck. I took a half step back. "Now wait a second," she said softly. Then, she took my collar in her big fingers, flattened it down, picked a piece of gray lint off my shoulder, showed it to me, and then flicked it to the floor like it was a dead bug. She followed that by brushing off both my shoulders with her huge hands. I didn't move. I just stared deeply into her eyes, and she stared deeply into mine while she "fixed" my uniform. "Mmm-mmm, now, that looks a whole lot better."

Her voice was so soft and maternal-sounding, and just for a moment, she wasn't a prisoner: She was a mother, a grandmother, someone of great feeling, someone trapped at the bottom of deep channel, flooded with desperate, unspeakable emotion.

LATER THAT YEAR, ON AN F-UNIT OVERTIME SHIFT, I WAS SUPERVISING an all-Hispanic work crew tasked with mopping the cellblock floor. One of the inmates asked me if it was possible to get a new mop because the one they had was filthy and falling to pieces. So, I went to the storage closet and got the crew a new mop head. The cleaners were delighted and made a big deal about the new equipment. I was amazed that the four women could place so much value on something so mundane. As the new head was attached to the handle, a barely containable excitement flowed between the women. While detergent and hot water filled the bucket, I said to the inmate holding the new mop, "Are you much of a dancer?"

"What'choo talkin' about, Mr. Reilly?"

"Why don't you turn that thing over and give it a whirl before it gets wet."

Puzzled but willing, the curious inmate turned the mop over. The new brilliant white cotton tassels fell on either side of the head and the handle. The inmate got it in a second and before anyone could say another thing, the mop and the inmate were in a passionate embrace, waltzing around the imaginary ballroom. The other women loved it. They cheered and clapped as the mop and the inmate charged clumsily around. As she danced, she called out to me over her shoulder, "Mr. Reilly, if you let me do this every night, I gonna lose some weight."

One of the other women jumped in and said, "Baby, you better keep on dancin', cause you lost at least a hundred pounds since you been up in this joint. Only problem is, it's the same ten pounds over and over again."

"Oh, shut up," said the dancer. "You just jealous coz I got a date with the only good-looking blond in the whole place."

One memorable morning, there was a lot of whispering and gossiping going on among the F-Unit staff. I asked around and soon found out what had happened. It was both hysterical and heartbreaking at the same time. The gossip concerned a husband and wife who were both third-shift guards. The wife had been away to visit friends or family and left the husband home alone. While she was out of town, the husband decided to have a little fun. He'd gone downtown and picked up a hooker, then taken her home for a barbecue and a game of Twister. A day or two later, the hooker had been arrested and thrown into prison. Imagine the surprise on the face of the guard when he found himself looking at his new, best, intimate friend after being assigned to work nightshift on F-Unit.

The hooker quickly realized through inmate gossip that her customer's wife was also a guard working the nightshift. She quickly made her move. When the guard made his next round, she told him, if he didn't pay up, she was going to tell his wife. He told her to stop being so silly or something along those lines, maybe not worded quite as nicely. It didn't take long for the wife to hear about the threatening hooker and decide to go and see what all the fuss was about. The wife didn't believe a word the hooker said until she described the inside of her house, down to the kind of curtains hanging in the bedroom and the exact type of toiletries she kept next to her sink.

This incident caused a lot of trouble and embarrassment for the couple, and I don't know what happened to their relationship. I do know the female inmate was quickly transferred to another prison on the western side of the state. I know this because a female member of staff and I were given the job of taking her there. Outside of the obvious stupidity of the incident, I started to wonder about if, where, and when the two worlds of prison and civilian life might cross or overlap for me. It felt like prison was a virulent disease and one way or another, if I gave it enough time, there was a good chance I would become infected.

1 2

The Naughty Table

ONE WAY OR ANOTHER, LIFE IS ALL ABOUT FIGHTING, BUT NOT everyone can fight or has the stomach for it. If everyone stuck up for themselves and had allies on hand to call in when the going gets rough, bullies wouldn't exist. But they do and they are everywhere, torturing others through a thinly veiled attempt to cover over some sort of torment visited on them by other bullies before. At its worst, once a bully has laid the groundwork, he or she can let off the persecution pedal, float phantom-like into the backseat, and let you do all the driving. The bully no longer needs to harm you, as your self-esteem reaches an all-time low, you'll be beating yourself up so badly, you'll be left with only two choices, either run away to get bullied elsewhere or knuckle up and fight back.

The prison was full of bullies. The warden seemed like a bully to me, some of the guards and inmates were bullies, and Sergeant G seemed like the saddest little bully of them all.

My first real bullying experience was at the hands of my first grade teacher, a man called Mr. Wheeler. I remember him extremely well. He was very young and had recently started teaching. Our class may even have been his first. He was tall, thin, and very quiet. I can never remember him yelling or threatening. He was calm, cold, and uncaring. In retrospect, he always seemed strangely detached. Wheeler had a "naughty table," and I sat there a lot. I was very young, six or seven. I remember being placed at the naughty table for flunking tests, talking or laughing in class, being late for lineup, and not knowing answers to quiz questions when called upon.

I did not do well in school. I was a poor student and a flop as an athlete. For the most part, I existed in a spacey world of my own imagining, a world that floated somewhere between fantasy and the occasional sobering dose of reality. My parents were desperately disappointed by my lack of academic ability. My miserable end-of-term reports made my mother sad and my father absolutely furious. I had special education testing at various points throughout grade school, but nothing conclusive was ever discovered. One teacher told my mother, "There's nothing wrong with him. He's just flat-out lazy."

I desperately wanted to do well, but trying to be successful in the classroom always felt like putting together a picture with the pieces from seven different jigsaw puzzles. On the outside, I just laughed it all off and pretended I didn't care, but on the inside, being a failure in school made me feel stupid and awfully lonely.

About once a week, Wheeler would call the class to attention and then tell the kids at the naughty table to get up and stand by his desk. In a quiet, calm voice, he would inform our classmates of the details of our latest failures and infractions. The other children thought this was great and loved the kangaroo court atmosphere.

Wheeler would then request the nearest child to him to bring their ruler up to his desk. The rulers were the twelve-inch, indestructible, wooden jobs handed out to each student at the beginning of the school year. In turn, Wheeler would then hold the wrist of each "naughty" child down onto the top of his desk with the flat of their palm facing up and then give their hand a good hard *whack!* All this was done with a great deal of deliberate showmanship. The audience loved it! Then, methodically, Wheeler would ask each child, one after the other, to bring his or her ruler up to his desk and hand it to him. The process was repeated over and over and over until we'd been hit with every classmate's ruler. This cruel corporal punishment happened countless times, to me and others. I always tried to hold out as long as I could. I didn't want to cry in front of my friends. But I could never make it more than six or seven whacks before dissolving into a blubbering puddle of tears and snot. All the while, Wheeler would be bearing down on my wrist, holding my palm skyward until I had been struck with every single student's ruler. I remember hanging like a ragdoll off the side off his desk, one arm dangling, feet thrashing, tears and mucus streaming down my face, just waiting for it all to be over. Afterward, usually for the rest of the day, my fingers always felt like overcooked sausages, swollen and ready to split open. In the wake of one of these bullying sessions, myself and another boy, who had just shared the same punishment, got in big trouble with Wheeler for having terrible handwriting and not holding our pencils properly.

The first-grade highlight of the week was Thursday morning swimming lessons. The whole class would get on a bus and go to Blackfriars swimming baths. It was an old Victorian public pool on its last legs. The entire place was tiled from ceiling to floor. The changing rooms were two levels of curtained cubicles around the edge of the pool, girls on one side and boys on the other. The water was always freezing, but I loved it. There was something about being in the pool that made me feel free and in a sort of dream state. For a very short period of time, probably only a few weeks, I was the only kid in the class that could swim a width of the pool under water. On one occasion, at the instructor's request, I performed this exercise for the class. I remember being absolutely thrilled, that for once, I was the center of attention for being good at something. As I pulled myself silently through the cool blue-green liquid, black and white tiles blurred below me, lungs threatened to rupture, hands and feet pulled, kicking and reaching out for the smooth wall and the trough that ran around the inside of the pool. I broke the surface of the water, gasping. The class, led by the instructor, cheered and clapped. But the first thing I saw was Wheeler. He was stood directly in front of the spot where I'd surfaced, his cruel arms crossed in front of his thin bony chest, his long unreadable face wearing a sick, tight-lipped smile. He was shaking his head ever so slightly and staring down at me in disgust. I looked at the cheering class and then back to the wicked Mr. Wheeler. I glanced into the trough, and directly in front of me, floating an inch from my nose was a gift left by some other swimmer, a large, brown, water-logged turd. And that was exactly how Wheeler made me feel about myself.

When the spirit moved him, Wheeler would walk over to me first thing on Thursday morning and whisper quietly to me, "No swimming for you today, Reilly."

I would rather have had the rulers than miss swimming. On one occasion I was so upset about not going to the pool, I told my mother and she came into school the next day and talked to Wheeler. He was as sweet as could be and told my mother everything she wanted to hear and assured her I would not be missing any more swimming lessons. Then, after she left, Wheeler walked me back to the class, told me to sit at the naughty table, and then informed me and the rest of the children, "Reilly will not be swimming again next week. And the more he tells his mother about what I decide to do, the less he will go swimming."

I never complained to my mother again.

During my teens I read and loved the book *How Green Was My Valley* by Richard Llewellyn. My favorite scene was when protagonist Huw Morgan's uncle comes into class and knocks out the bullying teacher who had been making his nephew's life a misery. I read this part of the book over and over again and flashed back and fantasized about my father coming into school and smashing Wheeler in the face.

Years later, on a camping trip, I met a teacher who worked at a school in the same district of Manchester I was raised in. At one point, the Wheeler stories came out. The guy stopped me midsentence, put his hand on my arm, and said, "No way! I went to teacher training college with that guy. I knew him! After graduation, I remember we were all amazed that he even got hired. Everyone knew the guy was some sort of weirdo. He should never have been in charge of children, ever. I am so sorry."

IN APRIL 2002, AFTER BEING AWAY ON VACATION FOR A WEEK, Sergeant G. was back. She strutted dutifully into the roll-call room at 5:45 a.m., with her clipboard tucked under her arm like a riding crop and a touch of the Gestapo in her step. The quiet chatter that filled the room turned to whispers and then silence. Someone behind me said, "Heads up, boys, the Bitch is back."

The room was full of bleary-eyed, hard-faced men and a few even harder-faced women. There was little they hadn't seen and even less that could surprise them. With the exception of perhaps me, the everyday drama of prison life was no longer a surprise to a single person present. However, what was a constant surprise was Sergeant G's ability to be a small-minded, overly officious, warden-worshiping micromanager. The things she came up with resided in the realms of the ridiculous. There wasn't a week that would go by without her pulling something completely nuts out of her hat.

It seemed to me that her moods all depended on just how much she wanted to impress the chief deputy or the warden himself. I always got the impression the chief deputy was a little embarrassed by it all, but the warden was another story: He loved it! Sergeant G was often spotted fawning all over him, yes-sirring and no-sirring him, and acting like a giddy cheerleader chatting up the starting quarterback.

Because it was Sergeant G's first day back from vacation, she wanted to get things going with a real bang. So, after reading out the morning assignments and a mouthful of monumentally boring "important memos from the warden," she announced with a Cheshire-cat grin that she had decided to have an on-the-spot uniform inspection. A series of low groans filled the air.

The entire shift got up, stood in line, and slowly filed past her as she sat at the front table casting her hawkish eyes over each and every guard's uniform. At least every third or fourth person had something wrong: a nametag wasn't on straight, no nametag, one guy had the wrong nametag on and couldn't explain why or where he got it, a shirt was untucked, a duty belt was too loose, and an undershirt was gray instead of black. She was doing great, building up enough speed to move in for the kill. Sergeant V, who was also at the roll call sat behind her with his head in his hands looking embarrassed and ashamed. Officer C stepped in front of her. She looked him up and down and then let out an overly dramatic sigh.

"Your boots, Officer C. What do you have to say about your boots?"

Officer C was a good reliable guy who took his job seriously, including his uniform. He had been in the army and was particularly fastidious about his appearance. His boots were always so shiny you could see your face in them. Today they were uncharacteristically scuffed and muddy. Officer C looked down at his boots.

"I stopped to help a guy push his car off the road and onto the breakdown lane on the way to work."

True or not, it wasn't good enough for Sergeant G.

"Those boots are unacceptable. I'm writing you up for failure of uniform inspection. Come to my office on your break to sign the paperwork."

She smiled a Wicked Witch of the East smile and rushed the rest of the shift through inspection and out the door. She was back and wanted to let everyone know it. And judging by the look on her face, she was delighted with how she'd started the day.

From 5:45 a.m. to 2:30 p.m., Sergeant G charged around the inside of the prison like a rabid pit bull chasing its own tail and barking madly at imaginary monsters. No task was too minute or mundane; no staff member was beyond reproach; whatever the warden or the deputy warden needed doing, there was always a sycophantic "Yes, sir, right away, sir!" Pant, pant, pant!

One of her favorite moves was to empower her position by telling the staff she had "direct orders" from the chief deputy, or, if we were all really lucky, from the warden himself, and that the job had better be done right. During one of these desperate attempts to impress everyone, she called me and three other guards into the sergeants' office.

"I have noticed a lot of hanging around, so I have decided to keep you four busy. I was just up in property and I discovered we are running low on underwear. I need an accurate count of all the underwear in the institution. Split into pairs and go through each housing unit, enter every cell, open every property box, and count every pair of underwear in the entire prison."

It was really hard not to laugh. After the first five cells in the very first block, my partner and I decided to abandon the task, take our time walking around, and just make up the numbers as we went. In my idling mind, I imagined coming across something wild and exciting like two hundred feet of rope made from beautifully braided prison-issue socks or perhaps a hang glider in a roof space made from well-starched, stolen prison bed sheets. While my co-workers and I pretended to check for five thousand pairs of stained prison-issue skivvies, the inmates were busy making shanks, taking drugs, constructing escape materials, stealing, raping, and beating each other up. When we reported our fabricated findings to Sergeant G, she seemed genuinely delighted.

THERE WERE A LOT OF RUMORS CIRCULATING ABOUT SERGEANT G. I don't know how many of them were true, but there was so much smoke, there had to be something burning somewhere. Rumor and gossip had it she was locked into a loveless marriage with a womanizing control freak who treated her like trash. If that was true, it wasn't much of a leap to see why she sucked up to the overlords and despised the underlings. Sergeant G was every male chauvinist's nightmare: a menopausal fear-filled man-hater with a big axe to grind and a point to prove. The funny yet sad thing was no one really took her seriously. And after I got over being annoyed by her, I just felt sorry for her and began to see her as a lonely, tragic figure. The way Sergeant G constantly lauded her supervisory status and paltry rank over the staff reminded me of something I once read: "Being a leader is like being a woman of virtue. If you have to keep telling people you are one, then you are not."

13

Family Ties

GROWING UP, OUR HOUSE ALWAYS FELT SAFE AND CLEAN, MY SISTER and brothers were wonderful friends, my father was smart and hardworking, and my mother was gentle, kind, and ever-present. I was never hungry, my clothes were always clean, our neighborhood felt safe, and there was always the overriding feeling that nothing bad could happen because my parents were right around the corner. I never witnessed my folks fighting or arguing. My grandparents were always at the house, and we were always at theirs. We went on a church camping trip every summer and had wonderful birthdays and Christmases. And while not remarkable in any way, my home and family life was normal, balanced, secure, and full of positive interaction. I was a very average kid with less-than-average academic and athletic ability, but I was a kid who lived in a great home with a great family.

So, as I worked my way through my crazy new job, I used my own childhood as a lens through which to view those I supervised. And often, when trying to understand difficult inmates with complicated problems, I'd play a quick game of What if/How now?

What if I witnessed my dad beat my mom? How now would I act

toward my own wife and kids when I was upset or feeling angry? What if my parents were drug addicts or alcoholics? How now would I act in front of my own kids if I didn't know what was and what was not reasonable behavior? What if my mom hadn't fed us good meals three times a day, kept us clean and clothed, and made us go to bed at the same sensible time each night? How now would I view nutrition, the need for regular meal times, and a cohesive structure in my own kids' lives? What if my dad was in prison or just not around, my mom had to work out of the house out of necessity, and I'd been left to my own devices? How now would I look at being a male role model for my own kids and what kind of work ethic would I have? What if, instead of being bullied by a sadistic teacher in grade school, I had been sexually abused by a controlling authority figure and never had the safety net of a great family to fall into? How now would I feel about my own sexuality and what effects would that have on my family and their future?

Not all the time, but often when I was in a difficult situation and things were escalating out of control, I'd play that quick game of What if/How now? And as soon as I realized how incredibly fortunate I was, and I reminded myself that if it wasn't for my family, and my wife's family, I might not be that different from the inmates I was dealing with.

THE MORE TRAGEDY AND DYSFUNCTION I WAS EXPOSED TO, THE more I kept thinking about my own upbringing. And the strongest, most profound feeling I kept having over and over again was just how unbelievably fortunate I was. Growing up, I did plenty of stupid things, but there were many, many times, I didn't get into big trouble and avoided even bigger trouble because I imagined my parents were watching me. The funny thing was that now I was a parent, I was avoiding trouble and making good decisions because I now imagined my children were watching me. Normalcy was the blueprint Sarah and I were both raised on, and whether it was conscious or not, that was the domestic and parenting plan we were now following.

This whole notion of parental modeling and expectation hit home hard when I witnessed a father and son meeting each other in one of the prison hallways. Neither knew the other was incarcerated. I wasn't supposed to, but I let the two men stop and talk for a minute. The father, in his fifties, wept. The son, in his mid-twenties, was embarrassed and told his dad not to worry, that he'd be OK. After a short while, I had to tell the two men to break it up because we had to move on. They understood, embraced awkwardly, and then went their separate ways.

On the way back to the block, I asked the son if he was OK. He said he was fine. He wasn't; he was shaken by this unexpected meeting with his father. But he told me that seeing his dad was not that much of a surprise. He said his father had been in and out of prison his whole life. I asked the young man how he felt about that when he was growing up. He said he lied to his friends and made out like his dad was some kind of big-time, tough guy gangster, but really, he was ashamed of his dad being a jailbird and wished he would come home and get a job. I asked the son if he ever talked to his father about it. He told me no, and he didn't really know his father. Then he told me about one occasion when his dad came home and tried to make nice with his mom after being in prison for some time. The son said he got mad and threatened his old man. In return, the father got angry. The son then punched him and knocked him down. The father got up and told his son, "The devil in you is stronger than the devil in me." Then he left the house.

Several years had passed, and the two hadn't met again until they saw each other in the prison hallway. It was heartbreaking. As my own blueprint was set, so was this guy's. Like my father, I was at work looking after my family. And like his father, there was a good chance this young man was going to spend most his life committing crimes and passing in and out of prison.

AS THE TIME FOR BABY NUMBER THREE GOT CLOSER AND CLOSER, I thought more and more about the children of inmates and the inmates as children. I was still having the bad dream about all the prisoners in my block turning into kids. Whenever I walked through the lobby and saw little ones waiting to visit their fathers, I thought of my own kids. I missed them after being out of the house for four hours. I couldn't conceive of not being there for them for long periods of time. There was so much bragging and bravado among the inmates surrounding how many kids they had, there seemed to be no sense of responsibility or caring attached to these conversations; it was a numbers game. Whoever had the most women and the most kids was the biggest man. It was also a foregone conclusion that the state would pick up the bill.

Nothing hammered this home as hard as when I found a photograph on the floor of J-Block. I found it right after the trustees who'd been sweeping up had returned to their cells. I figured it must have fallen out of one their pockets. There was no one else it could have possibly belonged to. After all, every other inmate had been locked in all morning. I'd done half a dozen rounds already. Surely, I would have seen it. It was right there on the floor, immediately below the stairs. After I picked it up, I studied the child staring back at me. It was a school picture. The first or second grader was posing uncomfortably at an old-fashioned schoolroom desk complete with cup full of pencils and fake wooden red apple. There was a slightly startled look in the child's eyes that made me think the kid was being bossed around by a jaded and impatient photographer, slighted by the menial assignment, unable to work out why he or she wasn't on the front lines documenting the real world for *National Geographic.* The little boy in the photograph was about the same age as my oldest child. Again, I immediately thought about going home after work and seeing my own kids, and I couldn't wait. Then, I wondered how long the child in the photograph was going to have to wait to see his dad.

There were six trustees. One white, one Hispanic, and four black. That narrowed it down. The child had to belong to one of the African American inmates. The four men all lived on the first floor. So I went over to the closest cell, keyed the door and stuck my head in.

"Wha sup, CO?" (Inmate slang for Corrections Officer.)

I showed inmate D the photograph, explained where I found it and then asked him if this was his child. Inmate D sat up on his bottom bunk, took the picture from my outstretched hand, looked at it for a few seconds, and then said, "Nah, I don't think so." He looked at it a second time, this time really poring over the image of the child at the desk. Shaking his head, he said "Yep, pretty sure this kid ain't mine." Then he casually lay back down.

After showing the picture to the three other possible fathers and coming up blank, I then went to every cell where an African American inmate was housed. There were a lot of answers and opinions about the picture, some funny, some not. One guy told me, "Nah, this ain't my kid. I already got six babies to six different bitches. I ain't interested in having another." His cellie laughed out loud and said "Six babies to six different bitches. Shit, nigga, you da man!" Then the two young inmates gave each other a high-five.

I probably asked forty or more men if the child in the photograph was theirs, but no one claimed him. Afterward, I couldn't throw the photograph away. Something stopped me from dropping it into the trash; so instead, I put it in the back of the filing cabinet in an empty folder. The act felt like closing the lid of a casket on a living child.

Sarah is almost always late and almost always in a good mood. I, on the other hand, am almost always on time and quite often in a bad mood on account of waiting for those who are late. On May 9, 2002, this was not the case. Sarah was not in a good mood because she was having contractions two weeks before she should. We called the doctor and were told to come in immediately. We dropped Josh and Lindsey off at our friend Vicky's house.

Vicky, a neighbor, close friend, and mother of three, took one look at Sarah and said, "You're having a baby today."

Sarah said, "That's ridiculous. I'm not due for another two weeks."

Vicky was right. The baby was coming. It didn't take long. It probably felt like a long time for Sarah, but from my imperfect perspective, everything started to fly.

After a brief period of labor, a baby boy arrived, but there was no crying or movement. The backside slapping and the towel rubbing weren't doing a thing. Silence filled the delivery room. Sarah stared at me with a desperate, questioning look. The doctor sent for the emergency post-delivery team. They arrived in seconds with machines on wheels and quickly took control. They inserted tubes up the baby's nose and down into its tiny mouth and started to suck out a black slimy mucus that was blocking his airway.

Sarah and I kept looking at the doctors and the baby and back at each other. It seemed too long for there not to be any sound. The nurses who had been helping with the delivery stood back with their hands by their sides and were quiet. Whenever I tried to make eye contact, they looked away. We waited and waited. The clock stopped, and all the air got sucked out the room just like the black slimy liquid getting sucked out of the little baby's nose and mouth.

14

"If It Wasn't For Us Criminals, You Wouldn't Have a Job"

BABY ZEKE CAME INTO THE WORLD FIGHTING, BUT WAS FINE. SARAH was fine, too. Joshua and Lindsey both had a little brother and we were now a family of five. When talking over the phone with my father about my new parenting responsibilities, he said "Don't worry, son; the first thirty years will be the hardest."

A week later, I returned to work to find I had been rotated into C-1, an even higher security block. Most of these inmates were older, tougher, and had plenty of prison smarts. There were no "kids" on C-1, and its atmosphere was very different than on I - and J-Blocks. I was initially rather anxious about my new assignment, but very quickly, I realized these much more serious inmates were much lower-maintenance than their younger counterparts. The other side of that was there was a constant air of seriousness on the block that led me to believe there wouldn't be many or any games played. I welcomed the change.

Blocks E through O were all part of the new prison built in 1993 at a cost of 23 million dollars. These large open cellblocks were designed under the "direct supervision" model where supposedly effective supervision by one competent staff member can manage and oversee forty eight single inmate cells surrounding a large, open dayroom area. This design was intended to encourage a community style of living. It all sounded good on paper until the idiots who ran the place put two inmates in each cell and now you had ninety six prisoners and one guard in a huge cellblock/insane asylum.

The A, B, C and D units were right out of the penal colony history books, old-world linear prison blocks with a dozen cells on either side of a dark narrow corridor. Built in 1932, the A, B, C, and D units were filthy, smelly, poorly lit, with low ceilings and no inside rec area to talk of. They were four enormous elongated petri dishes overflowing with hate, discontent, staph infections, antiquated practices, and the ever-present threat of something very bad happening. The guard's desk on C-1 was stuck in the middle of the corridor by the front door and once the prisoners were locked in, to monitor them properly, you had to continually walk up and down the corridor and slide a little steel plate up past a tiny observation portal in the middle of the old steel door and then peer into the cell.

The week I had been away from work had been a big one for my new charges. Every cell had passed inspection every day, and not a single inmate had been written up for a single infraction of the rules. This meant the blocks' residents received a big reward— movie night! This was a very unusual situation. There might be thirty or forty men locked down on C-1. Collectively, for them all to go through an entire week without failing a cell inspection, getting into a fight, being caught with contraband, abandoning an institutional work detail, or a dozen other things on a long list of potential derailments was quite an achievement.

A video was rented and piped in from one of the control centers to the cellblock's TV. The inmates were allowed to stay up late to watch it. This was the strangest babysitting gig ever. The movie chosen, without the inmates' consent or prior knowledge, was a modern romantic classic, *Scarface*, starring the great Al Pacino.

Considering that two thirds of the block's population was Hispanic, it was promising to be an interesting evening. I swear the sergeant who picked the movie either had a great sense of humor or must have been smoking crack cocaine.

But no one seemed to think it was a poor selection except for me. I would have gone with *The Sound of Music* or perhaps *The Muppets Take Manhattan*. But, anyway, the inmates were delighted, had already bought popcorn from the commissary, and had their chairs organized hours in advance. The top tough guys and their boys got the best seats front and center. The less pull you had, the farther back you sat. The exception to this seating arrangement was the chair reserved for Miss C, a flamboyant younger inmate who was a lot more woman than man. Miss C sat between the two top tough guys. The thugs shared their popcorn with her and laughed at all her desperate attempts at humor. Miss C was too stupid to recognize the setup. She loved the attention and her new-found minor celebrity status. Miss C was obnoxious and acted like an idiot, and while she talked trash and poked fun at other inmates, she was running up a line of credit that she was never going to be able to pay off. The tragic thing was, everyone knew it except for her. Once the interest-free protection ran out, the payments wouldn't be too bad at first. Just a few sexual favors every now and then, but as time passed, the payback rate would balloon to about 500 percent above primal fear, and she'd be working all the time just to stay alive. Eventually, when her novelty and "feminine good looks" faded, her former protectors would whore her out wholesale in exchange for pornography and their laundry done ahead of rotation. It wouldn't take long until Miss C, ravaged by disease and withered by weight loss, would start to resemble an extra from a zombie movie, an untouchable, a member of the living dead, waiting for a bed in the prison infirmary while the two top tough guys looked for a new sweetheart.

For some Hispanic inmates, the movie *Scarface* is a religious experience. I watched as the audience became totally absorbed and invested in the story. They sat in absolute silence and focused intently on the unfolding drama. I sat at ninety degrees to the TV and the viewers, watching the screen and the faces of the inmates in profile. Lots of them knew the dialogue and silently mouthed the lines as the show rolled on. The protagonist Tony Montana goes from Cuban immigrant ghetto rat to organized crime god in less than two hours. The felonious messiah blasts the hell out of everything with a huge machine gun while massive packs of cocaine and cash lie all over the place and hot-looking young women in expensive dresses run screaming from one room to the next.

I first saw *Scarface* when I was about sixteen. After the movie, I instantly returned to my real world with all its privilege, normalcy, and structure. Watching the inmates, I quickly realized that's not the case for them. To these guys, this movie is their version of the American dream. It's not a warning shot or a cautionary tale; it's a revival, a recall to the streets, a reminder of the real deal and an affirmation of life the way it should be. The forty-hour workweek, paid vacation, and health benefits are for the chumps and losers of this world. The real way of life is to be a gangster. Once again, it occurred to me: no one had ever told them or shown them that what they were watching was a great movie but not really the way to go. The inmates idolize the images, vicariously inhabiting the world of high-stakes, big-time crime and projecting themselves in to a place where violence, drugs, money, and misogyny earn the ultimate respect.

I must have been smiling as the credits rolled up because inmate F said to me in a fairly aggressive way, "What's so funny, man?" His voice sounded strangely like Scarface's.

Other inmates looked at me and waited for the answer I now had to provide. If I said the wrong thing and made light of the situation, I might be found guilty of blasphemy. So, I told the inmate, "I thought it was a good film, but my feeling is that showing this kind of movie is kind of ridiculous, considering where we are."

Emboldened by the film, inmate F became verbally hostile and fired back, "You think you are better than us. You are wrong. You are not better than us; you are nothing to us. You live your life by the rules and that don't mean shit to us, man. You got your shitty job and you probably come to work in a shitty little car and when you go home you probably go home to a nagging wife and a house full of screaming kids. When we are on the street man, we're the kings of the neighborhood. We do what we want when we want. We don't pay no taxes, we don't pay no attention to the cops. You, man, you live under the law, but us . . . we are above the law. You wanna know something man, you should be grateful to us; if it wasn't for us criminals, you wouldn't have a job."

I smiled and nodded and suddenly thought about Sarah's Uncle Bob. Whenever a discussion turned into an argument and lost all traction with reality, Uncle Bob would say, "Maybe so, maybe so."

I looked into the face of my inquisitor, channeled Uncle Bob, and said, "Maybe so, Mr. F, maybe so."

My questioning of *Scarface* had a very negative effect on my relationship with inmate F. He became surly and began to walk the line between begrudgingly complying and openly disobeying me. Whenever he was out of his cell, which was about half of the time I was on the block, he constantly watched me, tested me, and looked for any crack in my resolve to run the place according to the rules. I don't like to admit it, but I was intimidated by inmate F. It wasn't a physical intimidation; it was more of an awareness of his presence. There was something profoundly bad about him, and I could feel it and he knew I could feel it, too.

By chance, I happened to be in the intake-release area of the prison the day inmate F was sent back out into the free world. One of the older guards, who had admitted and released inmate F numerous times, joked, "Enjoy your time out there. We'll see you soon." As inmate F walked-swaggered out of the prison, he snarled and flipped the old guard the finger. The old guards words couldn't have been more prophetic. Inmate F was back in prison within a few weeks for brutally murdering his girlfriend while his children slept in the same room. Inmate F is currently and will be for the rest of his life a burden to the Pennsylvania taxpayers to the tune of about fifty grand a year. K–12 school students are allotted about fifteen grand a year.

15

Second Shift

August 2002

I HAD BEEN AT THE PRISON FOR A YEAR. IT WAS MONTHS SINCE I LAST played any music. Very occasionally, I would pick up my guitar or sit at the piano, but nothing would come out. My singing voice was thin and fading, and my hands were numb and useless. Expressing myself musically just felt foolish and sometimes I wished I'd never even started to play. I was thirty-five and had nothing to show for fifteen years of work. Well, that's not true . . . I had seven recorded albums and hundreds of unheard songs that no one was interested in listening to or buying. What compounded the feelings of failure was the cost of it all. My parents had truly believed in my music. And when parents support their children, it makes dreams seem possible. Their belief in me galvanized all my ambitions and every one of my mad plans. My parents paid, with their hard-earned money, for so much. They were so excited about every opportunity and supported me in every single possible way. My in-laws had done the same thing. I know they would have been happier if Sarah had married an accountant or a doctor or a teacher or, come to think of it, anyone stable and sensible. But Sarah sent all the sensible suitors away and chose me. But instead of objecting to their new son-in-law's crazy career choice, Barb and Zeke made me feel like one of their own kids and bought into my mad dream about making it in the music business. One night, I was playing at a bar in a part of town that really wasn't safe to be in after dark. About half-way through the second set, my in-laws walk in with a group of their friends, all dressed in tuxedos and ball gowns. They had been out at a bigwig business function uptown and instead of going home, they came out to the bar to see the band and drink beer.

But no one believed in me more than Sarah. She waited eight years to have the baby she wanted from the first day she said she loved me. She put her life and her career at the bank and her white-hot desire for us to have a normal family life on hold while I worked out the moves and tried to make the big time. She stayed home alone for years as I traveled and played in a thousand crappy nightclubs and recording studios. And all these things had run up an emotional and financial bill that was so big, I had started to think I'd never be able to pay it off.

Not long after my one-year prison anniversary, we went to visit my in-laws in Massachusetts. We had a great time, the kids loved seeing their grandparents, and we enjoyed a good old-fashioned beach vacation. Big Zeke had started to look and feel a lot better. The after-effects of his last chemotherapy were finally starting to wear off. Little Zeke was four months old, and everyone went crazy for him. Sarah took lots of pictures of Big Zeke and Little Zeke sitting together, and a really good time was had by all. Toward the end of the trip, the weather changed. A huge storm had swept in from the Atlantic, so I went for a walk along the top of the dunes to watch it firsthand. High winds and massive crashing waves roared up the steep, storm-raked sand. The ocean was so beautiful, violent, and incredibly intimidating. I loved all of its raw power and as I looked north and east, beyond the curvature of Earth, I thought about England and my family.

After my walk I went back to find the parking lot empty. The bad weather had chased everyone else away. As I approached the car, I saw Sarah slumped over in the front passenger seat crying.

I opened the driver's door and slid in behind the wheel. She was holding Zeke in her arms and clutching the cell phone in one hand.

"I just checked the messages at home. You're being moved over to second shift as soon as we get back."

This wasn't good news. It meant several major changes in our nice new routine. The biggest was Sarah was going to be feeding and putting three little kids to bed without any help. Then, after that, she'd be alone until I got back into the house at not much before eleven. For me, it meant my day would be much longer. On first shift, I showered and shaved the night before. I set the alarm for 5 a.m. and when it rang, I leaped out of bed, brushed my teeth, washed my face, dressed, made a cup of tea, and left the house by 5:20. I worked from 6 a.m. until 2 p.m. and got home by 2:30. I then had every afternoon and evening to be with Sarah and the kids. On second shift, you come home late, hungry, and stressed. So, you eat late and stay up even later watching crappy TV, then you get up late in a bad mood, and spend the next three or four hours clock watching until it's time to leave for work again. On second shift, it feels like you never really get a break.

There were other things about second shift that bothered me as well. The place changed once it got dark outside. After the administration and treatment staff went home and the warden left the building for his audience with the Pope or to give a lecture at the United Nations, the "correction facility" turned into a prison. This transition from politically correct treatment center to lunatic asylum-cum-gladiator school was due to all the inmates finally waking up and coming out to play. If you are an average incarcerated criminal, not too bright or overly ambitious, your usual hours of business are from roughly 6 p.m. to midnight. So, you get up, make it through morning inspection, then go back to bed and sleep through most of first shift. Second shift is where you rise and shine, do your thing, and try to make friends and influence people.

The other big difference was that the second-shift staffers were mostly young single guys with a lot of testosterone and a lot to prove. This meant a much more combative work environment. However, in stark contrast to first shift, the second-shift leadership was great. There was no bullshit, bullying, or micromanagement. There were just jobs to do and, from time to time, problems to deal with. I had no choice. I just had to get on with it. Sarah and the children were depending on me.

On second shift I was moved over to H-Block, another high-security, open housing unit containing ninety-six inmates. In some ways I felt lucky I'd had one year on first shift and had gotten to know most of the staff and a good number of the inmates. This gave me a huge leg up. I had also worked a fair bit of second shift overtime so I wasn't completely in the dark regarding the 2 p.m to 10 p.m. routine.

The stand-out supervisor on second shift was Sergeant D. He was in his mid-forties, well educated, had a wicked sense of humor, and did not suffer fools gladly. I was a little intimidated by Sergeant D, primarily because he was so popular with the tough-guy crowd, and I knew there was no way I was ever going to be a member of that club. Officer W, a second shift co-worker who was a great guy and just happened to be in the tough-guy crowd told me, "You have to be on point with Sergeant D. If he doesn't like the way you do your job, you'll be in the shit. But if he starts calling you by your first name, you'll know he thinks you're OK and he's got your back."

Despite the change of hours and the disruptions on the domestic front, the second-shift work was much more enjoyable. There was a feeling of camaraderie between the staff, and that was supported in a paternal sort of way by Sergeant D and the rest of the second-shift supervisors.

I also realized all the years of playing in nightclubs and bars turned out to have a rather useful secondary effect. Dealing with brainless bouncers and crooked nightclub owners wasn't all that different from dealing with inmates and, at times, some of the other guards. There was a lot less control in a nightclub. If you didn't get paid the right amount, you couldn't get on the radio and call in the goon squad to rough up the owner, beat down the bouncers, and get the rest of what you had been promised. There were many times I was stiffed money or promised one thing only to get another, but there were a few battles in the long-lost war that ended with sweet victories.

There was a place I played at fairly regularly that always had a good original music crowd. The owner was a snake, but the manager was a decent woman just trying to do a decent job. One night after a good show in front of a really good crowd, the band packed the trailer and I went up to the office to get paid. The minute I walked into the room, I knew something was wrong. The manager handed me an envelope and then sheepishly looked away. I counted the money and found it to be three hundred dollars short. I asked the manager why this was. She was embarrassed and said she wasn't sure, that was just what the owner had given her. There's no point shooting the messenger, so I asked to see the owner. I was told he'd gone home several hours ago. I insisted that the manager call the owner at home. The owner was quite surprised to hear my voice at two o'clock in the morning and even more surprised to be told that he wasn't to worry about the three hundred dollars, because while the boys were packing the trailer, we were going to take with us what I thought was about three hundred dollars' worth of tables and chairs. This would balance the discrepancy in the pre-arranged payment. I then put the phone down. The manager stared at me with a horrified expression. The office phone rang immediately; the manager looked at me with wide eyes, answered and then said a lot of yeses, OKs, and no problems. A minute later I had my three hundred bucks. All the years of dealing with nightclub nonsense and being a bottom-feeder in the music business had been good training for the madness of prison and especially second shift.

SECOND SHIFT WAS ALWAYS FULL OF SURPRISES. IT MIGHT BE A famous Russian ice skater, locked up for being drunk and crazy after a show at a nearby arena. Or a senior sergeant from another local prison, temporarily staying with us for reasons unknown. A minor-league basketball player passed through the facility and was given the five-star treatment including his own cell and permission to eat in the staff chow hall. A couple of ex-members of staff came back to stay for the wrong reasons and on the wrong side of the bars. The most flamboyant, openly gay inmate might beat up the guy who everyone including me thought was the toughest guy in the entire place. And when all ninety-six inmates were out of their cells, it was loud and chaotic. The African American guys controlled the TV, which was always turned up way too high. The Hispanic guys ruled the tables and the dominoes, slamming them down, shouting and arguing over who was winning or losing. The white guys played cards and sulked menacingly on account of being the minority, and no one ever knew what the Asians were up to.

Fights broke out all the time. The place went into full lockdown at least once a night. There were medical emergencies, fire drills, no-contact visits, and evening work details all to be taken care of. The power in the entire prison would periodically fail and throw the entire facility into blind danger-filled darkness. This would cause another much more serious emergency lockdown, often for hours and, on occasion, for several days. Lots of funny things happened, too. I watched an inmate fall down the stairs, all the way from top to bottom, like a mannequin tumbling down an escalator. When he got up, brushed himself off and realized he was OK, he yelled out angrily, "Shit! That was my big chance at the American inmate dream." Inmate lawsuits cost the taxpayers tens of millions of dollars a year.

One inmate who loved to sing, but wasn't very good, was told to shut up and not to think about giving up his day job. His response was perfect: "I ain't never had a day job." There were always flyers being made up for bus trips to strip clubs, casinos, and sporting events. Dopy inmates always signed up and wanted to know when the bus was leaving and if they could wear their street clothes on the trip. During one particularly manic second shift, while all sorts of prison madness and inmate movement were underway, a particularly gullible guard working in the housing control center was talked into making an institution-wide announcement about "Jewish Synagogue" starting in fifteen minutes in the gym. The radio response from not-amused supervisors was priceless. The big joke among the African American and Hispanic inmates was there were no Jewish guys in prison; they were all too smart to get caught.

At times, the prison became so overcrowded that "new commits" had to sleep on mats on cellblock floors, making a mockery of the security and classification system. During a minor crime spree in which seemingly half of H-Block had some of their meager possessions pilfered, two of my own pens went. It became clear that if something wasn't done and the thief was caught, something very bad was going to happen. Trouble was brewing. So, without asking for permission, I got all the inmates' attention and told them I was cancelling all their rec periods for the next week if the stealing didn't stop. I sent all the inmates to their cells and told them I would be running a risk-free, larceny redemption program. I would be visiting each cell with a black trash bag. Anything that "didn't belong to them" was to be put in the bag, and then I would make a list of what was stolen and match it with what I'd received. It was like some sort of crazy, upside-down, criminal Santa Claus show. It worked incredibly well, and most inmates got back their magazines, pencils, commissary candy bars, new socks from the property locker, and other priceless bits and pieces, including their rec. I got only one of my pens back. But after this rather ridiculous peacekeeping performance, one of the inmates who put most of the stolen property in the trash bag came up to my desk and said, "That was pretty slick, Mr. Reilly. You're just like Sherlock Homes, except he's from London and you're from England."

Second shift was prison life on full volume, speakers thudding, drinking from a fire hose, fifty pounds of potatoes packed into a forty-pound bag. Everything about two till ten was pumped up and always just about to burst.

16

Intake Release

Whoever was responsible for the design of the intake-release section of the prison should have been flogged in front of the staff and inmates at least once a week until he came up with a better idea. Intake release is the portal to the outside world where inmates enter and leave the prison. The emotional climate in that section of the institution was mercurial to say the least. There were always guys changing into their street clothes and getting released into the free world at the same time other guys were having everything taken from them and being processed into prisoners. These converging hot and cold fronts often caused dramatic outbursts.

One much talked-about incident happened when a young guy with huge muscles and an attitude to match was being booked and relieved of his liberty. The new inmate was a self-important young man who was trying hard to let anyone who would listen know exactly who he was and why he shouldn't be incarcerated. He was wearing a red, white, and blue track jacket and matching sweatpants. His hair had been dyed several colors so that it matched his outfit, quite a bold fashion statement. To the seasoned guards in the booking room, the guy was the subject of a great deal of mockery for all the obvious reasons.

Inmate Colorful took great exception to being the brunt of the joke and yelled out aggressively, "What are you laughing at?"

Silence instantly filled the room. The senior guard present, a huge muscular man in his late forties with massive arms and chest, narrow fighter's eyes, swept-back black hair, and a Stalinesque mustache—a man more gladiator than prison guard—crossed the floor menacingly and got right into the young tough guy's personal space and told him, "We're laughing at you, you little shit. And I was just telling the guys that I once had sex with a parrot and was wondering if you were my kid."

The room erupted into rounds of raucous laughter. Hard, uncaring men, both guards and inmates, who routinely witnessed all sorts of brutality, laughed and pointed at the ridiculous-looking inmate who'd run his mouth to the wrong man.

As the laughter died down, the mouthy inmate was told in rather unrefined terms to "Change into these," his new baggy prison blues. The young tough guy tried one more attitude-infused stare, only to be informed at full volume, "—or I'll strip you down like a bitch and make you."

That was all it took. The young tough guy vanished; a new scared inmate materialized and started to cry like a frightened child. After he changed, he was led away and placed in the prison's quarantine block with over a hundred other men who knew nothing but poverty, hardship, and crime, and would have no time for spoiled, loudmouthed pretty boys.

ONE EVENING EARLY IN DECEMBER 2002, WHILE WALKING THROUGH the intake-release area, I saw someone I recognized. The tall skinny man in his mid-fifties with short, gray, messy hair and a badly pockmarked face looked at me and smiled nervously. He was being handed over to the prison by local cops after a wild drunk driving

cat-and-mouse chase. The new commit was leaning unsteadily against the booking counter, still full of drink, but not being any kind of a problem.

"You gonna be OK?" the old bald booking guard asked.

"Yeah, I'm gonna be fine. I just don't like these prison-issue shoes. They're so uncomfortable. I'm going to get blisters."

"Boy, It didn't take you long to find your way back here did it," I said to the guy.

"What?" he replied indignantly. "I've never been in prison a day in my life,"

"Oh, you're full of it. You just left here a couple of weeks ago."

"I swear I've never been in this or any other kind of prison in my entire life, ever, I'm telling you."

As the man tried to defend himself in full sentences, he started to look bewildered, and then he began to tear up. I felt sorry for him. Then, a split second later, I thought about Sarah and the kids driving home from somewhere and this drunken idiot cruising around in his car, smashed out of his mind, looking for an accident to get into and a family to slaughter. Any pity I felt evaporated instantly.

The old guard at the desk looked up at me and said, "He's right, kid. According to the computer, he's never been locked up before, not that I can tell."

I stared hard at the guy. I knew I recognized him from somewhere.

"Where do you work?" I asked.

"I just got fired from T's barber shop this morning. After I left the shop, I started drinking, and it all went downhill from there." The light went on!

"You gave me a haircut last week. That's where I know you from."

As the convict barber was being led away, he called out to me, "Hey, er, excuse me, sir. What did you think of the haircut I gave you?"

I called back across the booking counter, "It's funny you should ask. When I got home, my wife said, 'What happened to you? It looks like a drunk guy cut your hair.'"

I wasn't particularly trying to be funny. It just came out that way, hard sounding and uncaring. It was the first time since I started at the prison I noticed I had said something that didn't really sound like me; I wasn't quite sure where it came from.

As the drunken barber was being led into his new sobering reality, several other men were changing out of their prison blues and putting on street clothes they hadn't worn in months or even years. It was cold out; winter was coming. One guy was putting on flip-flops, shorts, and a T-shirt. There was a party atmosphere as the inmates prepared to be free men again. One of the men putting on a ridiculous-looking shiny gray pinstripe pimp suit was complaining about how thin he had gotten and how baggy his clothes were. The brown paper bags with their wallets, watches, cell phones, and other personal items were being handed back and opened up. One of the men yelled out, "Hey, where's my money, man? When I came in here, I had a thousand dollars in my money clip."

A guard who was sitting behind a computer called out, "How d'you think I got to Florida last month?" Someone else called out, "Hey! Where's my Rolex?" The guard behind the computer didn't even respond to this one; he just raised his left hand and showed off his black plastic Timex watch. Everyone laughed.

I didn't know any of the inmates getting ready to regain their freedom. But it did occur to me: are any of these soon-to-be-ex-prisoners dangerous? A few weeks earlier, inmate F left the prison in exactly the same way these men were leaving, and days later he returned after he murdered the mother of his children while they slept in the bed next to hers.

About a week later, this thought was in my mind again.

I was at the bank waiting in line to deposit my check when I heard a voice call my name from the next teller window over.

"Hey, Mr. Reilly, how you doing?"

I looked up and was a little shocked to see one of the inmates I had supervised on J-Block looking right at me, smiling. I'm ashamed to say, I instantly thought he might be robbing the place.

"What you up to, Mr. Reilly?"

I searched for a name but came up blank.

"Oh, you know, banking my paycheck. What about yourself? What are you up to?"

The ex-inmate grinned at me. "Cashing mine. Going out tonight."

He waved a paycheck at me.

"Well, stay out of trouble, won't you?"

The guy grinned maniacally and nodded. "Take care, Mr. Reilly."

"Yeah, you take care, too."

As I stood in line, I watched the ex-inmate leave the bank and jump into a waiting white pickup truck. It was a weird feeling. I was only a couple of blocks from my house, my two worlds had collided. I felt a little unnerved; I had been standing only a few feet from him and if he hadn't said anything, I wouldn't have even noticed him.

On Christmas Day, 2002, because I was on second shift, we managed to have a real Christmas morning at home. I watched the kids opened their presents, called my family and friends in England, and enjoyed the feeling of normalcy. After we ate breakfast, we loaded up the minivan and went across town to see Big Zeke and Barb. Zeke was looking and feeling a lot better. They were excited about their upcoming trip to Arizona. We were all hoping the warm southwestern winter would bolster his recovery and get him back up to speed.

The Christmas day second shift was a complete non-event. From the 1:45 p.m. roll call to 10 p.m. shift change, a bleak heavy-heartedness hung in the air above everyone's heads. It didn't matter what side of the bars you were on, no one wanted to be there. I was back on I-Block for the night. There wasn't the slightest trace of a holiday anywhere. Most of the inmates stayed in their cells, and those who came out weren't in the mood to be talkative or friendly. The evening passed uneventfully beneath a cold, slow Christmas cloud of depression.

THE ANTICLIMACTIC DAYS THAT FOLLOWED CHRISTMAS WERE DARK and heavy. At one of the roll calls in late February 2003, Sergeant D read out my name.

"Here," I answered.

Fully expecting to be in a housing block with ninety-six nut cases for the evening, I waited to hear what my assignment would be.

"Utility float."

Utility float! Now that was much better. Apart from relieving a few staff for coffee breaks, all the utility float really did was hang out and wait for something bad to happen. Most of the time, it was the easiest job in the whole joint. But if all hell broke loose, the utility float better be there to help take care of things and assist co-workers.

A couple of hours into the shift, while sitting in the staff room watching TV, the radio crackled and Sergeant D's distinctive voice asked, "Officer Reilly, what's your location?"

Better not lie, I thought. "Staff room," I replied.

"Come to the sergeant's office, please."

Oh crap, I thought, am I going to get chewed out for loafing around and drinking coffee, which is exactly what I was doing. Until this moment, I had had very little interaction with Sergeant D, and that was fine with me. I kept a low profile and stayed off his radar. As I walked through the corridors toward the sergeant's office, I wondered what he was going to say to me and how I would respond. If I got chewed out for watching TV and sitting around the staff room, I would just admit my wrongdoing, apologize, and then keep out of his way even more than I had up to now.

His office door was open. I knocked on it and stepped inside. Sergeant D was sitting behind his desk, leaning all the way back in his chair with his fingers laced behind his head and his feet up on the desk. The soles of his boots were directly in front of his face. I stepped to one side to make eye contact. Sergeant D was the anti-Sergeant G. She tried way too hard to impress everyone with her own puffed-up projection of authority and vain attempts to bolster it by sucking up royally to the administration. Sergeant D had real authority, but never flaunted it, and I had the very strong impression he'd never sucked up to anyone in his life. In some ways, he reminded me of a younger version of my father.

Sergeant D looked at me, didn't move, and then said, "Do you know Officer P on third shift?"

I didn't. "No, I don't know any of the third-shift guys."

Sergeant D studied me for a second or two then said, "Well, last night he had one of your CDs with him. I listened to it, and I think it's really good."

Sergeant D smiled. I didn't know what to say except, "Thank you, Sergeant D."

"Robert, what did you like to listen to growing up? Are you a fan of The Who?"

"Yeah, I love The Who."

We then launched into a long talk about bands and guitarists, drummers and concerts, and the differences and similarities between British and American classic rock. Sergeant D also liked to grill me about growing up in the U.K. He always wanted to talk about the queen, why Prince Phillip wasn't king, and why couldn't Margaret Thatcher come to America and be president. Whenever I was a float officer, which started to become a regular work detail, if the prison was quiet, Sergeant D would pop into the staff room for a cup of coffee and watch the occasional *Twilight Zone* or *Seinfeld* with me and the other hardworking crime-fighting members of the prison guard community.

I'd tried to hide my music from the people I worked with because I felt I would be ridiculed, only to find out the most respected supervisor on the job had heard one of my CDs and enjoyed it. It was like a magic trick. Now he called me by my first name and was being a friend to me. It turned out Officer P on third shift was a friend of a friend who came to see one of the bands I'd played in from time to time. I had met him, but never knew he worked at the prison.

Being acknowledged by Sergeant D made the biggest difference to me being able to work second shift successfully, and it was a huge confidence booster. The hours were still bad, and the inmates were still a handful, but having a good supervisor looking out for me really made all the difference. I know for a fact Sergeant D had the same positive effect on lots of other staff members.

17

No Longer
the Rookie

April 2003

As spring slowly approached, second shift felt like it was getting longer and longer. The staff and inmates felt like they were changing a little, too, but in a good way; they were becoming a bit more manageable, more normal, or perhaps I was changing, becoming a bit more like them, assimilating.

Twenty months had passed, and two new classes had graduated behind mine. I was experiencing a feeling of being established, accepted, and actually knowing what I was doing. New guys were even asking me what to do. One evening, Sergeant G, who happened to be working a rare second shift, sent two new guards into the block I was working on to practice "cell searches." Their orders were simple: Look for contraband, don't leave a single stone unturned, and then when you're done with that, infiltrate organized crime syndicates and international drug cartels, and find out who really shot JFK.

Sergeant G was the butt of lots of crime-fighting jokes. There was the time she ratted out another sergeant to the chief deputy warden for bringing a soda can into the institution. She imagined there was a possibility the soda can might get stolen from the lunch box that was locked in the sergeant's office and fashioned into a lethal weapon! The thing is, she could only have known about the can by rooting through her co-worker's lunch box. She wrote another sergeant up for "looking mean" and another for not following the SOP correctly.

After this, the soda-sipping sergeant placed a pinch of oregano in a cigarette paper and put that in his lunch box to see what would happen. The trap was set. Sure enough, a couple of days later the sergeant was called into the chief's office to give a urine sample for a drug test and was told to explain himself. I have it on good authority that once the chief deputy understood what had happened, he thought it was both sad and very funny.

Then there was the time some of the older guards put a few work-release inmates up to "leaking" information to her about an alleged gun being dropped off in the parking lot. The good old boys wanted to see if and how long she would stake out the parking lot. The outcome was fantastic. She never failed to disappoint. She hid in her car and waited *all night* to bust the fictional gunrunners.

So, as Sergeant G's new guys started tearing cells to pieces, looking for grappling hooks and coils of rope, I sat at the desk and soaked in another general-population second shift. Suddenly, I heard a muffled yell from one of the new guys. Infiltrating organized crime syndicates and international drug cartels didn't look like it was going too well.

"Reilly! Reilly! Reilly!"

Then there was a series of heavy metallic banging sounds. The next thing I heard was a crowd of inmates roaring, laughing. The new guard, not wanting to be watched while he searched through the cell, closed the door behind him. The only problem was that the control panel was on the self-lock mode. The new guy had locked himself in.

"Rookie doin' such a shitty job, Mr. Reilly lockin' him in for the night!" yelled a delighted inmate.

As that was happening, the second new guy, who was only a few cells away from his locked-in partner, started laughing hysterically, and then called me over to the cell he was searching. These new guys were starting to infringe on my education. I was enjoying a wonderful collection of Roald Dahl short stories and had to put my book down to go and see what was going on.

"Hey, Reilly, check this out."

Before I closed my book and turned off the control panel, I pressed a button and released the first new guy. He emerged from the cell red-faced and sweaty and was met by a round of applause from the audience of convicts. I then went to see what the other guy wanted. As I entered the cell, my new co-worker beckoned me over and pointed down at the steel one-piece sink-toilet unit. He directed my gaze down to the biggest bowel movement I had ever seen. It was sticking up, several inches out of the toilet water like a sculpture of the Loch Ness Monster.

"All right, all right," I said. "I don't need to see that, thank you very much. Flush it!"

As I turned to walk out the cell, the rookie, still laughing went over to flush the toilet. And as he leaned over to press the flush button above the bowl, his spectacles slid off the end of his nose, fell into the toilet, and crash-landed into the side of the monstrous mound of fecal matter.

"Oh, shit! What do I do, what do I do?" he called after me, panic rising up in his voice.

"Get 'em out," was my response. I pulled a pair of surgical gloves out from a pouch on my duty belt and threw them at him.

18

The Mental Health Unit

IN JUNE 2003, AS I APPROACHED MY TWO-YEAR MARK, WHILE working as a float officer, I started spending quite a bit of time on the N- and O-Blocks, the mental health unit. That part of the facility was split into two separate sections: an inmate waiting room, with a nurse's station, and a patient area with gurneys separated by curtains. Beyond that, there was a restroom and a couple of offices, one for the nurse-practitioner and one for the prison psychiatrist Dr. A.

Dr. A should probably never have been hired to work in a prison. She was without doubt a troubled woman who in my memory wouldn't or couldn't make much eye contact with the inmate-patients and had an even tougher time talking to the guards. Short, squat, and in her mid-fifties with crazy, frizzy dark hair, big round glasses, mad darting eyes, and an almost ghostly whispering voice, she gave weight to the clichéd argument that most shrinks needed their own dose of clozapine and a couple of nights a week under the secure care of a professional friend. Unfortunately for Dr. A, her appearance made her the brunt of a great deal of verbal and emotional abuse from those she worked with and those she was hired to help. Another part of her personality that made her the subject of derision was her love of the TV show *Buffy the Vampire Slayer* and all things occult. Both staff and the inmates were aware of these facts, which didn't help her make friends or be taken seriously.

The second, inner section of the N- and O-Blocks was unlike any other cellblock in the prison: a two-story housing unit with a huge glass front designed so the inmate-patients could be seen from the guard's desk down in an open area on the first floor. The single cells that made up N and O were secure, steel-door containment spaces trying very hard to masquerade as hospital rooms. Some of the residents seemingly never came out of their "quarters," and others were allowed out from time to time to wander around the fishbowl corridor and watch the TV up where the end wall met the concrete ceiling.

I was shocked at how terribly sick some of the inmates were. Most of these people should not have been in prison. They should have been in the hospitals that the state couldn't keep open. The fact is, hospitals for the mentally ill are overcrowded and underfunded, they won't help win elections, and they're closing down quicker than gay bars in Kabul. New prisons are being built at about the same rate as new Burger Kings and Starbucks and definitely help politicians get votes.

Some of the things I saw on the mental health unit will be renting space in my head for a long, long time. There was one man who said the same thing to me every time I passed his door; sometimes, he would repeat it for hours on end. If I didn't enter the N- and O-Blocks for several days, then turned up again for some reason, he'd still be saying the same thing: "I'm glowing like a filament at the prospect of my neighbors being arrested and put in here with me. It's a scandal what they're doing to me in here. I'm very close to losing my mind completely, and then after that, there'll be nothing left."

One inmate would bite himself so badly he actually took lumps of flesh out of his arms and lower legs. After each biting incident, he would be bandaged up and put in the restraint chair for a few hours, then released back to his cell wearing nothing but a suicide smock, a thick nylon-covered blanket with two arm holes. The suicide smock is so thick and inflexible; it can't be turned into anything that might be used as a weapon or a noose. Some mentally ill inmates lived in empty cells wearing only a suicide smock for months at a time, and they were fed nothing but food loaf, a meal of mashed-up slop, baked into a semi-hard fist-sized lump and then handed to them through the tray slot in the middle of the door. Their drinking water was rationed out to them via an endless supply of small paper cups.

After this particular inmate was released from "The Chair" and returned to his cell, he would tear off all the bandages and gnaw at his limbs again. It got so bad he eventually had the suicide smock removed and lived naked and heavily medicated for months. I watched this inmate-patient cease to exist as a person and become a catatonic, hair-covered creature with horrendous scabs and scars all over his arms and legs. He spent most of the day perched on the end of his bed like a diseased crow, defecating on the floor and staring out the thin cell window into his own desperate, ferociously disturbed future.

Some inmates cut themselves with anything they could get their hands on. Others stood in their toilets all day, ate their own scabs and feces, or masturbated for hours on end. More than a few, whose emotions and childhood horrors seemed to be buried somewhere deep within them like unexploded depth charges, just stood at their cell doors staring vacantly out into space day after day after day.

The madness of the N- and O-Blocks seemed to be compounded by the on again/off again presence of the detached and unreadable psychiatrist Dr. A. From my limited perspective, her relationship with the staff had become nonexistent, while her relationship with some of the inmate-patients seemed out of balance, overly close and approaching the unprofessional. One of the senior female members of staff who worked the N- and O-Blocks a lot told the chief deputy warden she thought the doctor was becoming unstable and she was very concerned about her. The staff members' worries were elevated after Dr. A's dog died and she came to work in pieces, and then spent the day sharing her heartbreak and mourning inappropriately with those she was supposed to be counseling and treating.

One particularly memorable inmate loved to eat bathroom supplies—deodorants, shampoo, and toilet paper were all on his lunch list. Soap was his favorite. When confronted about his diet of personal hygiene products, he always became combative, started yelling, usually about "a terrible stomachache," then he stuck his finger in his eye. It wasn't just a quick attention-seeking poke to the pupil. It was a full triple-digit dig, right up to the knuckle. He'd shove it in, pull it out, scream about going blind, and then slide it back in there as if he was trying to bruise his brain. After a minute or two, he'd quit screaming, go sit on his bunk, pull his finger out, and then cry for the rest of the day. This unending horror show never slowed down or got any better. The guards that worked the N- and O-Blocks all the time seemed worn down and more exhausted than anyone else in the entire place. There was so much suffering and raw anguish on display down there; I often wondered, *What's the point? What are we hoping to achieve by failing to help these poor bastards?* There didn't seem to be any real treatment going on, just medication, sedation, and containment. According to what I heard, about ten days after her dog died, Dr. A came to work dressed as one of the characters from *Buffy the Vampire Slayer.* She was told by someone in administration to leave the facility. She did, and then she went home and committed suicide.

19

D-Block

Of all four of the old cellblocks, D-Block was by far the worst. It was the dirtiest, the smelliest, had the most violent inmates and was the last place in the prison I wanted to work. I was about to spend the next three months there, starting in August 2003. D-Block, the disciplinary unit, consisted of two floors and a BAU (Behavioral Adjustment Unit) that was behind a separate set of doors at the very back of the first floor. The BAU was reserved for the very worst of the very worst.

Those who couldn't behave in the real world went to prison. Those who couldn't behave in prison went to D-Block, Seg (segregation), The Hole, Solitary Confinement. Most of the inmates housed down there were so antisocial that living in a general population housing unit just wasn't an option. The majority of the D-Block prisoners had originally started in gen-pop, but almost always because of fighting ended up in The Hole. Although each inmate was housed separately, there was plenty of communication. The old steel doors that opened by sliding from left to right on an antiquated rail system had a quarter-inch gap down both sides and along the bottom. The gaps at the side of the doors enabled the inmates to get a very limited view up and down the dark, foul, germ-infested walkway. The gap at the bottom of the door enabled them to slide things from their own cell to the cell opposite, and then up and down the hallway, a process they called fishing. Carefully removed strands of thread were pulled from their mattresses, tied together into a line, and then attached to a piece of wet paper, folded, pressed, and dried into a square of hard card. The card and line were then flicked under the door to the opposite cell. After that process was complete, there was a long string connecting one cell to another. Depending on the level of cooperation, using the fishing system, inmates could pass messages or magazines all the way up the cellblock zigzagging them from one end to another. Verbal communication and signaling were also a big part of how inmates connected. D-Block was a two-story unit. The old 1930s heating system enabled upstairs and downstairs inmates to talk to one and other through the vents and tap pipes in a very crude, rudimentary Morse code–style message system.

For the most part, the majority of the D-Block inmates lay around festering in their own funk while life in the prison at large continued on without them. To a few of the fighters, who took regular trips to seg, it was a bit of a vacation. They got their own cell, with room service, and no inspections. It was also warm, often too warm. The heat in D-Block was permanently cranked up. For some of the regular visitors coming from the colder parts of the prison, a stay in The Hole must have been like a spring trip to Florida.

Most of the inmates had a long list of things they could not have and a very short list of things allowed. For most, a few clothes, usually just magazines, paperback books, pencils, and a writing pad. On the other end of the spectrum, down in the BAU, the ultra-violent prisoners, the ones who should have probably been in the N- and O-Blocks, but were just too aggressive, were stripped out and forbidden to have a single thing. They were deemed by the treatment staff and the administration to be such a threat to themselves and others that all they had to keep themselves company in the BAU cell was a suicide smock, and like their less aggressive N and O neighbors, food loaf to eat, passed through the tray slot in the middle of the door three times a day. The toilets in the BAU cells were turned off, too, because the inmates plugged them up with their suicide smocks and kept flushing them until the cell and then the corridor beyond began to flood. There were occasions when collectively, all the inmates in D-Block would actually plan a protest and all flood their toilets just so the staff would have to clean it up. Others ate anything and everything their bodies produced, threw urine at staff, refused to take showers and their meds, and tried to attack anyone they could whenever possible. There were hunger strikes, self-mutilation, endless hours of screaming, howling, and banging on cell doors and unquantifiable amounts of verbal abuse directed at any staff member who walked down the corridor. When being brought out of their cells, most of the D-Block inmates and all of the BAU residents had to be handcuffed behind their back, through the tray slot opening, before being let out. You didn't want one of these guys getting behind you, slipping their handcuffed wrists over your neck, and trying to decapitate you.

MY OWN PERSONAL CROSS TO BEAR WHILE I WORKED DOWN ON D-Block was at the hands (and mouth) of inmate QY. He hated me from the second he set eyes on me. Inmate QY was a tall, slim Puerto Rican gangster with a lot of tattoos, a lot to prove, a massive mouth, and an attitude to match. In his late twenties and in prison on drug charges, inmate QY had instigated and been involved in numerous brawls since entering the facility two years earlier. But there was something cowardly about him. He was always surrounded by "his boys" even when he was in seg, and the fights that he had been part of were always gang beat downs of one lone general-population inmate who never had anyone to lean on. A typical situation was after an inmate on a regular housing block received magazines in the mail or snacks from the commissary, inmate QY and his thug buddies would roll in, take what they wanted, and then beat the crap out of the guy. The other part of this was that the resulting disciplinary time in the hole made him and his boys look like hard men and only enhanced their reputations.

The first time inmate QY saw me, through the quarter-inch crack at the edge of the cell door; he called me over and asked rather quietly if he could have a phone call. I said "No, we're not doing phone calls right now." Within a second of my answer being airborne, inmate QY started screaming, "He just called me a nigga, he just called me a nigga. This skinny faggot just called me a nigga. I want to see a lieutenant. I'm writing you up, faggot." His neighbors all jumped on the bandwagon, slamming their hands on the heavy metal doors, screaming profanity and all repeating verbatim exactly what I hadn't said.

For the next three months, the abuse never let up. "When I see you on the block, I'm gonna fuck you up." "When I see you on the block, I'm gonna cut you." "When I see you on the block, me and my boys are gonna beat you down." "I'm gonna find out where you live." "I'm gonna burn down your house." "I'm gonna send someone to the school your kids go to." "I'm gonna find out what car you drive and blow it up." It went on and on and on. There were volumes of vile threats and accusations directed at my wife, children, mother, sister, and grandmother, all of it unrepeatable. Some days I laughed it off, other days I just ignored it. But never once did I engage, respond, or try to defend the character of my loved ones. The only thing I did to protect myself was open up the peephole in the door to make sure he wasn't going to throw some sort of bodily fluid on me when I handed him his food, mail, magazines, toilet paper, or his meds when the nurse was on the block. Some days were worse than others. Co-workers encouraged me to write him up. "Why?" I said. "He can't be punished any more than he already is."

During my three months on D-Block, lots of crazy things happened. There was lots of one-on-one, twenty-four hours a day, staff–on-inmate observations for suicidal prisoners. One inmate did manage to kill himself on third shift. There were the usual toilet floods, cell extractions, hunger strikes, mental breakdowns, inmates covering themselves in feces, and staff being abused. And on top of all that, inmate QY was there to mock, jeer, threaten, and insult me and my family.

I was working the evening that inmate QY was being released

from D-Block and sent (for the umpteenth time) back to general population. I had the pleasure of telling him to get ready to move. Although there were other staff on the second floor, I was the one who manually unlocked his cell door, slid it open, led him down the corridor and then out through another door onto the upstairs staircase that led down to D-1, the D-Block front door. As soon as the upstairs door closed behind me, I told inmate QY to stop, turn around, and face me. As he silently followed my instructions, I took a step back. It was just the two of us on the small square landing at the top of the stairs. There were no cameras, no intercom, and no other staff members present. "Now's your chance" I said. Inmate QY looked at me, but didn't answer or move. Although I was still in control, I was seething. I wanted to smash him, damage him, and hurt him so badly he wouldn't be the same afterward, ever. The last twelve weeks of bullshit was about to boil over. "I said now's your chance, QY. You want to fight, let's do it."

Inmate QY glanced down the stairs and then over my right shoulder at the door behind me. I was pretty sure he was seeing if there were other staff members lurking around. Perhaps he was going to go for it; I wanted him to. Still, he said nothing. As we stared at each other, I thought of all the evil, unrepeatable things he'd said and called and threatened to do to me and my loved ones. Then, all of a sudden, I thought of my dad again. What would the old man do? The answer came quickly. He'd do the right thing, that's what. I'd bet inmate QY had never even met his own father. So, I pointed at inmate QY and told him he was about to be moved to J-Block, and that I worked there regularly. And if he wanted to, I'd be as happy to fight him there in front of his boys, as I would be here in the stairwell with no one else watching. Then, inmate QY spoke, without profanity, insult, or bravado. He said in a quiet, almost boyish voice, "I don't want to fight you, Reilly." Then, with that, he turned around and walked slowly down the stairs to the D-1 door and waited for another guard to take him over to J-Block.

I saw inmate QY countless times after that, on J-Block and H-Block and back on D-Block from time to time. He was always quiet, said "please" if he had cause to ask me for something, and said "thank you" if I ended up handing him something he wanted.

||||||||||

I HAD TWO BRIEF BREAKS FROM THE DRAMA OF D-BLOCK IN AUGUST and September of 2003. The first was a series of hospital runs. There were inmates, often with a high-security classification, whose medical condition was beyond the treatment capabilities of the poorly operated prison infirmary. A dentist friend of mine had told me that I should always remember there were doctors, dentists, and nurses who graduated at the bottom of their class and that all these people worked somewhere. I was beginning to think they all worked in prisons.

The "hospital-run prisoners" had to be taken to the real hospital downtown, where they were watched over twenty-four hours a day, seven days a week by an armed guard. It was a nightmare for the shift commanders. Not only did they have to worry about what happened inside the prison, now they also had to worry about dangerous inmates out in public, with only one guard.

Prison policy dictated that the hospitalized inmate should be restrained at all times, either shackled and or handcuffed to the hospital bed. On one occasion, I arrived at the hospital to relieve the first-shift guard, only to find the inmate sitting on the side of the bed, free as a bird, talking to my co-worker. Instead of saying hello to my co-worker or the inmate, I went straight for the shackles in the black canvas bag at the foot of the bed. I threaded them through the plastic-covered metal frame, and then slapped them on the inmate's ankles.

"What are you doing?" yelled the inmate.

"My job," I replied.

The other guard, notorious for being relaxed and overly friendly said, "Oh c'mon, Reilly. He ain't going nowhere. The man's sick."

"You're absolutely right. He's not going anywhere," I responded.

The outgoing guard gave me the gun, holster, spare ammunition, and left without saying a word. The inmate fumed, turned on the TV and with the aid of the remote, landed on *The Jerry Springer Show*—I don't think so.

I held out my hand and said, "Give me the clicker."

"No, it's mine. I'm the patient, not you," responded the bedridden inmate.

I returned to the black canvas equipment bag, fished out a set of handcuffs, and told the guy, "You either hand me the clicker or you're getting cuffed to the bed as well as shackled."

Begrudgingly he handed me the remote, told me I was violating his human rights, and how, when he got back into the prison, he was going to report me to the ACLU and write to the warden and have me fired. I told him that Reilly has two Ls so as to make sure he spelled my name right, then we said cheerio to Jerry Springer and changed the channel to PBS. For the next eight hours we watched underwater volcanoes in the Pacific rim, an omnibus edition of *News Hour with Jim Lehrer*, a documentary on nonprofit doctors in the Sudan, a Masterpiece Theater version of Dickens' *Little Dorritt*, and then, to my great delight, a riotous question-and-answer session from the British House of Commons. Being controlling about the clicker wasn't just about watching PBS. It was about concealing my anger and resorting to passive aggression. I was furious that the inmate had lung cancer, the same as Big Zeke, and his treatment seemed to be going better than expected. The day before I had heard a doctor tell him there was a very strong chance he'd make a full recovery.

Later that same month we were back up in Massachusetts for a few days visiting Sarah's folks. It turned out to be a tense and stress-filled vacation. The kids were great but hard work. Anyone who's taken a one-, three-, and five-year-old on vacation knows there's not much relaxing going on. My mother always said, "Going on vacation with young kids is just doing the same thing you always do but in another place."

The children, however, were a great distraction. The cause of stress was Big Zeke's health. During a routine and scheduled checkup, the doctors had found something they didn't like and changed his medication. This change in treatment was having a terribly negative effect. Zeke's strength was waning, and his every waking hour was plagued with endless bouts of rough, rasping coughing fits. Barb was on edge the whole time and doing a bad job of covering up her fear. This new setback was a massive downer for all of us. It seemed like after the winter in Arizona and his last round of chemotherapy, he was out of the woods and well on his way back to a great retirement.

After we got back home, I prayed for Big Zeke. What else could I do? I prayed that he would be healed and the family would return to normal. I prayed for this great guy to have what was rightfully his—a long, fun-filled retirement, ending with him watching his grandchildren graduate college, start their own lives, and maybe even get married and make him a great-grandpa.

Escape Plan

November 2003

THE TONE OF MY CO-WORKER'S VOICE WAS MORE ALARMING THAN
THE announcement itself.

"Medical assistance on E- Block! Medical assistance on E- Block!"

The quivering voice broke the silence in the unusually still corridor. I just happened to be standing right outside the E-Block sally
port door.

Snatching my radio out from its holder, I keyed the mic, and
said, "Intake, open E-one."

The door clicked open immediately. I stepped into the sally
port, pulled the first door shut behind me, and waited for the second, inner door to open. In the moment I waited to enter the
block, my mind skipped back to a recent incident in exactly the
same cellblock. An inmate had been brought into the prison after
leading police on a high-speed chase through the surrounding
countryside, crashing his car into a tree, then fighting with the
arresting officers. After being booked and placed in E-Block, the
quarantine unit, he walked up the stairs to the second floor,

climbed up onto the waist-high handrails, and then swan dived head-first to his death, onto the concrete floor below.

The inner door clicked open. At first glance the block seemed completely empty, entirely locked down, the officer's station was unattended and the computer turned off. I looked around, then up to the second floor. I saw a co-worker standing outside an open cell door, leaning over the rail, rubbing his face with both hands. He looked like a seasick passenger on a cruise ship. I ran across the dayroom and bounded up the steel stairs. Other voices on various radios were calling for the E-one door to be opened.

I quickly approached my co-worker and asked, "What's going on?"

He didn't respond, just shook his head and pointed blindly over his shoulder into the open cell. I looked through the wide-open door. The inmate was sitting on a gray plastic chair in the middle of the cell, staring out the narrow, impassable window. His shirt was off. In his right hand he held a thin strip of metal, a shank. His left hand was doing a bad job of covering a huge gaping slice across his stomach. Visible behind his palm and fingers were coils and links of gray slimy intestines. It looked like he was holding ten pounds of raw, slippery sausages on his lap. He'd sliced his own stomach open.

"Help me out here," I called to my co-worker. He glanced over his shoulder, made eye contact with me, glanced at the inmate, then shook his head and leaned back over the hand rail again. The inmate was calm. I moved in front of him. I was now standing with the window at my back, facing the inmate, the open door, and the back of my nonresponsive co-worker. I told the inmate he was going to be OK and quickly removed a pair of blue surgical gloves from a pouch on my duty belt. Keeping an eye on the shank, I reached out and said, "I'll take that now."

Slowly, he extended his arm and placed the razor in my gloved hand. Surprisingly, there was very little blood. Heavy steps and panting were followed by several staff members and two nurses arriving at the cell door. I handed the shank to someone and proceeded to assist the nurse wrapping a towel and several broad bandages around the butchered belly of the suicidal inmate. At this point the inmate spoke for the first time.

"I wanna die. I don't ever wanna get out. I'll only do it again. I only stopped cutting cause it started to hurt too much."

The inmate, a convicted sex offender, then started sobbing bitterly.

Afterward, on my way to the staff room to write my report, I walked through the lobby. It was packed with old men, women, and children, all waiting impatiently to visit loved ones. As I weaved through the throng of anxious civilians, a little girl, maybe four or five, about the same age as my oldest, looked up at me and said angrily, "Are you a policeman? Did you lock up my daddy?"

Driving home that night, I thought about the coming holiday season: Thanksgiving, Christmas, the new year. Then, a few long months after that, I would be looking at my third year anniversary at the prison. Three years! Stonehenge was built in three years; Michelangelo sculpted David in three years; the *Titanic* was also built in about three years.

I was delighted that Sarah was happy and at home with the kids, and I was glad I was able to provide for them; that part felt a whole lot better than being a loser musician. But something inside me felt like it was changing. I had recently been on the edge of doing something illegal. I wanted to fight and badly hurt an inmate because of the things he had said. Was I slowly becoming the same as the two thug guards who'd wanted to beat up the sex offender just after I started working there? All of a sudden, that didn't seem so appalling. If that same incident had just happened, would I have said no, or would I have let my co-workers beat the crap out of him? Would I have wanted a piece of the action? After all, he's just a sex offender, right?

In December 2003, we started to talk seriously about moving. We had friends and family in New England and on the West Coast. We talked about how nice it would be to live near the ocean or in the mountains. We looked in magazines and online at the best small towns in America. We lived in a nice neighborhood with good neighbors. Our home had plenty of room for our growing family and was close to everything—work, schools, stores, airports, and Sarah's family—but we just didn't feel any sense of belonging.

It somehow always felt as if we were just camping. But whenever we talked about our great escape, a piece of me always felt it was motivated by failure. If I went some place new, maybe I could completely forget about music, maybe never write, play, or sing again, and in some way, that might make me someone different. When I was being honest with myself, I felt like a coward who wanted to run away because I was embarrassed about my lack of success in music. But the talk about making a big move was just that, and nothing more. My father-in-law's illness was at the center of all our family plans and activities. We weren't going to do anything until we knew exactly what was happening with Big Zeke. Christmas came and went, and Big Zeke's health continued to decline.

21

The Immigrant Guard

IN JANUARY 2004, I WAS STILL IN A STATE OF CONSTANT ASTONISH-
ment at what was happening around me and the worlds within the
world of prison. For me at least, one of the most interesting parts
of the job was trying to figure out what the warden was up to. His
ongoing battle with the Teamsters Union was an easy one to work
out. It was all about control. But there was something else, something bigger. He was always in the paper talking about expansion.
He openly had his eye on the county-run retirement home, down
the hill and across the road from the prison. There was a constant,
low-thrumming chatter about expanding the prison to include the
retirement home. And if it somehow ever became available, it
could easily be renovated and turned into another "secure facility."

From the get-go, this constant talk of increasing the prison and
its budget seemed to be entirely the wrong way to think. It felt more
like the warden was trying to build a business rather than be an
agent of positive social change. Surely, the thing to do would be to
work toward creating opportunity and education with all those mil-

lions of county dollars. But it appeared that these ethereal and naïve notions had no place in reality and existed only inside my mind.

It was hard to put my finger on it, but there was something conniving and contrite about the way the warden publicly appeared to be victimized by the institution's lack of money and resources. He seemed to cast himself in the light of "He with a heavy cross to bear." I personally thought it was all a rather clumsy, see-through sales pitch. Bad things happened all the time: suicides, violence, overcrowding, staff members with staph infections, unhygienic conditions, overtime wages threatening to blow the county budget, the staff/inmate ratio ballooning to ninety-six to one, the prison's entire electronic locking system failing for an entire week, or the volume inside the cellblocks being so far off the charts, it could cause hearing loss. And whenever anything bad happened, the warden donned a public persona of tireless civil servant, social crusader, mission-driven man of the people, short on resources but high on heartfelt hopes. The warden announced that he was trying hard to rehabilitate drug-addicted petty offenders and violent recidivist criminals. But I didn't believe a word of it. I was starting to believe he just wanted to expand the prison and get a bigger chunk of the county budget. His whole song-and-dance stank of thinly veiled self-promotion and a duplicitous bid for broader authority, a better seat at the big-boy table, and a louder voice in local politics.

During an in-depth discussion about prison expansion, I shared my theory with a senior member of staff who openly hated the warden. He told me, "Why would anyone want a bigger prison? A bigger prison means bigger problems. The warden can't handle what he has. Relax, Reilly, and stop reading so much. It's messing up your mind." But my friend and I had to agree to disagree. There was too much evidence of empire building. Behind the warden's faux PR performances, he constantly lobbied for more county money, waged a continuous war against combative union reps, promoted weak, ineffectual staff members who would never challenge him, and watched suspiciously over the shoulders of the good supervisors who posed anything that might look like a threat to his leadership.

Around this time, I also became aware that the prison had some sort of arrangement with INS/Homeland Security. As I said earlier, The A-, B-, C-, and D-Blocks were old, dirty, and dangerous. The A- and B-Blocks were full to overflowing with foreign nationals who'd been picked up primarily for the crime of being undocumented. Based on the conditions of the blocks and the appallingly poor services the A and B inmates received, I believe they were being kept for not much more than a few dollars a day. That was probably where the deal existed. The INS/government paid the prison X dollars a day to keep each inmate, and the prison spent Y dollars a day and pocketed the difference. At the time, I remember thinking, *Wow! I wonder if the prison is more about keeping the community safe or making money.* Squashed into the A- and B-Blocks were a couple hundred Africans, Chinese, Cubans, Russians, Pakistanis, and a lot of Central and South Americans. The obvious irony of me, an English immigrant, working that particular part of the prison was not lost on my colleagues or the inmates. At one roll call, I was told by the generally good-humored Sergeant T that my brother had been thrown into prison last night, so, during my shift, I was to make sure not to show any favoritism. Curiosity turned to hilarity when after seeking out my newly incarcerated sibling, I discovered inmate Reilly was a six-foot-four black man from West Africa.

There was no need for introductions. After we both looked at each other's nametags, I asked the inmate, "How is our mother?"

He smiled, nodded, and said, "She is well, but our father has still not come back home."

We both had a really good laugh and then the family reunion was over. The miracle on A-Block happened during a period of extreme overcrowding and high tension in early February 2004. A South American inmate who spoke no English had been refusing food and medical treatment for days. On the third or fourth day of his hunger strike, he upped the ante by barricading himself in his cell with chairs and mattresses. On top of that, he became belligerent and abusive, even though none of what he was saying could be understood. Some of the inmates and Spanish-speaking guards had tried to get through to him, but had been unsuccessful. Whatever dialect he was threatening us all in was a mystery to everyone. Eventually, a cell extraction was called for. It was decided the inmate had to be forcibly removed from his cell and taken to the mental health unit for observation and evaluation.

On this particular day, I was part of the extraction team. I was tasked with cuffing the inmate's hands behind his back once we had subdued him by pinning him to the bunk, wall, or floor. I had done half a dozen of these extractions by now, and they always went the same way. No matter how you cut it, one guy in a confined space can't fight four guys wearing helmets and riot gear. On one occasion, however, I had been a part of an extraction where a tall, amazingly muscled Jamaican inmate actually did fight with the team for well over five minutes. On that day, I was the fourth member of the team and by far the smallest guy in the group. I remember thinking, as we thrashed and fought to control the inmate, that if we were on any kind of level playing field, this guy would kill us all.

We moved in single file down the corridor. A sergeant with a video camera filmed everything, while a couple of nurses stood by, ready to administer first aid should the inmate need it after the "planned use of force" was over. The corridor of the cellblock roared and rumbled. It filled with screaming and maniacal laughing; metal doors and desks being pounded on; and voices in half a dozen languages yelling, screaming, and cursing at us as we approached the barricaded cell. Moving into position outside the dirty cell door I suddenly became aware of how badly the inside of my visored helmet smelled. Sweat, nicotine, and bad-coffee breath oozed out from the dense foam padding. Beneath our stab-proof vests and helmets, we all wore matching black fatigues and ski masks, so we couldn't be recognized by sharp-eyed inmates looking for revenge later.

The sergeant gave the inmate one last chance to put his hands through the food slot, cuff up, and come out peacefully. The inmate's response was an incomprehensible rant. The rest of the block's population sensed the moment of truth drawing near and raised the volume and intensity of the screaming, pounding, and chanting to a near-deafening warlike roar. The sergeant checked his video camera. The nurses nervously stood back from the cell door. Officer N, the number-one guy, huddled the four of us together. He suspected the inmate knew what we were up to and was standing inside the door against the wall waiting for us to rush in, giving him a shot of rushing out or doing something worse, especially if he had a weapon. Office N, a tough and very well-respected guy, told us to give him a split second. If the inmate was hiding to the left of the cell door, he would pull him out into the hallway where it would be much easier for all of us to get to work. It made a lot of sense: Pull the guy out into an open space, or we'd end up like four pit bulls in a box, all trying to bite the same rat.

"Ready," the sergeant said loudly. We all nodded, put our heads down, and placed the flats of our hands on the back of the guy in front of us. I did a quick pat check. The cuffs were in the square Velcro pocket on the front of my stab-proof vest. The sergeant raised his radio to his mouth. Then, over the din of the near-riot-ous cellblock I heard him say, "Control, open cell fifteen."

The door in front of us hissed and made a heavy clanking sound and then quickly slid from left to right. Officer N's intuition was spot on. The inmate was pressed against the wall to our left, ready for us to storm in and hopefully miss the target. We gave Officer N the split second he asked for. Instead of rushing in for the usual pig pile, Officer N grabbed the inmate by the shirt with both hands and cordially invited him into the corridor for a game of Twister. The inmate hit the floor with a heavy thump. The rest of the block's population erupted, screaming and beating at their doors. The four of us leaped to it. The inmate decided to fight. This was a bad idea, and mainly a show put on for the benefit of other inmates. A good performance was very important. If a prisoner wanted to maintain his reputation, he had to be seen to fight.

The sergeant ordered the inmate to "stop resisting." The inmate continued to struggle, scream, and curse in his unintelligible native tongue. The sergeant gave the order again. The inmate continued to thrash around wildly. The sergeant leaned down and then blasted him in the face with a prolonged shot of pepper spray. As the pepper spray worked its magic, in what can only be described as a feeling of having several red-hot screwdrivers rammed into your eyes, nose, and mouth, Officer N got the wrist lock he'd been looking for. At that same moment, the rest of us got the other wrist and ankles just where we needed them.

Then, the miracle happened. In perfect English, the inmate screamed out, "Stop! Stop! You're going to break my arms. Stop! Oh, God, stop it! You're killing me!"

"I JUST WANTED A BETTER LIFE FOR MY FAMILY." THAT'S WHAT A Mexican inmate in A-Block told me one day when I asked him if he was OK. I had been watching him for a little while. He looked terrible, desperate, like he was about to do something crazy. His story was all too familiar. After refusing to leave his wife and young children, as a family they worked their way north, following farm work all the way from Florida to Pennsylvania. He had recently found employment at a mushroom-growing plant just outside town. One day a couple of weeks prior, the cops arrived to check everyone's papers. In another post–9/11 roundup, the guy was thrown into prison, not for criminal activity, but for being an undocumented alien. The fact that he was working and contributing to the economy didn't matter.

He told me, "Señor Reilly, I feel terrible. I don't know what is going to happen to my family."

I felt every bit of his anguish and desperation. Homeland Security had told him, after they processed his paperwork, they'd be deporting him back to Mexico. Until then, his wife and children would be stuck in a terrible house in a horrible neighborhood. Once he was back in Mexico, he'd somehow have to perform the impossible by conjuring up enough money to enable his loved ones to return home. That's if he could contact them, find out where they were living, and get the cash safely into their hands. He was probably going to be in prison for close to two years.

"I'm so worried about them, Señor Reilly. Is there any way you can help me?"

I hated doing it but I told him the truth: I said there was absolutely nothing I could do. The only thing I could do was think about Sarah and our children. I tried to imagine what it would be like for them to be in that situation. What if I was an illegal immigrant? What if something bad and out of my control had happened and I was locked up while they were stuck in some ghettoized hellhole without money or my protection. It would be beyond terrible. The very thought of it made me feel anxious and sick.

The A- and B-Blocks were full of people like this guy: men who weren't criminals in the real sense of the word, just men who existed outside the framework of the traditional employment infrastructure, economic driftwood, poor people trying to catch a wave, trying to make a buck and provide for their family and not sink along the way.

While I was playing music, one of my many crappy part-time jobs was working at a department store distribution warehouse. I worked there for about a year, Monday through Wednesday, second shift. The place looked like someone had welded six windowless aircraft hangars together and then filled the massive building full of brown cardboard boxes, hundreds of miserable workers, and a series of sixty-watt light bulbs every thousand square feet. The packages whipped around inside the dim, cavernous building on a complex set of overhead and ground-level conveyor belts. It was loud, dirty, and a desperately depressing place to work. The boxes that were too big for the conveyer belts were moved around inside the building by a fleet of forklift trucks. At the countless conveyor belt termination points were dozens of loading docks. The trailer bay must have been about a quarter of a mile long. Dozens of tractor trailers backed up to the dock and got filled with the merchandise that was to be taken to the various regional department stores. I hated the job intensely, but I needed the extra money. Just before I quit, for a slightly better part-time job, I remember looking at the miles of conveyor belts and the hundreds of thousands of brown cardboard packages getting loaded into the dozens of trailers. I thought to myself, these packages are going to keep coming and coming for as long as I live. I could work here for the next forty years loading trucks and watching packages move through the system on hundreds of miles of aluminum rollers. Immediately after speaking to the Mexican inmate, I suddenly started to feel that the prison was just the same as that monstrous warehouse. The inmates were just going to keep on coming and coming and coming and never stop.

ONE OF THE MOST ENTERTAINING, HIGH-MAINTENANCE INMATES IN the A- and B-Blocks was inmate U. To the best of my knowledge, inmate U was being detained by the government for bank fraud and tax evasion. After his arrest, it had been discovered that he was not a legal resident. Inmate U had been living under the immigration radar in the land of the free and the home of the brave for most of the thirty-one years he had been alive. Apart from a strong Pakistani accent, inmate U was as American as Microsoft and Walt Disney, but as far as Uncle Sam was concerned, he was a foreign national without documentation. He and his family had been residing and doing business in a predominantly Pakistani neighborhood in a large northeastern city for decades. Apparently, inmate U had been slowly bending the law for years, until one day it finally snapped and thrust him into the white-hot post-9/11 Homeland Security spotlight.

Inmate U was a royal pain in the ass. He complained about everything: the lack of special diet items, the limited access to the law library, the cramped and dirty living conditions, the lack of privacy when he showered, and the inability to practice his religion properly. He also complained about the volume of the TV in the dayroom, the material the prison-issue clothes were made of, the rash he had been getting from the soap he had to use, and on and on and on.

According to gossip filtering down from the admin office, inmate U's family had hired a lawyer who had been sending a landslide of nasty letters to members of the prison board and the warden regarding the inhumane treatment of his client and how his basic human rights were being denied. Also, according to gossip, the warden was terrified the mighty inmate U might actually get somewhere with his proactive legal lobbying. If there was so much as a whiff of racial, sexual, or religious inequality within the walls of the institution (not to imply that sort of thing would ever happen in a prison) and a sympathetic media outlet got their hands on the story, the warden may as well hang himself.

It was said that inmate U and his lawyer were well aware of the warden's fear and were riding him like a rented mule. Whatever the truth was regarding inmate U's lawyers and their hardball legal lobbying, the net result was that inmate U got about half of what he wanted, including personal visits to his cell by the warden himself and his entourage of doting deputies, secretaries, and social workers, all of whom appeared to be in training to be the warden's next proctologist.

Inmate U became a bit of a prison celebrity, offering financial and legal advice to other inmates, bringing dozens of his new friends to become faithful followers of the Islamic faith, especially during Ramadan, when, courtesy of the warden, bags of fresh food were handed out to all the true believers twice a day. Inmate U had also managed to acquire extra time in the law library each week. And, of course, he was accompanied by a dozen or so other inmates who had requested the same privilege under threat of legal action of their own. The guards joked that inmate U was the new warden. Inmate U liked the joke and thought it was very funny. It was rumored the warden knew about the joke, but did not think it was very funny.

Inmate U had been a guest of the government and the INS for nearly two years. His case dragged through the courts at about the same pace as a slow-moving glacier down a mountainside. In a strange way, both the guards and the inmates grew to hold inmate U in quite high esteem. There was no doubt he was a difficult, demanding, high-maintenance troublemaker, but the only trouble he really caused was the kind that gave the warden a migraine and career indigestion. Both guards and inmates liked this because they all detested the warden equally. The guards detested him because he gave the inmates too much, and the inmates detested him because he didn't give them enough.

One cold March evening, the old phone in the A-/B-Block control room rang loudly. The bell was as abrasive as the atmosphere in the A-/B-Block. It was hard and jingly and always sounded like emergency music. The voice on the other end informed me that two agents from the Department of Homeland Security had arrived to take inmate U home. This news was completely unexpected. According to inmate U, he was on the cusp of having his case heard by the Supreme Court, and when he was released, he was going to sue everyone in the Northern Hemisphere wearing a uniform or holding any kind of state or government-appointed position. But it looked like the Supreme Court had passed on this particular case, and inmate U was about to receive his get-out-of-jail (not quite free) card. I hit the button on the intercom, "Mr. U, two sixteen. Mr. U, two sixteen. You are being released. Please bring your property down to the booking office."

The news traveled through the cellblock like a shockwave. From behind the glass of the officer's station a cheer could be heard reverberating throughout the entire housing block. Various recently converted Muslims leaped up from their big, plastic, riot-proof armchairs and dashed into the dirty cell-lined corridors to make sure inmate U had heard the good news, the great news!

Other recent converts shouted things like "Allah is most merciful!" and "Our brother's chains have been broken." But they didn't move until the white pickup truck they were watching on *Cops* crashed into a convenience store and the driver was pulled out and pummeled by several burly police officers who were all well and truly tired of the redneck wild goose chase.

Fifteen minutes later, the victorious inmate U, pumping his fists into the air and waving his arms like a long-shot underdog who'd just won the title, entered the dayroom surrounded by a throng of supporters, carrying his tote, laundry bag, and numerous boxes of legal materials. As promised, he had won his fight and was about to regain his freedom.

I looked at inmate U and thought that he and I were not too dissimilar, both uneducated immigrants looking for a way out of the same harsh reality. I thought about how I had come to know him a little bit over the last few months and how he was now getting out, escaping from prison, just like he always said he would. I realized I wanted to escape as well. I wanted to leave this town and this lousy job, go home, collect my family, and drive away to Washington State, Colorado, the Florida Keys, or up to northern New England and find a new job where I wasn't exposed to the worst parts of the worst people every day. I had a flash daydream about a little house near the beach or the mountains. My kids and I were playing outside. The children were running around without shoes on, and I was spraying them with a hose. We were all laughing. Sarah was smiling at us, watching from a big backyard deck.

As inmate U walked toward the booking room, he talked over his shoulder to the other inmates, "I vill not forget you my brothers. Ven I get home I vill continue the fight. Sa vite devil vill be brought to its knees!" I smiled. I had heard this speech so many times I almost knew the lines by heart. Whenever an inmate leaves, they are always full of vows to keep in touch and do this or send that. The words are full of nothing but bravado. Everyone knew it, but the inmate U show had to have a closing act, and a victory parade, full of powerful promises and rhetorical threats.

On the whole, inmate U's relationship with most of the guards was good, despite his overly annoying barrage of questions and requests. Inmate U knew, rather like himself, that most of the guards would much rather be somewhere else. He understood that inmates get trapped by the law, and prison guards get trapped by economics and lack of education. Most of the men and women who work these jobs fall into this line of employment out of financial necessity. Prison guards look at their job no differently than any other factory worker looks at his job. The only difference is the product in the prison factory is living, breathing flesh. The shifts are the same as every other factory, but in this line of work, there are never any layoffs or cutbacks, because there's never a recession in crime. Smart inmates like inmate U learn this quickly and intuitively understand the guards are generally not the enemy.

Before entering the release room, inmate U stopped and rooted through a light brown legal folder he was carrying under his right arm. He pulled out a *Playboy* "college girls" calendar and handed it to a withered old African American man who had been carrying his laundry bag. The old man put down the laundry bag and took the calendar with a wide-eyed grin that lit up his tired, toothless face.

"Thanks, man. Y'know, I always loved dat ting. Oh yeah, Miss September's so fine, she make me wanna sign up for some college classes myself."

As the old man held up the calendar and leafed through it, looking for the lovely Miss September, inmate U put both his hands on the wrists of the old man and said, "Remember, ven looking at girl from September, make sure you only use von eye, just in case you're struck blind."

Inmate U and the old man exchanged a coy smile. The door to the release room automatically clicked open. Inmate U and I disappeared into the sally port. After the door slammed shut, the noise of the busy dayroom was behind us, muffled and barely audible.

Inmate U grinned at me and said, "I told you so, Mr. Reilly. I vill be vindicated and dis great injustice vill be corrected, mark my verds."

I nodded, smiled, and channeled Uncle Bob, saying, "Maybe so, maybe so, inmate U."

Inside the release room stood two tired, slightly untidy Homeland Security officers. They were there to take inmate U out of the prison and back to his home. Both men looked like they were doing too much overtime and not getting enough exercise. The younger, slightly cockier officer stepped forward, presented inmate U with a folder, and told him, "Everything in the bottom right-hand corner marked with an X has to be signed before we leave the facility. Do you understand me?"

The Homeland Security officer overemphasized the "do you understand me" part, like he was talking to an imbecile. Inmate U bristled at the officer's tone. I felt it, too, but obviously said nothing. I suddenly sensed the onset of one of inmate U's militant victory speeches. He was about to lash the proud ears of the arrogant infidel. My gut feeling was validated.

"Let me tell you something, my good fellow. Do not talk to me like I am idiot. I am businessman and have many connections. I see your nametag and you too vill be named in very large lawsuit that vill bring you and your people to your knees. If you vish to treat me like animal, then you are vanting but you are not getting. Oh no, no, no! All my life I have vorked and been a part of your precious American dream. I vork hard, I pay a few taxes, and I even donated big check to your president, Mr. George Bush, and this is how I am treated, like common criminal. Let me tell you something, because of people like you, I hate America and its hypocrisies. I am very angry vith you and your government—very, very angry indeed. This place is sheet, America is sheet, and ven I get home there vill be justice, names vill be named, and da guilty vill be held accountable!"

The two Homeland Security officers looked at each other. Their facial expressions didn't change but their eyes clearly said, "Can you believe this shit?"

Inmate U angrily signed the pages, one after another, scrawling his proud signature boldly above, below, and across the entire neat little line in the bottom right-hand side of the page, a last act of noncompliance.

"The vite man has ruined dis country. You so busy enforcing stupid laws, you fail to see dis country is being taken over by man vith colored skin. And von day soon you vite men are going to be the downtrodden outcasts and vee, da men of color, vill rule America. America is sheet, its courts are sheet, and its law enforcement is sheet. I hate you, and I am hating America!"

Finally the older of the two Homeland Security officers, a rugged-looking man in his early fifties, walked up to inmate U and asked him in an aggressive growl, "Have you quite finished, because you are starting to piss me off."

This guy meant business, and I could tell he was not far from making inmate U understand him in a much different way.

I interjected, trying to be the voice of reason. "Mr. U, please. All you have to do is sign the paperwork, and then you're out of here."

Inmate U ignored me and raged on. "Oh no, I have just started. You people take two years of my life away and you expect me to be happy! Happy, ha, ha? Vell, I am not happy. I am vanting phone call to let my family know I am coming home and I am vanting to call my attorney. You bastards have no idea who you are dealing vith. I am hating you, and I am hating America!"

The two Homeland Security officers stepped up to the counter to the left and right of their prisoner. The mood in the room instantly turned hostile, leaning toward physical. The younger of the two Homeland Security officers opened the pouch on the left side of his belt and got out his handcuffs. Mr. U glanced down at the cuffs and then rapidly finished signing the last couple of forms. He was visibly seething. His signature became erratic and scrawling. As he finished signing the paperwork, he said loudly and forcefully, "I am vanting to make phone call!"

The older of the two guards said, "Mr. U, you will not be able to make a phone call before we take you home."

Mr. U whipped around. "Vat are you saying? I must have phone call. It is my right, you do not understand. My people are not knowing ven I am coming. Dey must know I am free and coming home. You don't understand."

The two Homeland Security guards gave each other a sly look. The younger of the two sneered. The older man continued, "Oh, I think it's you who doesn't understand, Mr. U. When I said we're taking you home, I meant we're taking you back to Pakistan. You're application for a visa has been denied. You're being deported. In a few hours, my partner and I are boarding a plane with you in custody, and tomorrow we will be getting off the plane in Karachi."

The two Homeland Security officers smiled at each other. Inmate U became frozen solid, a statue of incredulity. The words were seeping into him like black ink on a white linen sheet, reaching into his heart, turning into the sharp steel teeth of a nightmarish trap quickly closing around his known world, shutting out the light, crushing the future, separating him from all the memories and experiences that had brought him to this point.

"Oh no! No, no, no! Please, don't take me, no don't take me. I cannot leave, I vant to stay, I vant to stay! I love America, I love America! God bless America, God bless President George Bush! Mr. Reilly, please can you help me?"

Inmate U was dragged out of the prison handcuffed, kicking, screaming, and professing his love for America. Minutes later, in the back of a Homeland Security van, he was on his way to JFK International Airport. Next stop, Karachi International Airport, Pakistan.

In the wake of inmate U leaving for Pakistan, I started thinking about returning to England and seriously began to consider "going home." Sarah said it was up to me. She'd move back to the U.K. in a second if I wanted to go. The easiest way to make that possible would be to ask my parents for a job in their business, which was now being run by my youngest brother Paul. It was so much to think about, selling the house, packing up the family and all our belongings, traveling back across the Atlantic. The whole idea would be a huge undertaking. It also felt like another open admission of defeat. I had just applied for citizenship; Big Zeke still hadn't fully recovered. Our kids would have a huge readjustment period. Could I work for my father and my youngest brother? I wasn't sure.

Then, a conversation with a relative put the whole thing to death. I was asked, "So, when are you going back to England?" The question caught me off-guard. I felt like I was having my mind read. I hadn't shared my thoughts with anyone except for Sarah. "Why do you ask?" I responded. "Well, I thought that since you'd failed in the music business, it wouldn't be long until you went home to ask your father for a job." That was all it took. Suddenly, the idea of going back to the U.K. on my knees, begging my parents for work just wasn't an option. I'd stay put, fight it out, and see what I could do on my own. My smug, condescending relative could go to hell.

22

Lights Out

THE PRISON WAS HAVING PROBLEMS WITH THE POWER. IT WAS AN ongoing problem. And it seemed like it always happened during violent storms. Occasionally, just to keep everyone on their toes, it happened during extended periods of clear, calm weather. But, on this occasion, the gale-force gusts and heavy rain battering the entire eastern side of the state seemed to be the culprit. Outside, in the darkness, beyond the high walls and the prison's outer perimeter fence, the howling wind and near-horizontal rain were trying to tear down the barbed wire and drown the ground. From the narrow cellblock windows, flashes of white electric light and powerful gusting winds were illuminating the high chain-link fences, flexing the millions of coils of razor ribbon and making the Frankenstein night look "alive!" Just as I was thinking, *What a great night it would be for an escape,* all the lights flickered off and on a couple of times. Then, the entire facility was plunged into a pitch-black, blinding darkness.

I was sitting at my desk, writing notes in my pocket diary when the power went out. I'd started to keep copious amount of notes, almost from day one. Seeing as Sergeant G didn't want me to read, which I was still doing at every single opportunity, I jotted down, with as much accuracy as I could, all the details of my daily escapades. The cellblock was completely black. I literally couldn't see my hand in front of my face. Then, for a brief moment, the lights came back on, and, a second later, went out again. When the lights didn't come back on, the inmates went wild. The radio crackled to life: "Attention all officers. Lock in. Lock in. Lock in. Lock all inmates in."

I was lucky. The only inmates I had out were four trustees who were cleaning up after another nutritious evening meal: a delicious gray-brown mystery meat, tapeworm noodles, and a dollop of corn starch pudding for dessert. Those who were locked in, ninety-two of them, all went ballistic and started pounding on their doors, screaming, howling, and making animal noises. I've no idea why they did it, but whenever there was some sort of drama, you could always count on hearing at least one cow, a couple of pigs, and a chorus of barking dogs and yowling cats.

A mock female voice yelled out, "Oh, mother, help me, help me! He's trying it again."

In the complete and total darkness, I quietly opened the desk drawer and got out the flashlight, standard issue on all cellblocks. Before I turned it on, I reached behind me and opened the staff restroom door. The staff restroom was directly behind the desk. Its concrete walls and heavy metal door would be a real refuge if you needed to stay safe. That's if you could reach it in time. The initial noise died down a little, and I heard footsteps not far in front of me. I didn't want to put the flashlight on. I knew if I couldn't see them, then they couldn't see me. A crash of thunder and a slash of lightning cast a blinking flash of white into the cellblock through the narrow second-floor windows. In that brief moment I saw four silhouettes standing around my desk. Then, from a cell very close by, a deep whispering voice uttered, "Fuck up the CO."

Then another voice from another cell yelled out, "Yeah, man, fuck him up."

I could hear footfalls close by then the wooden clack of a mop handle hitting the floor, followed by the thunk of an inmate walking into a mop-bucket. That was immediately followed by the

sound of water sloshing across the floor in front of my desk. I got a
warm waft of hot water and institutional detergent, pine scented. I
checked the restroom door again. It was ajar. I placed my hands
over my keys to mute any sound, stepped in front of the desk,
flicked on the flashlight, and swept its beam from left to right. All
four inmates were standing in a semicircle directly in front of me.
One of them stood in a big puddle of soapy water. The other three
stared and blinked repeatedly as I passed the white shaft of light
over their squinting faces.

The anonymous voice called out again, "C'mon, man, what ya
waiting for? Fuck 'im up."

I broke in, calling each inmate by name, telling them they had
to go to their cells and lock in. Because the control panel was
down, I walked each prisoner to his cell, manually unlocked the
door, told him to go in and then locked the door behind him,
thanking each man for his cooperation. I did this four times.

Just as I locked the last prisoner in, a supervisor's voice came
over the radio. "H-Block, Reilly, are you secure?"

"All secure on H-Block," I replied.

It felt like a close call, and I was glad it was over. What I was
really glad about was that all but four of the inmates were locked
in. I used the feeble beam of the cellblock's only flashlight to read
a couple of Roald Dahl short stories, and finished the rest of the
night without power, in full lockdown mode. Shortly after ten
o'clock, third shift arrived.

I drove home slowly over storm-wrecked roads, my car pummeled by torrential rain, violent, shuddering wind gusts, lifeless
traffic lights swinging like church bells to the deaf, fallen trees,
and blacked-out neighborhoods full of dark shadowy houses. As
soon as I got home, I walked all around the house looking for
storm damage, then went inside and checked on the children. All
three were sleeping peacefully and looked so beautiful, oblivious
to what was happening outside. I undressed in the darkness,
placed my clothes over a chair, and slid into bed next to a sleeping
Sarah. And as I lay under the covers, listening to the rain drumming against the windows and the roar of the gale-force winds,
pounding the house, flexing and flapping the darkness like the

canvas of some enormously evil black tent, I closed my eyes and hoped deep in my heart that by the time I woke up, the prison would be blown off the face of the earth by some unexplainable act of God. The next day, when I arrived at work, I was not in the least bit surprised to find the power still out. After roll call, I, along with several other members of staff, were armed and sent out to patrol the institution's perimeter. We were told by a near-ecstatic Sergeant G to be on "high alert for escape attempts and a visit from the FBI." This day had the potential of being the greatest of Sergeant G's life. The very notion that she might be able to supervise the shooting of a couple of convicts and meet a real-life FBI agent was visibly almost more than she could bear. She was positively glowing with self-importance, expectation, and the sort of euphoria reserved for saints immediately prior to a prearranged visit from the Almighty.

The potential escape issue was a thing of absolute fantasy. All the inmates were secured behind doors that were manually locked the old-fashioned way, with keys. Some of the oldest doors in the disciplinary unit had even been chained shut, just for good measure. The looming FBI visit was on account of an accused murderer from New York City, currently incarcerated in the prison and scheduled for an interview with the Feds.

As luck would have it, I just happened to be patrolling the parking lot when an official-looking dark-blue sedan car with New York plates cruised up the prison driveway and pulled into an empty parking space. A slim, average-sized, fit, middle-aged man in a dark suit got out of the car, with a briefcase. As I approached him, carrying my shotgun, he smiled, told me his name—Agent G from the New York City FBI—and then pointed to the breast pocket of his jacket and said, "Just going to get my ID out."

He opened his sport coat and I saw a handgun and holster attached to his belt. He showed me his FBI ID and said he was here to interview inmate M. I introduced myself and told him about the power outage. He gave me a slightly confused look, then we shook hands and I led him to the intake-release area. I was very impressed by the guy. He was warm, talkative, and very polite, not at all like the fictitious, unapproachable media Feds. As we walked to the door that led to the secure inner section of the prison, I told him he would have to place his pistol in a locker in the outer hallway.

"No guns or ammo inside the facility."

"No problem," he said. "Just let me know what I need to do."

I radioed ahead to the lieutenant on duty, making sure I skipped over Sergeant G, who was now probably foaming at the mouth knowing I had met the real-life FBI agent and passed him to her supervisor. Before the FBI guy walked inside the prison, he extended his hand again, shook mine, and then thanked me by name for meeting him and being so helpful. The pleasure was all mine.

THE PRISON'S POWER WAS DOWN FOR AN ENTIRE WEEK. IT TURNED out the oil tanks that fuel the facility's backup generator had recently been emptied during a recent service but not refilled. When the generator kicked on, giving us that brief flicker of light, it promptly burned out some kind of widget that could not be replaced immediately. Apparently the replacement part had to come all the way from New Guinea, transported to the prison by a one-armed man in a leaky rowboat. Personally, I thought the warden sent a confidante from the maintenance department down to the local hardware store the next day, bought a big fat fuse that would get everything back online, but kept it on his desk for a week so he could squeeze as much political capital out of the power outage as possible.

I was now certain the warden secretly loved anything that made his job look difficult. I imagined he fantasized about newspaper headlines that might read, "Another Tough Week for the Prison," accompanied by a photo of the himself looking anxious and a subheading that read something like, "A great public servant shoulders more than his fair share of the community's burden."

It seemed to me that the prison was like a rather large sewage treatment plant, a place the mass majority of the general public don't care about. That is, unless disaster strikes and the contents of its holding tanks somehow gets out and starts running down Main Street.

23

The Good Inmate

WHATEVER I NEEDED, INMATE RO WAS ALWAYS THERE: EXTRA HELP during cleanup, standing in as a worker on the food line, scrubbing the showers when the job wasn't done properly, and giving me a heads-up if something troublesome was percolating. In short, he was a hard worker and an informant whom no one suspected of being a rat. Whatever I needed, he was always there to oblige. After my initial period of suspicion wore off, I actually got to like inmate RO. He was so helpful and so straightforward, I was kind of impressed by him and wondered why he wasn't having success in life. I even asked him about it.

He told me he grew up in a bad neighborhood without a father, got in trouble after high school, and caught a couple of small prison bids for stealing. Then, after going straight for quite a few years, he bought a bag of weed from an undercover cop and ended up getting locked down again. Inmate RO seemed sensible to me. He was in his late twenties or early thirties, was fairly articulate, wasn't covered in tattoos, worked out, kept his cell as neat as a pin, and genuinely seemed full of regret for getting busted for buying weed. I honestly felt sorry for him.

On a couple of occasions, inmate RO really helped me out. Once, an argument between several inmates quickly escalated into a near fistfight. There was a lot of cursing, pointing, and pre-brawl posturing. I stepped into the middle of things, but it was like I wasn't there. I yelled for the inmates to settle down and back off, but no one was listening. Realizing things were close to escalating out of control, I pulled out my radio, raised it to my mouth, and was just about to call for assistance when the burly figure of inmate RO walked into the middle of the fray and yelled out, "C'mon, cut it out."

For whatever reason, the group of five or six men stopped yelling at each other and walked away in opposite directions. I was impressed inmate RO could do something I couldn't, and he seemingly didn't think it was a big deal. I spoke with him later and told him how much I appreciated what he did, but he shrugged it off and wouldn't really accept my thanks.

On another occasion, a group of inmates was watching the Miss Universe pageant. I was surprised by the respectful tone and content of the conversations regarding the contestants. The inmates commented thoughtfully on the girls' outfits, singing, and dancing abilities. One of the young women was interviewed and said she'd just gotten into medical school. This really got the viewers excited. One of the inmates said something foul, boring, and unfunny about the pre-med beauty queen giving him a physical. Inmate RO took exception to this, reprimanded him in front of the other inmates, and sent him away from the TV for being disrespectful to women. Again, the only thing I could be was impressed.

When inmate RO left prison, we shook hands and I wished him the very best and hoped he continued to act in the same way on the outside I'd witnessed him acting on the inside. I remember telling him, if he continued to conduct himself the way he had been doing, he'd be on the right track.

Several weeks later, Mr. RO was inmate RO again. He was back in prison for raping and murdering a sixty-nine-year-old Sunday school teacher. I can honestly say, of all the bad, mad, and crazy people I had met and experiences I'd had since I started working at the prison, the inmate RO incident got to me the most. It made me second-guess myself on a very deep level. I was convinced I had a really good feel for people and great gut-feeling about who I could and couldn't trust. The whole thing made me feel like a first-week rookie all over again. In subsequent weeks, I worked on the same block where inmate RO was housed. I could barely look at him. I definitely couldn't speak to him. There were a couple of occasions when he tried to catch my eye, inviting me into some sort of interaction, but I couldn't do it. He had completely fooled me.

24

Big Zeke

On February 10, 2004, Big Zeke was in the hospital again. The last few months of physical decline had developed into full-blown pneumonia. That evening, after taking Joshua to his swimming lesson, I went over to the hospital. It was close to the end of visiting hours. I was the only person there. When I walked into the room, Zeke was awake, lying in bed and staring blankly into space. I took my coat off, draped it over the back of a chair, and then sat down on the bed beside him. He looked thin and gaunt. All his strength was being stripped away. He worked up a smile and reached out with both of his hands for mine, as we held hands he glanced at the video camera I'd brought along with me and asked, "What do you have there?"

"A video of Josh swimming; I thought you might like to see how he's coming along." We watched the video several times. He said he thought Josh was going to turn into "a fine young man." It sounded so final, like something he knew would happen but would never see.

A few days later I called the hospital from the prison staff room. I knew Sarah was planning to be there all morning. Someone else answered, but Sarah quickly got on the phone and asked me if I could get out of work. She said her dad was going downhill fast and the doctor thought he could pass at any time. I called the shift commander's office and spoke to a supervisor. I explained the situation and said I need to leave work as soon as possible. They told me it would take about half an hour to find a replacement. They were right: about thirty minutes later I was relieved by someone who told me he was sorry to hear about my father in-law, but was delighted I had to leave because he really needed the overtime.

Big Zeke lay dying in his hospital bed; it was about 10:15 a.m. The curtains covering the window allowed the brilliant February sun to enter the room around the outside edges of the glass, giving the illusion of a highly polished silver frame around the window itself. The only electric light was in the far corner of the room. It was dim and yellow, forty watts perhaps. There was a dull hum of forced air being blown through an AC vent and a constant hiss of oxygen being released into the mask covering Big Zeke's nose and mouth. And apart from the extraneous sounds of hospital life going on outside an almost closed door, the room was quiet and smelled of detergent and fresh-cut flowers.

Zeke was laboring under great strain for every single breath. His eyes were closed, but he was conscious; I just knew he was. I stood at the foot of the bed but couldn't speak. Any words I might have wanted to say were trapped in my throat; I had the sensation of a child's wooden building block being wedged in my esophagus.

DURING THE DRAMA OF SICKNESS, BIRTH, AND DEATH, THE WOMEN do all the emotional heavy lifting. They give themselves entirely to the process while the men become helpless bystanders, inarticulate onlookers. Around the bed sat Sarah, her sister Allison, sister-in-law Susan, and Barb. Each clutched a hand or lower leg in their hands. The four women sat in perfect symmetry, hunched over, exhausted by grief, and awaiting the inevitable—desperately holding on while their husband, father, and father in-law slowly and agonizingly let go. Oh, God, I prayed silently inside my own head, did you love Lazarus more? It's not too late, we know you're there, a miracle, please, we beseech you.

Someone came into the room. My silent prayer evaporated.

Hours passed. The four women in waiting didn't move. Big Zeke continued to try and fill his one working lung. A minister and various family members hovered restlessly outside the door in the busy hospital hallway. His good looks and strength were almost gone now: His wisdom and wit, his sense of humor, his unassuming, easygoing character were all, like the daylight, failing fast.

The next morning, Valentine's Day, I got up early and called off work. As I was feeding and dressing the kids, the phone rang. Sarah's sleep-deprived, exhausted voice filled the receiver. Her dad had fought all night, became alert during a visit from a doctor, and said he wanted to go home. I couldn't believe it! The physician agreed to Zeke's request and as we were speaking, an ambulance was being called. I told Sarah I'd dress the kids and come over right away. The miracle must have happened. The news was amazing.

It took me ages to get the kids dressed and ready to go. Just as we were leaving the house the phone rang. I put down baby Zeke, two carseats, and a diaper bag and answered it. There was a long silence, then sobbing. Sarah told me her dad had been brought into the house, put into his bed, and after a few short minutes, he had passed away. He was only sixty-eight. And that's how it happened: on his own terms and with equal measures of dignity and modesty, he was gone.

A MONTH AFTER ZEKE'S PASSING I RECEIVED AN OFFICIAL LETTER IN the mail informing me that all my paperwork was in order and I was to report to the city courthouse on March 24 to be sworn in as an American citizen. In the wake of the recent events, it was hard to get excited about anything. I got the day off from work, polished my shoes, put on a suit, and with my family in tow, headed downtown. I wasn't sure what to expect. I suppose I thought I would be sworn in, in an anteroom with a handful of other immigrants. I was surprised to find a near circus-like atmosphere in the county's main courtroom as seventy-six people, and an enormous audience of families, from literally all over the planet were becoming U.S. citizens. I found the ceremony extremely moving. The speaker told us new citizens "to carry the burden of freedom as though it were a child and nurture it by voting."

25

Fall Guys

AFTER ZEKE PASSED AWAY, GOING BACK TO WORK AT THE PRISON felt terrible. I didn't care about a thing. I found myself wallowing in a bad attitude and trying to get away with doing as little as possible. Most of my co-workers and all the inmates lost all their personality, and I became one of the "us and them" guards. I thought about Big Zeke constantly and felt angry every time I became aware of prisoners receiving medical treatment and getting cured, knowing full well what they were in for and what they were doing while they were locked up. I remember thinking: *They should just let these guys die in here.*

In May, I was sitting at the desk in J-Block. The dayroom was almost empty and very quiet. A spell of good weather had taken most of the inmates into the yard to enjoy a spot of outdoor rec. My radio, which I had sitting on the desk facing me, burst into life, blaring, "Fight in J-Block yard! Fight in J-Block yard!"

Crap, that's me! I quickly turned off the control panel, clipped my keys to my belt, grabbed the radio, and ran for the rec yard door.

"Control," I called into the radio as I ran, "Open J-Block rec yard door, J-Block rec yard door."

Whoever was in housing control was right on it. I sprinted across the dayroom and as I approached the door, it clicked open. It was so bright outside, my eyes had to adjust from the dim interior of the cellblock. The yard was packed with well over sixty high-security inmates. Squinting down from the steps, I glanced over the heads of the prisoners and through the fence. Officer I was on perimeter duty. He pointed excitedly to a knot of men in one corner. I ran across the yard, burst through the circle of inmates, and found two prisoners knocking lumps out of each other.

"Break it up! Break it up!" I yelled as I reached the fighters. I pulled the two men apart. One of them, bleeding from the nose and mouth, fell limply to the floor, like a pile of wet laundry. The other, still raging and in full fight mode, surged forward. I grabbed hold of his shirt. He pulled away, screaming, cursing, and pointing at the man on the ground. I pulled back on his clothing, grabbed him in a headlock, leaned forward, and flipped him. The inmate sailed over my back, his momentum took me off my feet. We both landed on the blacktop hard, me right on top of him. A second later, we were surrounded by dozens of chanting, hostile prisoners.

I heard the weird stereo effect of Officer I's voice coming from behind the fence and also out of the radio attached to my belt. He yelled, "Is anyone coming? Reilly's in there by himself!"

The inmate continued cursing and swearing, his gasping face next to mine. I hung on for dear life, squeezing down on the headlock as hard as I could, moving my body around to keep my weight on top of his. The fighter tried desperately to wrench himself free. He growled and hissed at me as we made brief eye contact.

"If you don't let me go, I'll fucking kill you."

I thought he was going to bite me. I pulled my face away from his. The radio went off again, this time the voice was yelling, full of urgency, "Assistance in J-Block yard! Assistance in J-Block yard! Officer and inmate fighting!"

From where I was lying on the deck of the rec yard, holding on tight to the inmate, all I could see were dozens of feet shifting from left to right, surging toward me and then pulling back. A thought and an image flashed through my mind, if these guys start kicking me, it's all over. The image was of a fight I had been in during high school. After weeks of friction between me and another kid, things came to a head one night and erupted into fisticuffs. As with most unskilled fights, like the one I was in, it quickly turned to wrestling and went to the ground. It went rapidly downhill from there. The friends of the boy I was fighting and, funnily enough, his older sister, circled around me. I couldn't get up. My opponent held onto me, his superior weight and strength pinning me down. I kicked, punched, wriggled, and squirmed. The circle of friends moved in closer and then put the boot in. They kicked me until I was black and blue and almost senseless.

The door of the housing unit flew opened. A dozen screaming prison guards rushed out. In seconds, all the inmates were sitting with their hands on their heads. As I stood and brushed myself off, the two fighters were cuffed up and taken to medical for a checkup and then off to The Hole for unsportsmanlike conduct.

The guy I flipped suffered a broken clavicle as a result of me landing on top of him. A nurse told me about the broken bone. She heard my name mentioned by the inmate when he was talking to a trustee who worked in the infirmary. The nurse said she wanted to give me a heads-up because it wasn't beyond the realm of possibility for the inmate to try and get some sort of lawsuit going with my name all over it. And, if that happened, the warden would ask for my head to be severed, placed on a tray, and then given to the lawyers as a peace offering.

Not wanting to be one of the warden's fall guys, the next day, I went down to The Hole to see the inmate and ask him about his injury. After speaking with the nurse, thoughts of lawsuits and revenge had been cycling regularly through my mind. But when the inmate saw me at his door he called out, "Hey, Mr. Reilly, how ya doin'?"

I looked at him in his arm sling and said, "Sorry about the shoulder. You didn't really give me much of a chance out there yesterday. Anyway, what was all that fighting about?"

"Oh, don't worry about this." He pointed at the sling with his good hand. "Dude kept bumping the chess board, and all the pieces kept moving off the squares. I just got mad and lost it."

As I processed the response, I pointed at him and said, "I hope you and I aren't going to have any problems when you get back on the block."

The inmate laughed loudly. "C'mon, Mr. Reilly, you kidding me. This had nothing to do with you. You were just doing your job."

ON TOP OF THE DAY-TO-DAY INMATE COMMOTION, THERE WAS ALWAYS plenty of staff gossip. Was the warden secretly profiting from the trustees who worked on his own little private farm project? Which deputy wardens were stealing from the county and having sex with which junior staff members? Who was entertaining themselves on third shift by letting inmates out of their cells at night to fight each other? Which female guards were being seduced by which inmates? Which female guards were seducing inmates? Which third-shifters were sleeping all night? Which staff members were drinking on the job? And which staff members were getting written up by Sergeant G this week and why? Much to the amusement of some of my co-workers, Sergeant G had recently written me up for being shirtless in the staff gym. I was changing from one T-shirt to another when she walked in. "We have a locker room for changing in, Officer Reilly," she said rather venomously. "Oh, I'm not changing; I'm just putting on a new shirt." It didn't matter. The next day I was called down to her office to receive my write-up and told once more, "This write-up is going into your personnel file." I thanked her and then walked back to the block I was working on and filed her write-up right down the lavatory. One particularly troubling morsel of gossip that had been leaked from the spies in the administration office was that the warden was on the warpath and out to get Sergeant D fired. Everyone knew Sergeant D should be promoted to deputy warden and then get the big job. His education, experience, and leadership certainly qualified him. There was no way Sergeant D's popularity and respect had escaped the warden's egomaniacal attention. He was far too insecure and had far too many toadying ass-kissers running to him with "news from the trenches," people like Sergeant G, who all but openly detested Sergeant D and would love to send Sergeant D off to the warden's fall-guy guillotine at the first opportunity.

The battle between Sergeant D and the warden had actually started twelve months earlier, incredibly on one of Sergeant D's days off. A high-risk inmate was being removed from his cell in D-Block to be seen by a nurse and receive medical treatment. The supervising sergeant ordered a guard in the disciplinary unit to bring the inmate out of his cell. Now, as I mentioned earlier, standard operating procedure when dealing with these kinds of violent, assaultive inmates is to cuff them through the tray slot with their hands behind their back. Only then, when the inmate is secured and handcuffed behind his back is the cell door to be opened and the inmate removed. Again, violent inmates cuffed in front can turn restraints into a lethal weapon in a split second. Just imagine a physically powerful, angry, and emotionally unstable inmate gets behind you, and in a flash slips his handcuffed wrists over your head, and starts using the chain attaching the cuffs to saw through the soft tissue of your neck!

The inmate refused to comply. The sergeant told the guard to cuff the inmate in front instead. The young guard reminded the sergeant of the "cuff behind the back" policy. The young guard was told to do it anyway. Immediately upon the door opening, the inmate attacked the nurse. The young guard laid into the inmate and gave him what might be described as a good, old-fashioned dose of physical Christianity. From the perspective of the nurse and her family, I'm sure they appreciated the protection. The young guard, jacked-up by the whole situation, probably came on too strong for too long, but in the process, he definitely prevented the nurse from receiving a savage beating and perhaps even saved her life.

The following Monday, Sergeant D got to work and found out about the incident. The on-duty sergeant had written up the young guard for "excessive use of force." A chief deputy warden asked Sergeant D for an opinion. He suggested a written reprimand and two days off. Sergeant D then asked about the other sergeant: What type of discipline was he to receive? If he had followed prison policy, the incident would never have happened in the first place. Sergeant D was told that was none of his concern.

According to several well-informed sources, the warden, worrying about a lawsuit, quickly decided to reduce his culpability and fire the young guard. If the inmate sued, then the warden could say, "I've already taken care of it and fired the guard responsible." Then, the union got in the middle of it, and the whole show went to arbitration. For some reason, the worrying warden told Sergeant D that he would have to testify at a hearing. Sergeant D explained to the warden that he was out the day that the incident occurred. The warden said that point was irrelevant and as the senior sergeant on second shift, he should be very grateful that people value his opinion. Sergeant D told the warden he'd testify to what he knew, which meant stating that the on-duty sergeant failed to follow written policy and gave an incorrect order, an order that actually initiated the incident and put members of staff in a potentially deadly situation. By all accounts, the warden went ballistic, pitched a fit, and started screaming at Sergeant D. In response, Sergeant D didn't take any of the warden's petulant shenanigans, and defended himself and his own position at high volume, and then left the warden's office. A year later, on May 20, 2004, Sergeant D got to work a little before 2 p.m. to find that a disturbance on H-Block was about to escalate out of control. Sergeant G and the other feckless first-shift leaders needed Sergeant D to go down to H-Block and deal with the volatile situation, because they could not handle it themselves. Sergeant D went down to H-block with a half-dozen handpicked men, settled things down, and then left. He returned to his office to find the warden along with several members of his personal proctology club waiting for him. The warden informed Sergeant D, "You're fired." It took the warden a whole year of stewing in his own juices to finally fire Sergeant D, for not being involved in an incident and not be a sniveling, sycophantic yesman, and actually having the audacity to say what was on his mind. In my mind, the main reason Sergeant D was added to the warden's fall-guy list was for being a legitimate leadership threat.

The good supervisor who becomes a fall guy became a running joke among the staff: The warden wouldn't stop firing and hanging out to dry all viable successors until he retired or died. Until then, his authority would not be questioned, by anyone, ever! He would mold the leadership of the prison in his own image and only appoint and promote weak and inexperienced staff members into senior positions. And, in turn, they would be grateful for their seat at the table and not rock the boat.

"Being a prison guard requires a lot more brawn and bravery than it does brain." That's what an ex-Marine with over ten years' prison service under his belt told me. He was talking about the young guard at the epicenter of the trouble that resulted in Sergeant D getting the chop. My co-worker was right. Forcing hard, violent men to do things they don't want to do is a very dirty business and sometimes stopping them from doing things they shouldn't be doing, like trying to kill defenseless nurses, is even dirtier. Force is often the only option, and the level of force needed to control a situation fluctuates dramatically according to the nature of the incident. It's no secret that young, hard men full of testosterone can act unpredictably when feeling threatened or defensive, no matter what side of the bars they are on. But it's these men, both in guard and supervisor positions, who actually ensure that prisons function and very bad men are kept under lock and key and away from the public. Someone once said, "People sleep peaceably in their beds at night only because rough men stand ready to do violence on their behalf." Whoever said that was absolutely right.

26

New Commit

WHEN A "NEW COMMIT" WITH NO PRIOR PRISON EXPERIENCE ARRIVES on the block, it's a good idea to keep a close eye on him. The prison parasites are always on the lookout for a "new fish" they can reel in, play nicey-nice with, and then squeeze for any number of things that could be considered currency.

One hot afternoon in summer 2004, a young guy just out of quarantine arrived on the block. He was not quite ready to spend his first day in general population. He was a good-looking kid, maybe twenty, maybe a little older, but not much. He had been locked up for a string of car thefts. It was easy to tell by his slim build and nervous disposition that he wasn't a violent criminal or a guy who was much of a fighter. After I showed him to his cell and explained what was expected of him, I told him to watch out for some of the older, more streetwise guys, who at the least would make a fool of him and at the worst would turn his stay into a nightmare. The young man thanked me, but I could tell he was in for a rough ride just by the way he was looking at everyone who passed him, trying to make eye contact, nervously looking for a friend before establishing himself in some meaningful way.

As the shift progressed, the new inmate hovered around the bookshelf, which just happened to be close to my desk. I was sure that he felt being close to me was the best way to stay out of trouble. He was right to a certain extent, but it was a plan that would only work for so long.

Whenever I rotated in to a new housing block, the first thing I did was move the bookshelf as close to my desk as possible. I did this for two reasons. The first reason was, whenever new books were brought into the block, I wanted to get to them before the inmates. Occasionally, there would be a literary gem to pilfer. I often wondered if stealing books from prison was considered literary larceny. The second reason I kept the bookshelf close to my desk was to trick Sergeant G. After being on the job for a couple of years, I'd developed a good rapport with most of my co-workers. We all helped each other out, especially when it came to dodging and dealing with the dreaded Sergeant G. I would be reading, the phone would ring, and any one of a number of guards would tell me, "Reilly, G's coming." I would leap out of my chair, turn off the control panel, close my book, walk a couple of steps, slide my read into the bookshelf, then start walking around like I was about to bust up a mass escape. Sergeant G would enter the block and always find me strolling, patrolling, and looking fully engaged, just the way she liked it.

While the new commit hung out restlessly around the bookshelf, an inmate called Pig Food—a huge slob of a man who worked in the kitchen and got his nickname from eating inmate leftovers out of the plastic pig buckets that fed the warden's swine—sauntered over and introduced himself to the new guy. Pig Food's posse watched with interest from a nearby table, where they were doing a bad job of pretending to play cards.

"First day?"

"Yeah."

"Done any time anywhere else?"

"Nah. A couple of months' juvie, that's it."

"Oh, well, not to worry, it's not too bad in here, most everyone gets along. Hey, do ya like movies?"

"Yeah, I do."

"Well, on Sundays, we all watch the early movie, right here on the block TV. It's a really good time. Do you like basketball?"

"Yeah, I use to play a little in high school before I dropped out."

"Oh, that's great. Every Monday we have a pickup game in the yard. Most of the guys go out and play or watch. It's awesome."

"Yeah, that sounds like a good time,," replied the new inmate. Pig Food continued.

"Then on Tuesday, it's Italian night. They serve spaghetti every Tuesday night. Do ya like Italian food?"

"I love Italian food. My father's Italian."

"See, it's not going to be too bad. It's nothing you can't handle. Then, on Wednesday we get commissary. If your people send you in a few bucks, you can buy candy, soap, and Snickers bars, shit like that."

The new boy nodded. A wary smile stretched tightly across his face. I could see him visibly trying to relax. Contact had been made, a clique was calling. Maybe things weren't going to be too bad. The kid was moving around a little now, shuffling, rubbing his hands together, nervously attempting to look cool, not wanting to make a wrong move.

Then, Pig Food put his huge, pink, blubbery arm over the kid's shoulder and asked him as plainly and as loudly as could be, "Hey, are you gay?"

The kid pulled back in shock, jerking away from Pig Food, steadying himself on the bookshelf, eyes wide with horror.

"No!" the kid exclaimed. "No, I am not gay."

"Oh dear," said Pig Food. "Then you're not going to like Thursday nights much . . ."

Pig Food and his friends, and I'm ashamed to say, myself all roared with laughter.

27

Wake-Up Call

October 2004

DURING AN ADVANCED STAFF TRAINING EVENT AT THE FIRING range, the warden decided to join the rank and file and share with us some of his extensive and considerable firearms knowledge. He started the class with an informal conversation designed to discover who owned the most guns and had the most experience, be it military, law enforcement, hunting, competitive target, or trap shooting. We were all shocked, thrilled, and surprised to discover that the warden knew more about guns, owned more guns, and was a better shot than everybody present. I, on the other hand, was last in all categories. Prior to the compulsory NRA course I had taken during training, I had virtually no firearms experience whatsoever. Finding myself surrounded by the servants of the Second Amendment, I tried to shrink away from all questions and hide my semi-liberal light under a conveniently discarded camouflage cape. For a moment, during a particularly spirited debate about hollow-point bullets and the transient nature of ballistic coefficients, I thought the warden was about to ask us all to strip to the waist, cover ourselves in mud and blood, and chant the name of Charlton Heston until the moon came up.

As the afternoon progressed, we cycled through the three weapons the prison used. The AR-15 assault rifle, the Mossberg pump action 12-gauge shot gun and the Smith & Wesson 9mm semiautomatic pistol. Toward the end of the training, the warden had a brilliant idea! He suggested we have a bit of a competition. The idea was well received, and everyone seemed to think it would be a fun way to wrap up the afternoon, me included. The rules were simple: Use all three weapons to hit a series of targets at various distances in an allotted amount of time with a limited amount of ammunition. The field quickly narrowed to four men: two serious, well-respected shooters; the warden; and me, the only guy there who openly admitted to liking classical music and knowing nothing about guns.

By some fantastic fluke, the gun gods must have decided to have a good laugh and hand out fourth place to the warden, third place and second place to the serious shooters and first place to me. I had the winning score, with the best time and, to add lacerations to the losers, a few rounds to spare in the clip of the pistol. The two serious shooters, both avid hunters, great shots, and good men you'd definitely want in your corner when the fudge hits the fan, laughed, shook their heads and then shook my hand, congratulating me on some fine shooting. As I proudly turned away

from my co-workers, the warden was walking right past me. I extended my hand in the spirit of good sportsmanship, expecting a little flesh pressing and maybe even an "attaboy." Instead, he glared right at me, refused to shake my hand, then walked off the range, climbed into his truck, and drove away.

THE INCIDENT AT THE SHOOTING RANGE; THE OPEN WARFARE WITH the union, the supporting of ineffectual staff, and the firing of excellent supervisors like Sergeant D served as a loud and clanging wake-up call. It occurred to me that what the warden withheld and denied from those who worked for him were the very things he craved most of all: acknowledgement and respect. The warden's actions made me think about my father, who fought his way from being a working-class motorcycle cop to a successful business owner and community leader, and who always said, "Son, if you don't like something, vote with your feet."

It was time to go, Sarah agreed. The job paid the bills, kept the family's head above water, but I was working in a micro banana republic. I strongly felt that my boss was only interested in a self-serving program of prison expansion and creating more of a problem than a solution. Maybe I was naïve to think this way, but all the same, the sensation was so strong, I couldn't ignore it. So, I started to look for an escape route in earnest. I had been working at the prison for three years and three months. New England, the West Coast, and Colorado were all places we liked and thought we might want to move to. It was an exciting proposition, and suddenly anything seemed possible. Our idea didn't seem too unrealistic: We wanted to move out of the suburbs, away from the city, in the mountains or by the ocean, and find a nice little country school for the kids. But first I had to get a job.

I decided to look for work using my developing people skills, even if they were incarcerated people skills. So, since the only thing I was qualified to do was work at a prison, prison employment became an integral part of our search criteria. On every department of corrections website, they all say the same thing:

Hurray! We are hiring! Come on down! Recession-proof work, competitive wages, fabulous benefits, paid time off, stress-induced heart disease, and free psychotic mood swings for anyone who manages to make it more than five years with the department. So, I thought, how bad could it be? If it got us to a better place, where a better future was more of a reality, I'd take another prison gig. And then I'd bail out as soon as I could find a decent job.

Washington state, California, and Oregon were all hiring, but the cost of living was too high. Upon closer examination, Colorado was landlocked. We briefly widened our search to the Southeastern coastal states but realized we wouldn't be able to handle the heat. So, New England it was. If we stayed in the Northeast, we would still be able to visit Sarah's mom in Massachusetts and have access to East Coast airports for trips to see my family in England. By a series of geographical and financial eliminations, we were left looking at the great states of New Hampshire, Vermont, and Maine.

I applied to all three departments. Vermont responded immediately, and I went up for testing and interviews. I passed the tests and was quickly offered two jobs: one in St. Johnsbury and another at a prison near Newport. After the interviews, I drove all over the area and tried to imagine my family living there. My gut reaction was strong. I just didn't feel it. When I returned home, I received a package from the Maine DOC. Mid-coast Maine actually seemed like it would meet all our needs: I could get work, and there were mountains, the ocean, quaint little towns and villages, four definitive seasons, low crime, and nice schools for the kids.

Sarah called a real-estate agent, and I called the Maine State Prison. She got a few appointments to view houses and I was assigned a test date.

On November 1, 2004, our friend Laura came to the house to look after the children, and Sarah and I traveled up to Camden, Maine. I took the tests at the Maine State Prison in Warren while Sarah looked at houses with a real-estate agent. The prison was fairly new, less than ten years old, a replacement for an older facility in the neighboring town of Thomaston. That prison had been condemned and knocked down. The new prison's façade was a fake-friendly construction job that said, "Look, we're just like a high school." But, just past the customer-friendly lobby, polished floors, and spotless public restrooms lurked something altogether different.

The testing was in three parts—a physical fitness test, followed by a written test, and then an interview. After the weeks of waiting and all the hoops I had to jump through for the Pennsylvania job, this seemed strange. If I passed, would they offer me a job on the same day? The PT test was a piece of cake, a timed half-mile run, followed by a dummy drag. My mother could have passed it wearing her nightgown and slippers. The written test was unmemorable and then I waited for the interview.

After about fifteen minutes of waiting, I was called into a windowless room and asked to take a seat in front of two captains. They ran me through a series of "what if" questions and scenarios. After the last three years, I knew exactly what they were looking for. Deliver a good strong handshake, look the interviewers in the eye, and speak clearly and confidently. As a guard, when in doubt, I should contact a supervisor and act according to standard operating procedures. I should be straightforward with inmates and co-workers. I should be punctual, reliable, and a good team member. Ten minutes after the interview, I was called back into the room and told that they would like to offer me a position in the Maine State Prison. Could I start training in December? I said yes. We were moving.

WE WENT HOME FULL OF EXCITEMENT. THE TRAINING CLASS started on Monday, December 27. We had a little over seven weeks to sell the house, find a new one, and move. Sarah had seen a couple of homes she thought might work out, so she threw herself into a sale, packing, and relocation frenzy while I handed in my notice. It was very anticlimactic. The chief deputy asked me why I was leaving. I told him about the new job and the big move. He gave me a tired, world-weary smile, and said with a great deal of kindness in his voice, "Good luck, Robert."

At 10 p.m. on Thursday, December 9, 2004, I walked out of the prison for the final time. As I left the building, a third-shift supervisor was playing AC/DC's "Highway to Hell" at full volume through the institution's internal PA system. Perfect.

POSTSCRIPT

During one particularly remarkable roll call, the sergeant reading out the assignments, somewhat embarrassedly, told the entire shift, "The warden wants all staff to now refer to the inmates as clients." The roomful of tough blue-collar guards stared at the sergeant in stunned disbelief and then started to laugh openly. The sergeant quickly extinguished the mockery and naked incredulity and told everyone to settle down. I raised my hand.

"Yes, Reilly, what is it?" The sergeant sounded annoyed.

"Clients, that's the same as customers, right? So, does that mean the next time I have a disagreement with an inmate/client, I should keep in mind the old axiom, the customer is always right?"

The sergeant gave me a dirty look and barked, "Reilly! That's not funny."

The sergeant was right: The language she was using wasn't a joke; it was the harbinger of a new era in corrections, the era of inmates becoming a revenue stream, customers.

My suspicions about the warden wanting to expand the prison were ultimately confirmed. The old county nursing home across from the prison was acquired and converted into an immigration holding tank. After the bars went on the windows, the prison started turning undocumented families into big-time detainee dollars, internment for profit. See the edited articles in the appendix for more information.

28

Out of the
Frying Pan

THE NEW MAINE STATE PRISON, BUILT ON A LARGE TRACT OF STATE-owned coastal land in Warren, an hour and a half north of Portland, opened its doors in the winter of 2002 and, according to an article in the *Bangor Daily News*, "cost about 85 million dollars." The Maine State Prison houses approximately 825 inmates and has roughly 410 members of staff, half of them administrators. Just imagine a state-funded school built on that kind of budget, with a ratio of roughly one staff member for every two students. I arrived at the prison on December 26, 2004.

During the Maine State Department of Corrections' six-week long training course, I stayed at the "old warden's place," a once-grand, dilapidated old home in the center of Thomaston, opposite the site of "the old prison." I and one other new hire from out of state stayed there during the training. The others, all locals, went home every night. For many years, the home had housed a long line of prison wardens and their families. It was now pretty much empty apart from a few rooms full of old metal bunks, a filthy kitchen, and a couple of bathrooms that should have carried a public health warning.

With a couple of exceptions, the training course was a complete and utter joke. It was almost entirely classroom lectures, written tests, and a few pathetic practical instructionals. In comparison to the course I'd taken in Pennsylvania, which was fairly interactive, it was excruciatingly boring, poorly presented, and taught primarily by a woman who was very nice, but surprisingly enough, had never actually been a prison guard. I knew these academic excursions were so unrelated to the real job, it was almost impossible to maintain even the lowest levels of interest. So, I sat at the back of the class, asked the occasional question, and I'm ashamed to say, fell asleep from time to time. A month and a half of sitting in a warm, windowless classroom listening to MDOC lectures felt like I was having all my fingernails pulled out in slow motion while being under some sort of mind-numbing anesthetic.

Throughout the six week course, there were only a couple of memorable interactions. One was with an overly officious instructor living for the day "the terrorists" attacked the prisons and the facilities' security would be compromised. He assured us, even if we were off, we would all have to somehow come into work, and if we were already at work, we would not be allowed to leave. The guy was hilarious. The idea of the prison being attacked by terrorists made him visibly excited. In his mind he was projecting himself into a modern-day Alamo, a dystopian last-stand shootout where good battles evil at the Maine State Prison. I found myself unable to control my tongue. It felt like I was having a bout of common-sense Touretts's. I raised my hand. The instructor pointed at me and said, "Yes, you at the back."

"Let me just get this right, something terrible has happened and the state of Maine is under attack. I'm at home with my family, and you're telling me I have to come to work or, if I'm at work, I'm not allowed to leave to go home to protect my wife and children."

"Yes, that's exactly right. Your number one priority is to protect the facility," replied the instructor excitedly.

"Yeah, I don't think so," I replied. I'm pretty sure this was not on the instructor's list of acceptable fantasy responses.

The other memorable moment occurred during OJT, on-the-job training, where we, the NOBs (New On Board), were generally met with poorly veiled disrespect and a mild amount of mockery. But I didn't feel in the slightest bit intimidated. The last three years had erased any trace of the person who once might have been bothered by bullies and loudmouths.

I was standing with my training officer, a decent mild-mannered family guy, and a group of guards in the recreation building (the gym). The inmate band in the "music room" was playing a terrible, passive-aggressive, nonstop version of Eric Clapton's "Cocaine." As the gang of guards joked around about a woman whose photos were featured in a confiscated *Playboy* magazine. One rather large, mouthy guard said, "Her face looks weird. Nah, no way would I have sex with her."

Again, I couldn't help myself. I told the guy, "That's unfortunate, because it's my understanding after reading the accompanying article that the *Playboy* model in question is actually looking for an overweight, middle-aged prison guard with a bald spot and four kids for a bit of no-strings-attached casual sex."

He didn't think it was that funny, but the others did, including my training officer.

While we waited for the inmates' rec period to be over, the conversation took a dark, bigoted turn, delving into what "faggots and queers" should and should not be allowed to do. I wanted no part of the discussion, but there was no way I could have walked away. I had to remain with my training officer at all times. Then, out of the blue, the overweight, middle-aged prison guard with a bald spot and four kids said, "What do you think, Reilly?"

It was said aggressively and meant as a challenge, something to test or demean me in front of the other men, a retaliation for the earlier joke. I asked him, "Do you have any gay friends?"

There was silence, followed by an emphatic, "No! Of course, I don't. Do you?"

"Yes," I said, "I have quite a few gay friends, and they're exactly the same as the rest of us. They're people!" My inquisitor was struck dumb. He made a face like he was trying to do some sort of complex mental arithmetic, then he waddled off. A few minutes later, he returned with another guard I'd already met. He was a fat, foul-mouthed, bullying pig of a man who put himself up as an enforcer and a tough guy. As he strutted toward me and the group of guards, he pointed and said loudly, "Hey, Reilly, rumor has it you're a homo lover."

The inquisitor waddled behind the bully, grinning maniacally in silent support. The bully strode right up to me, got into my personal space, pointed a fat sausagey finger at me and said, "Are you a homo lover, Reilly?"

We looked romantically into each other's eyes. I had a brief flash of anger. I knew this useless lump of lard didn't have more than thirty seconds of gas in his engine. If I could avoid getting knocked out, I'd cripple him in less than a minute. So, I said, "What if I am a homo lover? What are you going to do about it?"

The bully was struck dumb. The inquisitor looked to the bully, confused. The prison band hit another chorus of "Cocaine." The inquisitor and the bully looked at the other guards for some sort of support, but there was none. Then, while they were thinking, I said, pointing right at both of them, "I'll tell you what you're going to do if I'm a homo lover. You're not going to do anything." Neither talked to or came near me again.

ON EVERY OJT DAY, WE WERE TOLD BY ALMOST EVERY SEASONED guard and supervisor that half of you won't make it six months and half of that 50 percent won't make it through an entire year. The prison I had just left ran a training class once or twice a year. The Maine State Prison ran a training class every six weeks, one right after the other. No wonder the testing was such a joke. There was something slightly weird going on; two members of our training class had already quit. At graduation, the warden, a six-foot-four, sixty-year-old, Ken-doll stunt double appeared out of nowhere, mispronounced most of our names, shook us all by the hand without looking us in the eye, and told us he was absolutely delighted we were ready for work, and then abruptly left. We wouldn't see him again for six months.

On the last day of training, we had a lottery for job assignments. I came in second to last and pulled second shift with Tuesdays and Wednesdays off. It couldn't get much worse. I didn't say anything to Sarah about the specifics of my work detail. I told her I'd be working two till ten, but I would see what I could do about a first-shift position as soon as I could work out how things operated. Sarah was upset, though she understood I was going to have to put up with it on account of being a rookie all over again. On the home front, Sarah had a million things to do, moving into our new home, finding her way around a new area, getting the kids dialed in at their new school, and missing her father terribly. All while staring out the window at three feet of snow blanketing the entire world.

29

SMU

February 2005

"DUE TO THE LACK OF EMOTIONAL AND FINANCIAL RESOURCES, THE light at the end of the tunnel has been permanently turned off." Those encouraging words of wisdom were printed on the side of one veteran guard's lunch box. He was standing immediately in front of me in the crowded, stuffy, windowless briefing room. It was my first roll call at the new prison, and it was just the same as the other place: a room full of grumpy, world-weary prison guards waiting for their names to be called and their assignments to be read out. The only real difference was there were only two women and one African American man. Apart from that, it was all white guys.

"Reilly."

"Here."

"SMU." *Oh, how wonderful!*

The Special Management Unit is like a dungeon below a Roman circus. It has three separate units, which house about a hundred fifty inmates. Pandemonium often rules. Many of the prisoners are mentally ill. Most are locked down twenty-three hours a day, getting only one hour of rec in a "dog run," an iso-lated, elongated cage about thirty feet long. That's if the weather is good. SMU prisoners are not allowed any electronics or human contact, except with prison staff. Their cell lights stay on all the time. Their bland, unsavory food is served through a locked tray slot in the cell door, and their physical and mental health needs are almost entirely overlooked. Some inmates are so violent and so dangerous they never come out of their cells, ever. They just lan-guish there in a windowless purgatory, waiting like animals to be fed, medicated, or transferred. And while they slowly waste away, they pace around their cold concrete boxes like psychotic canni-bals in a horror-movie mental hospital, keeping one eye constantly open for anything that looks like opportunity.

The SMU is filthy and loud. It smells of blood, feces, body rot, and caustic institutional detergent. Inmates yell and roar at one another through heavy metal sliding doors. Their screaming, sob-bing, maniacal laughter and depraved verbal abuse are awash with deeply tormented sexual and religious subject-matter. Their pro-fanity fills the dark corridors like clouds of poisonous gas. Mounted metal boxes full of shackles, restraint belts, and handcuffs hang on the walls. Cold, moldy, single-stall showers drip water down cracked tiles. An Orwellian desperation and hopelessness fill the dank air, and wall-mounted cameras watch over every inch of every grim, fear-filled section of the unit.

That first evening, I worked with Officer F. He was about ten years older than me and had an easygoing way about him. He immediately seemed like a decent guy. I was just glad not to be teamed up with some macho meathead intent on proving to me just how tough he was.

"What did you do before you came here?" asked Officer F.

"Worked at another prison in Pennsylvania."

"Did you work the disciplinary unit?"

"Yeah, but it was only one unit. It was a lot smaller than this."

"Do I need to give you the full lecture?"

"I don't think so, but I'll take any pointers."

"OK, you're the new guy. They're going to fuck with you as much as you let them. So, do more listening than talking and, more than anything, just watch out for the shit shake. It's their favorite form of initiation. Remember, a bunch of these guys have AIDS, Hep-C, and God knows what else, so make sure you don't get any of that shit on ya."

The shit shake consists of the inmate's bladder, bowel, and all other bodily secretions deposited into a disposable plastic cup. They nip their skin with their teeth to add blood to the mix (a new cup comes with each new meal). After the ingredients are deposited into the cup and mixed up into creamy bio-hazardous soup, the inmate waits for the tray slot to be opened, and then the contents of the cup are thrown into the new guard's face. Welcome to the SMU!

The bulk of the evening's work would consist of feeding all the inmates; serving and then collecting trays; escorting the nurse during the medication handout; getting some of the inmates out, one at a time, for showers; getting other inmates out, one at a time, to clean their cells; and then taking a couple of the long-term inmates to their noncontact visits. It was going to be a busy night. I was going to be tested and I knew it. These guys had nothing better to do than mess with the new guys. The insults and the trash talk started the second they saw me. I remember thinking, *My poor mother, if she could hear what was being said about me, she would cry*. If she heard what they were saying about her, she might well have a heart attack.

When it was quiet, which wasn't very often, I spent as much time as I could looking at the logbook and checking out what had transpired on the unit over the last few shifts. I wanted to understand the general pattern of things, get an idea in my head of how the place was run, and see if there was anything that resembled a rhythm.

The radio crackled. The food cart was on the way. Dinner was about to be served. The big aluminum carts came into the block on an elevator. Officer F said he would take one side of each corridor while I took the other. At each cell, the inmate waited like an animal at the door for his food. I made a big deal of not talking too much, but looking through every window to see if they were holding anything to throw at me. On a couple of occasions, I told the inmate to "show me your hands" or "step away from the door, please." It was straightforward stuff to let them know I was there to do my job and nothing more. The foul jokes and insults poured out and spilled from one cell to the next like overflowing sewage. I ignored it all and did everything I could to make Officer F know he had a co-worker with him, not a rookie who needed handholding. One inmate, when told to stand away from the door, moved back. Then, as I opened the tray slot, he lunged forward in a flash, and spat through the opening, hitting me on my shirt. I went and changed and then returned to work. I would be lying if I said I wasn't a little tense at times, but I managed to keep it covered up.

A few of my classmates hadn't been so lucky. Officer V, a large African American woman, was having a terrible time. She had no one to turn to or relate to. Being thrown into an almost all-white prison in Northern New England didn't look like it was going to work out for her. There were also plenty of guards and supervisors who wanted to help her fail. A couple of the guys from my class were just flat-out scared and in way over their heads. The inmates knew it, and so did the veteran staff. On the blocks they were assigned to, and completely unprepared to run, they cowered behind their desks while the lunatics took over the asylum. One guy was totally out of control. He pressed his emergency response button a couple of times every shift and became a standing joke among both staff and the inmates. He was going to get someone killed. He didn't last long. A couple of other guys got assaulted, and after a few weeks they just didn't show up for work. Officer V vanished as predicted. The administration seemed to be completely absent. A few decent staff members held down the fort while a few decent supervisors tried to hold up the staff. But I was starting to think the old guys were right: Not many new hires would make it.

Another thing that made the job increasingly difficult was the mandatory overtime. Because so many people kept quitting, the prison was woefully understaffed. If there weren't enough men to fill the next shift, they pulled from the existing shift. You could be getting ready to leave, looking at your watch and saying to yourself, in half an hour I'll be in my car and on my way home, or at my kid's baseball game, or going out to dinner with my wife. Then, the desk phone would ring and a voice would tell you that you have to stay and work the next shift. If you worked second shift, like me, it meant that you had to work all night and wouldn't be able to go home until 6 A.M. A couple of nights into second shift, I was on my way out of the block after handing over my keys and logbook to a particularly cadaverous-looking third-shift guard when the phone rang. The third-shift zombie answered it and then said, looking intently at my name tag, "Er, Reilly, it's for you."

A captain announced himself and said, "Reilly, you're mandated. You're not going home. You're staying in the SMU all night."

Then, he hung up the phone.

That first third-shift mandate was a very long night. I drank a gallon of bitter, bile-like black coffee. Putting any milk in it would have just insulted the cow. By about 2 in the morning I felt sticky and sweaty. It felt like the worst jet lag ever: prison lag. By 4 a.m., my eyelids and limbs had turned to lead. The coffee burned inside my bladder like gasoline and made me pee every half hour. But it was the only way to stay awake. Sitting down was lethal. The second I stopped moving I just started to nod off. Sleeping on the job was a firing offense. Getting fired wasn't even worth thinking about. Sarah and the kids were counting on me.

This cycle of SMU second-shift and third-shift mandates was my new reality. I tried hard to come home and be a happy dad and a caring husband. I didn't want to tell Sarah about the work conditions because she was also working really hard herself to make the move work. Josh was at school; Lindsey and Zeke were at home and needed all their mother's attention. Complaining wasn't an option. I did my job and, just like the prisoners, kept one eye on keeping myself safe and the other eye on anything that looked like an opportunity—in my case, a better job.

Keeping my radar on and staying safe was a major preoccupation. One of the SMU prisoners with a sizable reputation was a transfer inmate from out of state. He had been the ringleader of a notorious riot in the Southwest. He and another inmate had taken two guards hostage in what turned out to be one of the longest prison standoffs in the nation's history. One of the guards was a woman. Throughout the course of the long, horrifying ordeal, the two inmates raped and abused her repeatedly. This particular inmate was never allowed out of his cell. He never spoke to staff and never wore clothes except for his underwear. He was huge, powerful, covered in elaborate tattoos, and extremely menacing. His size wasn't the work of a supplement-fueled weightlifting lifestyle; it was the burly, natural brute strength of loggers, ironworkers, stone masons, bloodthirsty Vikings, and grizzly bears. I knew the only way I could defend myself and my family against a man like that was with a shotgun. It was while I was working in the SMU that I started to think seriously about buying a firearm. Depending on the situation, killing another human being suddenly didn't seem like it would be something I'd have to think more than a split second about.

I served the inmate in question his dinner every night for several weeks. Every time I pushed the tray through the oblong slot in the middle of the cell door, he just stared out of the small Plexiglas window, right through me, out into some sort of dark distance, years into his own hellish future. Whenever I fed him, I was always very cautious. I'd push his tray into the cell with my fingertips. I knew if he got a chance to grab my wrist, he could easily shatter my entire arm, bite huge pieces of flesh out of it, and probably rip it out of my shoulder socket. One evening, while serving the inmate his food, I was distracted by someone screaming in an adjacent cell. I glanced at the screamer, who was standing on his sink, bending over, and pressing his bare ass against the cell door window. As I instinctively but foolishly turned my head to look at what was happening, I pushed the tray through the slot a little too far and the back of my hand rubbed slowly and smoothly against the back of the inmate's huge hairy hand. I felt an incredible surge of negative energy. The jolt ran right through me like a low, pulsing electric shock. I inhaled a strong whiff of bleach and cheap rehydrated food. I slowly slid my hand back out of the metal mouth of the open tray slot and looked into the cell. The inmate monster stared into my eyes. He'd felt something, too. It was probably his first human contact in months. I stared back at him and slowly rubbed my hand. He smiled ever so slightly, terribly. A dim light glowed momentarily in the back of his dark, dull-looking eyes. Then, just as the light was about to go out, I asked him, "Inmate X, do you believe in God?"

He stopped, tilted his huge head to the right slightly, and squinted until a puzzled expression slid fully across his broad bearded face. Then, he said in a low, barely audible growl, "I only believe in myself."

A couple of days after this, a heavily armed SWAT team came into the prison, removed inmate X from his cell in shackles and battleship chains and took him out of the facility. No one really knew where they were taking him. According to an Associated Press article I found, inmate X is serving seven life sentences for kidnapping, assault, sexual assault, and a slew of other heavyweight charges.

There were other men imprisoned in the SMU, too. Men who were so far gone and whose crimes were so depraved, they had to be put somewhere. If a thing or a person is damaged or cracked in some way, with skill and caring it can be fixed and put back to use. But if a thing or a person is so broken and smashed beyond all realistic repair, all you can do is put the shattered pieces in a secure container and place it in some sort of storage. I quickly realized the SMU/Supermax was a storage unit for these broken, unfixable human beings. The state of Maine has no death sentence.

30

There's No Such Thing as Life in Prison, Only Existence

ALL WORK ASSIGNMENTS AT THE MAINE STATE PRISON WERE PERMA-
nent positions. A staff member can keep a job for as long as he or she
wants. As staff left (in droves), got fired (hardly ever), or occasionally
promoted, various positions became available. If you had enough
seniority and you watched for jobs to open up, you could move your
way into an easier, less stressful post as time went on. Because the
turnover was so high, new posts were opening up constantly.

For men with a few years of service and no ambition, the most
desired post in the institution was in the infirmary. Virtually nothing ever happened there. It was eight hours of sitting and snoozing
in a quiet, moderately clean play-hospital environment. Occasionally, you had to enter into the logbook that this nurse or that maintenance man entered and left the unit, but that was pretty much it.

The reason nothing ever happened in the infirmary was because the administration sent almost every inmate with more than a toothache to the hospital in town. The administration was more concerned about a medical malpractice suit than putting staff and the general public at risk. Taking inmates out of the prison to see a doctor was a disaster waiting to happen.

In March 2005, wanting to catch up on my reading and make some easy money, I volunteered for a first shift of overtime in the infirmary. An entire shift went by, and I didn't see a single soul except the one old convict who'd been put there to die. At one point, I heard him moving around in his bed so I went to see what was going on. I stood at the door and looked at him. He was wide awake and staring at me like he had been expecting a visitor.

"Are you OK?" I asked.

"It's my nerves," he said.

He held up his hands. They fluttered like a pair of poisoned pigeons. His eyes were as dull as scuffed marbles and his hair, sun-bleached straw. Skim-milk skin covered his ruined arms, which were ruptured by bulging purple veins and faded blue-green tattoos.

Half a century ago, he'd killed two men and probably would have killed more if he hadn't been caught. Apparently, he was so wild they threw him in The Hole for nearly five years. While in there, his hard case apparently calcified even further. When they let him out, he almost killed a guard. A gang of club-wielding screws beat him back and nearly killed him in return. He probably didn't feel a thing. As I looked at him, I tried to imagine a man, not as a near-ghost, but as a terror, a beast boiling over with violence and hatred. I wondered what happened to him when he was a child. Now he just reminded me of an old piano teacher I once knew who couldn't play well anymore because of his terrible, uncontrolled trembling.

At the end of the shift, on the way out, I asked an old nurse how long the dying man had. "Not long," she said casually, as if she was waiting for a bus. A thought popped into my head, and I asked the nurse, "Hey, when was his last visit?" The nurse looked at me, shrugged her shoulders, and said, "Way before I worked here. We both came over from the old place."

"How long have you been working for the prison?"

"A little over twenty years."

As I finished the overtime shift in the infirmary, and then went to my regular assignment in the SMU hellhole, I thought about the old inmate and his journey. I was spending sixteen hours of my day in prison, which felt like a long time. This guy had spent almost all of his life locked up, and a good portion of it torturing himself and others. My mind wandered and I wondered what he might have become, what he had missed the most, where it all went wrong, and why no one ever came to see him. Did he think about these things too? The next day, while on break, I slipped into the infirmary. The same nurse was on duty, and she was sitting at a desk reading something when I walked in. She raised her head slightly, smiled and said a brief hi before returning to her magazine. I found the patient's room empty, the bed stripped of sheets and blankets, the room dark. I went back to the nurse and asked about the old man, "Where is he?" She looked up at me again, closed her eyes, pursed her lips, shook her head, and then returned to her magazine. During the night, the geriatric inmate had finally escaped prison, for good.

BY THE MIDDLE OF MARCH, I WAS LOSING TRACK OF WHO FROM MY training class hung on and who dropped out. A big scandal had also come to light. A guard in the class right behind me, who, rumor had it, had actually been a convict in another state (can anyone say "background check"!), had taken a job at the Maine State Prison as a way to expand sales in his heroin and marijuana business. His new marketing plan was great: Sell contraband to a clientele without any other retail choices. He'd been bringing in thousands of dollars' worth of dope a month. He was busted in a sting operation by the DEA. It was in all the papers and on TV, and the guards of the Maine State Prison were famous.

One afternoon, as I walked into the roll-call room, I did what I did every day: I looked at the posting board. There was a position opening up on first shift in the Medium Custody Unit. The

Medium Unit held inmates with the most freedom and usually, but not always, those who'd behaved well for a decent amount of time. Or, in some cases, those close to release. The bottom line: The Medium Unit inmates were out of their cells a lot. They had institutional work details, classes to attend, and were, on the whole, a younger, more active group of men. I asked around. It looked like no one had put in a bid. No one wanted the job because it was the unit where you had the largest number of inmates, the most work to do, and if all hell broke loose, potentially the least amount of control. The Medium Unit typically saw the most general population activity and the most trouble. I put in for the bid.

Lots of guards and a few supervisors asked me if I was serious about wanting to work in the Medium Unit. I told them the truth; I wanted first shift because of family commitments and, if I was on first, I could only be mandated to work second shift. It would be a damn sight easier than having to work second shift and then forced to work the night shift. Normal people can be awake and fully functioning between 5 a.m. and 11 p.m.

So, on March 27, 2005, after working the prison for only twelve weeks, and for the love of my family and my own sanity, I'd somehow managed to perform an amazing magic trick, landing a permanent post on first shift. However, it must be said, I was the only member of staff in the entire place to bid on the job, so they gave it to me. No more forced night shift, ever.

There were no surprises for me as I transitioned into my new first-shift job. The inmates were active and demanding, and there was a good amount of troubleshooting and fires to be put out, but it wasn't anything I hadn't already dealt with or couldn't handle. The men I worked with seemed, on the whole, like a decent group of guys. Most of them were in the same boat as me: family guys who wanted to be home for dinner. The first-shift supervisors who ran the Medium Unit seemed like good guys. The head man, Unit Manager W, also seemed easygoing and laid back. He was keen to talk to me one-on-one to find out where I was at and why I wanted the job no one else did. I was straightforward about why I had applied, and I believe he appreciated that. The two sergeants running the shift, Sergeant T and Sergeant B, also seemed like really good guys. Between the three men, they had about sixty years of service. They all had families, and all three appeared to be under no false impression about how the prison was being run. These guys were just smart enough to realize that they were further in than they were out, so for them, there was no point rocking the boat or trying to reinvent the wheel. They were playing by the rules and taking care of their families, and that was that.

It was on my lunch break during one of those first few days that something interesting happened. I was walking out from the Medium Unit to the staff chow hall. Although it was the first week of April, it was still very cold and large piles of snow were mounded up on either side of the walkway. As I approached a group of guards who were waiting to direct inmates, I heard my name: "Hey, Reilly" Then, wham! A snowball hit me right in the face. I managed to see who had thrown it. I didn't react. I wiped the snow out of my eyes, spat it out of my mouth, and kept walking toward the gang of guards who were now all laughing hysterically. I got within a foot of the guy who threw the snowball, dropped my lunch box, lunged at him, and hit him with the flats of both my hands right in the chest. He was quite a bit bigger than me, but was taken completely by surprise. As he staggered backward, a snow bank hit him behind his knees. I gave him one more good shove, and over he went. I followed, grabbing his coat and bearing down on him. He balled up and covered his face with his hands. I let go, climbed back over the snow drift, picked up my lunch box, and went to eat. After I finished my break, I returned to work, walking back down the same walkway and passing the same group of guards. When I approached, there was a lot of laughing and good-humored teasing directed at the snowball thrower. He smiled sheepishly at me. I returned the smile, extended an arm, and we shook hands and both laughed. Toward the end of my shift, during a late coffee break, I heard my name being called.

"Officer Reilly, come into my office please."

It was the serious-sounding voice of Unit Manager W. I entered his office. A stern-looking Sergeant T stood against a wall with his arms folded in front of his chest.

"Reilly, I heard a rumor that one of my officers, who has only been working for me for less than a week, is already getting himself in trouble with other veteran officers. Is that right?"

Oh crap, I thought. *Here we go.* So I told Unit Manager W what happened and as I was explaining myself, he and Sergeant T broke out into huge grins.

"Why didn't you punch him in the side of his big stupid head? Well done, Reilly."

And with that, it was made plain that I was welcome in the Medium Unit and among friends.

Things were looking up. I was now on first shift, developing up a good rapport with the scheduling sergeant, volunteering for overtime when it suited me, and, for the most part, staying off the dreaded mandate list. The winter was winding down, and there were some signs of spring in the air. The kids were settling into our new home, and Sarah was starting to meet other mothers and make connections.

The mid-coast of Maine is absolutely beautiful. On my days off, it felt like I was on vacation. We had hills to hike and bike on, amazing woodlands to walk through, and spectacular ocean views, beaches, and several picturesque harbors, all just minutes from the house.

31

Jail Bird

IN MAY 2005, ONE OF MY CO-WORKERS, A SLOVENLY MAN WHO HAD the personality of a bulging colostomy bag, and loved to tell terrible sex jokes, usually at the inmates' expense, made a big discovery. During a routine search of a laundry room, he'd found a plastic one-gallon jug in the back of a tumble dryer. The jug was full of homemade hooch. The yellow liquid, with its white milky streaks, looked like a urine specimen from an infirm camel. Cocktail hour had been cancelled. And not surprisingly, no one was taking responsibility for the container full of block-boiled booze. Happy hour was over before it even started. My co-worker was delighted with his big find and was putting on quite a show, walking around the block, running his mouth, and bragging about his brilliant detective skills.

He walked from the block into the rec yard, ceremoniously calling out loudly as he went, "Does anyone here know who this shit belongs to?" Myself and half a dozen inmates followed him. Once outside, he flamboyantly poured the contents of the jug onto the ground. The yellow fermenting fluid spilled through the air and splattered on his scuffed black leather boots and stained uniform pants when it hit the concrete. It looked and smelled exactly like citrus-infused vomit. The inmates, now about a group of twenty, looked on silently. Some looked at me for a reaction. I refuse to acknowledge them. I was too busy watching my co-worker putting on "the big man show" and making a complete ass out of himself.

As I looked on in disgust, I saw a small, dirty-brown seabird land on the chain-link fence that capped the rec yard. I then watched as it somehow magically managed to squeeze through the links and enter the capped concrete space. The brazen bird, obviously used to getting snacks, clattered down to earth, all flapping wings and slapping feet. The visitor from the free world immediately started stabbing at the chunks of prison party slop, greedily choking down the swill. My co-worker stood back, put his fat hands in his stretched-out pants pockets, and watched. For a minute or more, the bird binged, gorging itself. My co-worker, the inmates, and I all watched the visitor with amused amazement. A weird silence settled over all of us. Then, the bird stopped, cocked its head to one side as if suddenly becoming aware it was the center of attention. It side-stepped from left to right and then back left again. Something was wrong. The bird bobbed its head and shuddered unnaturally. Then, embracing the sudden urge to fly, the dirty bird beat down against the ground and jauntily lurched up from the concrete. It swerved sharply from left to right, searching for a line. The wall was too high, its top covered over by tight lattice of steel links. Suddenly, it was going too fast. It couldn't stop or turn. Someone said, "Oh no." Then the bird spied a huge hole in a wall. It flapped madly toward it. The hole closed, the sky lied, and the bird's world turned into bulletproof glass. The visitor's fatal collision with its own reflection was met with cheering and applause from an audience of men, most of whom would also die within these same walls, including my co-worker. He laughed the loudest and longest.

THAT SAME DAY, ABOUT HALF AN HOUR BEFORE THE END OF MY shift, the phone on the desk rang.

"Officer Reilly, hate to tell you this, but there's been a whole rash of call-offs. You're mandated into second shift. Report to the SMU."

"But . . ." Before I could say anything, the line went dead.

I was about to say, "But I worked mandatory overtime yesterday."

I called the sergeant's office right back and explained my situation. There had to be a mistake. "I know, I know," said the stressed-out sergeant. "I can see your name on the list. We've been through all the staff and we're back to you already. Sorry, old boy." Then the line went dead, again.

I called Sarah and gave her the bad news. She was mad at first and then told me she loved me and to stay safe. I got over to the SMU and found out I had to spend the rest of the afternoon and evening in A-Unit. A-Unit is basically a holding tank for the worst of the worst sex offenders. These guys live in a concrete and steel cocoon, far from the macho madness of general population. They have to live separately, and at great expense, from other inmates for their own safety. They have single cells, a TV, a little kitchen, a vending machine, books, and board games galore. They also attend about a hundred different self-help classes each week. Outside the dayroom, they have their own special little rec yard with a cute wooden picnic table and a basketball hoop. The picnic table is where they gather to giggle and talk among themselves about their favorite things, almost like any group of men who share the same interests.

When we read in the paper that a terrible crime has been committed by a released sex offender, everyone pretty much says the same thing: "Oh, no. How could this happen? Who let them out? Why didn't we know they weren't cured? Who's responsible?"

Well, this is how it happens. These diseased animals commit the worst crimes imaginable. They get locked up, usually for less time than a poor African American man who gets caught selling a big bag of weed. Then, while they are incarcerated, they get to stay in Hotel Hell and take classes in an environment completely disconnected from reality, where there's no real accountability or threat of physical danger. These kinds of criminals, on the whole, don't carry guns, rob banks, sell drugs, run rackets, or behave like dangerous tough guys. But they do rape and murder women and children. So, by the law of averages, some of these guys, way more than you'd like to think, pass all the tests, complete their treatment programs, and never get into any kind of trouble or get written up while they're incarcerated. They become "model inmates" and after a few years, bingo! They get released back into our neighborhoods "fully rehabilitated." Then, when they're sufficiently confident, comfortable with their surroundings, and refilled with demonic desire, they go out and do the unthinkable . . . again. And then we all say, "Oh, no. How could this happen? Who let them out? Why didn't we know they weren't cured? Who's responsible?"

A good friend of mine who currently works in a Pennsylvania prison recently told me about a convicted murderer/pedophile who lives in incarcerated bliss and enjoys hormone treatments because, more than anything in the world, he now wants to become a woman. And some brain-dead shrink and imbecile prison administrators agreed to his requests and signed off on the deal. What about the needs of the victim's family? I wonder what they want more than anything in the world. I wonder how they would feel when they realize some of their tax money is paying for a sex change for the animal that raped and murdered their child. Those wants will never be met.

That night, during my mandated shift, the inmate antics of A-Unit made me feel extremely angry. By the time I left work I was seething and felt fully capable of doing something terrible and violent. It was an awful way to go home to my family. I felt sick to my stomach.

WHEN I WAS HOME I FELT RICH AND WONDERFULLY LUCKY FOR ALL I had. But always, in the back of my head, like a nail being scratched against a thin piece of tin, was the thought of returning to work tomorrow or in two days. When people asked me where I worked, I started to feel embarrassed. I didn't want to tell people I was a prison guard.

Back at the fun house, a guard who had been working in another area of the prison joined the Medium Unit day-shift crew. This guy was nuttier than a squirrel turd. He was one of those people who simply made up whatever he didn't know. Wherever you go, there's one of these guys in every group. But because of the environment we were working in, his personal interpretation of the truth seemed more ridiculous than anything I, or anyone I was working with, had ever heard. However, it was often very amusing.

This guy's lies were almost always connected to MW, a small town way up on the Canadian border, his birthplace and family home. He seemed to love the place so much and talked about it in such glowing terms, it made me wonder why he just didn't go back up there and work for the office of tourism. If you said you'd been on an archeological dig of the Middle East and rediscovered the Hanging Gardens of Babylon, this guy would say, "You do know they designed the Hanging Gardens of Babylon after Rene & Pierre's Big Moose Motel on the north side of MW?" If you said a neighbor of yours was a biathlon champion and had been in the last winter Olympics, he would say, "You know the biathlon was invented in MW after two drunk rifle-carrying Canadian border guards crossed into Maine on skis in pursuit of a black market maple syrup salesman." Whatever you said, this guy would top it with the most outlandish pack of lies you'd ever heard and some-how, all his stories started and finished in good old MW.

On one occasion, he was regaling everyone with the details of an astronomy class he'd taken while at junior college in . . . MW. No one was sure if there even was a junior college in MW, but any-way, he admitted that he'd failed the class because it was a lot harder than he thought it was going to be. I told him, "Perhaps you spent too much time studying Uranus." He assured me that the coursework didn't cover the planets in that particular solar system.

One morning, I'd had enough. Just as roll call was wrapping up, our supervisor asked if anyone had anything to say. Knowing full well that Officer MW didn't watch or listen to the news or read the paper, I said, "Hey, did anyone listen to the news this morning?"

"No," was the general grumbled response.

"Oh, there was a really terrible accident up in MW last night. It was all over the 5 a.m. National Public Radio news."

Officer MW turned around so quickly, he nearly gave himself whiplash. "What was it, Reilly? What did the news report say?"

"Oh, it was terrible. It appears that the Canadian air force was doing some sort of low-altitude night maneuvers, and you know how windy it was last night?"

"Oh, yeah, I did notice that. It was wicked windy last night. I'd say it was easily over thirty miles an hour."

"Yeah, well, apparently the fighter jets got blown off course, and by mistake they bombed the hell out of MW. According to the news, the entire town has been leveled, wiped off the map, devastated. There's nothing left. The reporter said there might be as much as five hundred dollars' worth of damage, and the cleanup is going to take until at least until lunchtime. They did say that the library had been saved and that all six of the books had been rescued before the trailer burned down."

MW stood up abruptly, glared at me, and then stormed out the room to a chorus of guffawing prison guards. On my coffee break, Sergeant T called me into his office and told me to close the door and sit down. He then said, barely holding it together, "Officer MW made a complaint about you and said he didn't like being teased like that at roll call, so don't tease him anymore. He's very sensitive about MW. Do you understand me, Reilly?"

"Yes, sir. I understand you clearly."

"Good, now get out of here."

As I left Sergeant T's office, I could hear him and Unit Manager W in the back office laughing their hats off.

Losing Faith

SHORTLY AFTER MOVING TO MAINE, I STOPPED GOING TO CHURCH. There was so much horror and misery at work. In my mind, I just couldn't reconcile that an almighty God could allow a man like Big Zeke to die and let the evil men I watched over receive treatment, be cured, and then go back to doing the same terrible things all over again. I'd never really questioned the existence of the Almighty, but now I did. If God was out there, where was He? How could He let this happen? The notion of an all-powerful, loving, caring God was becoming an increasingly dark mystery. I was losing my faith.

It was hard to tell Sarah what I was thinking. She was still grieving the loss of her dad, looking after three young children, keeping the house up, and making a whole new life in Maine. If I told her I was questioning the existence of God, starting to hate work, and feeling violent, I don't think she would have handled it too well.

To make matters worse, as the summer got underway, the forced overtime started to become ridiculous. One afternoon—it just happened to be a Friday the thirteenth—thirty-one staff members were mandated from the first shift to cover the second shift.

Of the forty-two guards needed to run second shift, they only had eleven. Something was terribly wrong, and the administration seemed oblivious to it.

The root cause of the problem was twofold. First, the number of inmate programs the department ran was ridiculous. Despite desperately dangerous staff shortages, the warden and his cronies refused to increase cell time for inmates. They insisted, at great risk to the stressed-out staff, that the prisoners have art, music, woodworking, weightlifting, indoor rec, outdoor rec, morning rec, afternoon rec, evening rec, drug and alcohol counseling, horticulture classes in the greenhouse, Native American ceremonies, NAACP meetings that were predominately attended by white guys, church meetings, prayer meetings, library groups, adult education classes, computer classes, and intramural basketball tournaments—and all while staff shortages passed critical levels and morale disappeared into a black hole.

The second part of the problem was the massively top-heavy management structure. There were so many staff and so few guards. There was the phantom warden and a troop of useless deputy wardens, most of whom had already retired. They were drawing large state pensions, but had hired back on and were now getting large salaries, too. These guys were known as "the double-dippers." There was a mess of unit managers who were more like deputy wardens, but actually did some work, and more captains than you could shake a stick at. On top of all that, there was a Correctional Emergency Response squad that wasn't allowed to do anything except train and play SWAT Team dress-up. There was a Greek chorus of mental health counselors, treatment counselors, drug and alcohol counselors, sex offender counselors, criminal investigators, firearms instructors, training instructors, an army of maintenance men, and more secretaries than a large Washington, D.C., law firm. The combined cost of all of these appointments and positions, a good number of which were redundant, must have been astronomical and created a huge financial hurdle that prohibited a better hiring policy and an increase of pay for good security staff.

Then, there was also a pathetically porous full-contact visit policy. This meant all general population inmates who were "well behaved" were entitled to face-to-face, full-contact visits from friends and family. On one memorable occasion, staff became aware through a snitch that an inmate's wife was going to bring a gun inside on her visit. She was going to attempt an escape with her convict husband. They would take hostages and shoot their way out. On the day of the planned escape, the wife was arrested by state cops on prison property. She was carrying a concealed and loaded pistol and was ready to go through with the plan. The impotent Correctional Emergency Response Team had to stand idle on the sidelines polishing their helmets while the State Police took care of business. It was suspected that the Correctional Emergency Response Team were not, or ever would be, allowed to participate in any serious tactical situation, in case their actions initiated a lawsuit that might incriminate the warden.

THE UNMANAGEABLE FULL-CONTACT VISIT POLICY ALSO FLOODED the prison with drugs and other contraband. Visitors were seldom patted down. Women and children were never touched. Drugs were placed cleverly in clothes, especially children's, exchanged orally when inmates kissed loved ones, and passed surreptitiously from hand to hand. All this happened while one or two exhausted, stressed-out guards tried to keep an eye on several dozen inmates and their families in a room about the size of two tennis courts. I found myself asking, "What kind of administration allows maximum-security prisoners to have full-contact visits and then complains about contraband coming into their facility?"

The drugs, usually placed in balloons or condoms, were swallowed and then passed into the toilet the next day or two. After the drugs were fished out and their packaging cleaned off, they were used, sold, and traded. On one occasion, I found myself yet again mandated, this time to monitor a suspected inmate smuggler. The inmate was being held in a solitary observation cell in the SMU. It was standard operating procedure to strip the inmate down, place him naked except for a sheet in a cell, and then wait for him to have a bowel movement. The prisoner was to be watched at all times, 24/7. The guard was, in turn, watched via a security camera by another guard in central control to make sure he was constantly watching the inmate. It was all very Big Brother and a spectacular waste of precious manpower.

Well, midway through my forced overtime shift, the moment of truth arrived: "Officer Reilly, I've got to go."

So, I got on the radio and called the supervisor, who quickly arrived with a couple of his henchmen. Then, we all stood around and watched the inmate defecate into a bedpan. I'm sure the experience was as inspiring and uplifting for the inmate as it was for me. I, however, have the distinct impression the sergeant and his two goons thoroughly enjoyed the show.

"C'mon, Reilly," said the sergeant. "You know what comes next." Unfortunately, I did.

The two goons giggled with glee as the sergeant handed me a pair of rubber gloves and a couple of wooden tongue depressors. The inmate covered himself back up with his sheet and retreated to the back of the cell, crouching in the corner like a beaten child. I then had to dissect his feces and look for balloons filled with dope. There were none.

After the Sergeant and his two ass-kissing companions left laughing, the inmate said, "I'm so sorry you had to do that, Mr. Reilly." He was very genuine about it.

I told him I was sorry, too. All I could think was *What would my family say if they could see me doing this?*

After the mandated shift was over, sometime around 10 p.m., I showered in the locker room before leaving work. When I got home, I took another shower, but it was no good. No matter how hard I scrubbed, I couldn't get the prison off me. It was in the follicles of my hair, under my nails, between my teeth, on the back of my tongue, in the pores of my skin, and it was slowly slipping into my vocabulary. After I dried off from my second shower in one hour, I got dressed, went into the kitchen, pulled a six-pack of beer out of the refrigerator, turned on the TV, sat down, and started drinking.

THE STAFF TURNOVER WAS SO HIGH AT THE PRISON, IT WAS ALMOST impossible to keep track of who was who and how long they had been employed. It was clear to me by now how the warden was running the place. Conduct a training class every six weeks, try and get a dozen or so candidates into class, jump them through a bunch of half-ass hoops, and hope a quarter of them make it. The administration was sick. I found myself asking, why would these "double-dippers" want to alter the status quo? They wouldn't, because it wouldn't behoove them to do so. They seemed to be operating under the rule of: "If it's broken, don't tell anyone because they might send someone in to fix it."

Working at the Maine State Prison was like being trapped in a Kafkaesque movie. There was something surreal and constantly threatening about the illogical bureaucratic baloney and the bewildering, inexplicable way the place was regulated. It felt like the guard staff had no voice and was at the mercy of controlling conspiratorial overlords who only cared about themselves.

IN JUNE 2005, AFTER SIX MONTHS AT THE MAINE STATE PRISON, I had my first real interaction with the warden himself. As far as the other guards and supervisors went, I was completely off the radar: I hadn't done anything that might attract attention or had any real write-ups, apart from teasing the guy from MW, but that didn't count. The night I met the warden, I had been mandated *again*. The phone rang and a tired voice said, "Heads up, Reilly. The warden's coming into the block. Make sure you're all squared away."

Then, the line went dead. There was nothing to do. Everything was shipshape and all the inmates were being relatively well behaved. My work area was neat and tidy, so I stood up, pushed the chair under the desk, and waited. A moment or two later, in strolled the warden. He entered the block, attended by his entourage. I came around from behind the desk, stood in front of it, waiting to say hello, answer questions, or show him anything he wanted to see. The warden walked right past me, within five feet, completely ignoring me, and went over to speak to a couple of inmates. He visited with them for a few minutes, and then on his way out walked right past me a second time without even looking at me or saying a word. Then, he left the block.

Wow! I remember thinking. *Did that really happen?* It seemed incredible that the guy didn't look at me, say hello, or even ask how things were going. After all, I was one of his staff. Was it me? Was I being egotistical? Or was that arrogance personified? Again, after sixteen hours of maximum-security lockup, eight hours of which were forced overtime, I went home angry. I found out the next day that he'd walked past all the other guards in all the other blocks without acknowledging any of them. It seemed both unbelievable and at the same time so emblematic of the larger problems the prison faced under his laughable absentee leadership.

33

Civility Costs Nothing

"CIVILITY COSTS NOTHING AND SOMETIMES GETS YOU EVERYTHING."
I said it a hundred times to a hundred guys, both prisoners and
guards just before they were about to blow a gasket. Or "Treat me
the same way you want me to treat you and we'll get along just
fine." It was the Christ part of Christianity I still had faith in. "Do
unto others . . ."

Ninety-nine point nine percent of the time, with guards and
inmates, this simple psychology worked like a charm. There was,
however, a group of people who couldn't and wouldn't be told how
to be reasonable. It was the guys doing a lousy job, especially the
bullies and the cowards. These guards were easy to spot. When
they were on their own, in close proximity to the inmates, they
were overly familiar and didn't keep respectful boundaries, and
then when they were around other guards, they treated the
inmates like crap. This made me crazy.

On one occasion in October 2005, I had been ordered to take

an abusive prisoner from the Medium Unit to the SMU. When we got down there, all hell was breaking loose. An ineffectual sergeant and a huddle of rookie staff were getting the royal runaround by the always hard-to-handle SMU inmates. A new guard I didn't know was threatening and insulting an inmate who was refusing to give up his food tray after chow. The guard was acting like an idiot. He actually called the inmate a "fat bastard," demanded the tray, and threatened disciplinary action, even though the inmate in question was on months of extended disciplinary action already. The inmate retorted, "It's better to be a fat bastard than be a stupid asshole like you."

The idiot guard wasn't smart enough to see it coming and played right into the inmate's hands. He said, "Oh, yeah, why's that?"

The grinning inmate said, "Well, I can always lose weight, but you'll always be a stupid asshole."

The guard completely lost it and became irate. The other inmates listening to the exchange howled with laughter, which only infuriated the guard even more. At any moment, the laughter was going to end and something very bad was going to happen. So, I walked up to the cell door and recognized the inmate. He was happy to see me and said, still surfing the wave of comic victory, "Hey, Officer Reilly, how are you? What you doing down here?"

"Oh, ya know, someone was misbehaving in the Medium Unit and has to come down here to cool off with you guys for a while. What's happening? What's all the fuss about?"

He proceeded to tell me what I knew, that the guard standing right behind me was being a real dick and wasn't doing what the inmate considered to be a good job.

In a soft, calm voice, I said, "Well, listen, you know me, and you know I'll be straight with you. The nurse can't come on to the block to do meds until all the trays have been collected. So, give me your tray, then you and the rest of the guys can get your meds, and everyone will have a nice, easy day. What do you think?"

He looked at me for a moment and then yelled at the trouble-causing guard behind me, "See, you don't get any respect down here because of that stupid fucking uniform. You get it because of how you act! Sure, Officer Reilly. No problem, here's my tray."

With that, he handed me his tray and went and sat down on his bunk. Immediately after I locked the tray slot, Officer Stupid tapped me on the shoulder and said, "I want to have a word with you."

"No problem," I replied, "but not here."

We walked away from the cells, out of earshot of the inmates, and he said aggressively, pointing his big fat finger in my face, "Do you think I'm scared of these guys?"

"No," I replied, "I just think you're treating them the wrong way."

That guard left work a couple of days later and never came back.

CHRISTMAS DAY 2005, I WAS OFF, EVEN THOUGH I WAS SUPPOSED TO work. I worked it out with one of the older guys who just happened to have the holiday off. He would come in, work for me, get his pay, plus my holiday pay. And on top of that, I gave him a hundred bucks. He needed the money, and I needed to be at home with my family. It was worth every penny. On Christmas Eve we got the fire roaring, ate homemade pizza, watched movies, and then after we put the kids to bed, laid out their presents below the tree. Christmas Day was bittersweet. It was a first for Sarah without her dad. We all missed him terribly.

The winter's months rolled on. Then, in February 2006, after a particularly big storm, the warden asked one of the sergeants to round up a couple of trustworthy trustees to clear the snow from the patio area outside his office; why and what he planned to do out there in sub-zero temperatures no one will ever know, but that's what he wanted. The two trustees were carefully chosen, handed shovels, and then taken to the work site. The snow was knee-deep, heavy, and wet, and it was going to take quite a while to clear, so, because it was bitterly cold, the sergeant left the two workers outside in the frigid February air and went inside to wait and keep warm. A good while later, the inmates came back inside, met up with their sergeant supervisor, and told him they were finished and that everything looked great. The sergeant readily believed his two charges, relieved them of their shovels and sent them back to their respective cellblocks. That afternoon, when the warden returned to his office, he immediately went to his window to see if his request had been taken care off. The snow had indeed been removed and had been piled up in a rather creative way. Staring at the warden as he looked out of his office window, like a giant polar peeping Tom was a massive snowman, with an enormous snowy penis, pointing right at his window. Rumor has it, he was not amused.

34

You Just Never Know What's Gonna Tip a Fella Right Over the Edge

March 2006

A SPLIT SECOND AFTER THE PANIC BUTTON ON A-BLOCK WAS HIT, the entire facility went into emergency lockdown. The loud speakers in all areas of the prison blared: "Man down in A-Block! Man down in A-Block! All inmates lock in!"

The handful of prisoners who were out—cleaning the hallways or on their way to or from rec, medical, or the case worker's office—were all herded at high speed back to their respective housing areas and locked in. All available guards, sergeants, and captains dropped whatever they were doing and went running as fast as they could toward the emergency.

As I sprinted down the corridor toward A-Block, the thunderous pounding, rhythmic and tribal, got louder and louder. The closer I got, the more intense, mob-like, and barbaric it became.

Officer NW was a legend of sorts. He was a crusader of cleanliness, a dictator of decorum. He saw things only in black and white: things that were allowed and things that were not allowed. In his world, the rules and regulations of the institution were akin to acts of God, and God should be obeyed at all costs. Officer NW never opened himself up to any interpretation of the rules. There was no latitude or leniency. If an inmate could not follow the rules, he found himself on the shit-list. And being on Officer NW's shit-list put an inmate under an almost unimaginable amount of scrutiny. Once on the list, the constant microscopic inspection and unabated monitoring always resulted in one of two outcomes: The inmate either adhered to Officer NW's edicts and got with the program, or they'd internally combust, suffer from some sort of emotional meltdown, and get dragged off to the hole, foaming at the mouth and screaming death threats to an unperturbed Officer NW.

Officer NW stood about five foot eight and weighed close to two hundred pounds. If someone was to say he was in shape you'd have to agree: pear shape. Although not a prime physical specimen, the former soldier's uniform was always immaculate: His boots shined like polished glass, he smelled of soap and cologne, and his nails were as clean and trimmed as his moustache was groomed. Officer NW's radar was constantly on. If he picked up any strange disturbances in the controlled atmosphere, he'd crane his neck one way then the other, twitch his neatly trimmed moustache like a hunting dog pricks up its ears, and then, alerted that perhaps some rumpus was afoot, he'd jump up from behind his desk, tuck his thumbs into his duty belt, narrow his eyes, and go check out the laundry room, the janitor's closet, or any number of random cells. He would stroll and patrol nonstop through the block with supreme authority and a no-mercy attitude that let everyone know exactly who was in charge.

If cloning was a reality, the Department of Corrections would never need to look for staff ever again. They would call the lab and order thousands of Officer NWs and have thousands more on standby for whenever the old ones broke down or became unserviceable after being destroyed by inmates.

The truth is, I quite liked Officer NW. I liked him because you always knew what to expect and consistency from a co-worker is a good thing in prison. I was in his block visiting with him once and we started to talk about music. He told me how much he liked classic rock.

"Me, too," I responded. "Do you listen to anything other than classic rock?"

"Yeah, a little country now and then, and a little pop. The only thing I won't listen to is rap music. All that fucking swearing and shit really bothers me."

That made me laugh a lot.

Officer NW had been assaulted numerous times. The most recent assault took place after an inmate refused to lock in, then attacked him and tried to gouge out one of his eyes. Officer NW took a couple of days off, got patched up, stitched up, and came right back to work within the week. Officer NW was a living legend.

The cavalry arrived expecting the worst. We rushed through A-Block's open door only to find every inmate, all sixty-four of them, locked safely in their cells. From behind their doors they were calling Officer NW's name in a brutal rhythmic warlike chant. Officer NW was standing behind his desk with his back against the wall looking pale and shaken. For a second I thought he'd been stabbed. Then, he started shouting into an empty dayroom, "Stop it! I said stop it now or I will keep the entire block locked down for a week! This is not funny. I said stop it. This is not funny!"

Officer NW yelled at the top of his lungs and pointed his finger at one cell after another. The inmates howled, laughed, pointed, and yelled through their doors, chanting Officer NW's name riotously.

The bullfrog must have weighed at least half a pound. It somehow found its way into the greenhouse and by all accounts had been living there for quite a while. The trustees who worked in there had grown quite attached to their big bug-eating amphibian friend. Anything creeping or crawling that could be caught was crippled then carefully placed on the gravel in the cool damp corner by the hose pipe. Within seconds, the distressed buzzing and flapping would bring the big frog out for his snack. The greenhouse workers were very protective of the frog. It was well-known that should anything happen to him, there would be inquiries made and blood spilled. This was a very real threat. The trustees who worked the greenhouse were all long-timers and lifers, most with murder charges. These men were not to be fooled with or taken lightly.

The frog sat on Officer NW's desk, croaking forlornly and blinking slowly as it tried to shrink back into its own slimy skin, while the noise of the pounding and chanting reverberated throughout the cellblock. The frog made a small jump forward, defecating on Officer NW's desk in mid-hop, and then stopped again.

"Get that out of here! Arrrgh! Shit, I hate those things. Hey, you, yes, you, in two-twelve, you think this is funny? Just wait, you just wait!"

The kidnapped frog had almost certainly been smuggled through security in the front of some pervert's underpants, and as Officer NW was doing one of his many rounds, the frog had been placed surreptitiously in the top drawer of his desk. Every inmate knew that once Officer NW finished his rounds he always sat back down at his desk, opened the drawer, removed the logbook, and made several entries. The trap was set and everyone in the block knew about it. The only thing the inmates didn't know was that Officer NW was deathly afraid of frogs.

Upon completion of the round, Officer NW returned to his desk, sat in his chair, and leaned back. He put his hands behind his head and listened. It was a little too quiet. The cleaners were mopping a little too conscientiously; the domino and cards gamers were less animated than usual; and there was no one at the desk asking stupid questions. There was definitely something going on. Officer NW could feel it in every fiber of his being. He slid open his drawer without taking his eyes of the inmates. His hand reached in to remove his logbook and felt something cold and wet.

He told me later, the first thing that sprang to mind was excrement. Then, whatever it was moved and slithered under his fingers.

"Oh, shit!"

Officer NW jumped up, pushing his chair away with the back of his knees. The chair rolled wildly backward and slammed into the wall behind him, stopping with a loud clatter. The open drawer revealed the big bullfrog in all his glory. The terrified amphibian croaked loudly enough to be heard by every inmate in the block. Officer NW screamed like a Girl Scout at a scary movie. The frog leapt up out of the drawer and landed on the big red panic button at the bottom right-hand corner of the control panel. The weight of the frog was enough to depress the button. This sent an instantaneous message to central control that a major incident was in progress and to lock down the entire facility. The inmates erupted. It was turning out better than they could have possibly have hoped for. The frog croaked again. Officer NW screamed for a second, third, and fourth time as the whole facility went into emergency lockdown. Over eight hundred inmates were herded into their cells, and an emergency count went into action. Without being asked, every A-Block inmate ran to their cells and locked themselves in, knowing that in seconds the goon squad would be on scene and wouldn't be handing out invites to the warden's garden party.

Afterward, the bullfrog was returned safely to his home in the greenhouse and no threats of bodily injury were issued from his keepers. Officer NW was counseled by a senior member of staff about taking his work too seriously even though it was a serious place to work. Another senior member of staff confided to Officer NW that during high school he really got into biology and during that period he must have dissected hundreds of frogs. This appealed to Officer NW's pitiless side and momentarily made him feel a bit better. But, for weeks after, wanted posters for the bullfrog bandit magically appeared on Officer NW's desk and on the A-Block notice board. They were torn down and destroyed immediately by the embarrassed and ever-vigilant Officer NW. And for the following few weeks, anytime the inmates were locked down, for count, for the night, or for any kind of emergency, as soon as silence settled over the cellblock, the mimicked sounds of bull-frogs could be heard ribbiting just loud enough and from just enough cells that Officer NW, try as he might, could never work out where they were coming from.

Not long after this incident, the legendary Officer NW, like dozens of other good men reached breaking point. The excessive mandating and crass incompetence of the administration forced him to take a job elsewhere, at another state institution.

You Seem
So Unhappy

IN MAY 2006, WE WENT BACK TO ENGLAND FOR A TWO-WEEK vacation.

"How the hell does a prison guard with a wife, three kids, a mortgage, and a car payment manage to pay for a two-week European vacation?" That's what most of my co-workers said. I answered with the truth: "Because of my parents, that's how. They pay for the kids' tickets, put us up in a rental cottage they own, let us borrow a car, and feed us. If it wasn't for them, we wouldn't be going."

Sarah and the kids were so excited about the trip. I was looking forward to seeing my family and a few friends, but I was feeling numb. On the way to the airport, I remember thinking, Oh no, in fifteen days, fifteen short days, I'll have to go back to work at the prison. My job was casting a dark, depressing shadow across all of my thoughts and immediately, across my trip to England. Living in Maine was great. Sarah and the kids were wonderful. They kept me going and gave me something to live for, but I was beginning to feel bad all the time. I wasn't in control of my life and I had become deeply unsatisfied. The ingrained negativity and the daily horror show of prison life were getting to me.

While in England, I felt mildly depressed most of the time. When anyone asked me about my work, I didn't want to talk about it, being on vacation, but unable to shake the thoughts of going back to prison felt sickening. My parents kept asking if I was OK and if I was doing anything with my music. That just made me feel worse. I told them I didn't want to talk about music either.

During the vacation we were invited to go down to London to stay with two of my oldest and closest friends, George, and his wife Flik. But the day before we were supposed to leave, I concocted an avalanche of lame excuses that I'm sure George saw right through. I told him we just couldn't make it. So, we didn't go. We didn't go because I didn't want to talk about my job and I was feeling jealous of George, who after a series of hardships and setbacks in his own life, was now running a successful business, fighting the good fight and coming out on top. The unflattering truth is, while I was wallowing in the sworn enemy of happiness, self pity, I was pushing away family and invaluable friendships.

The whole time we were away, I felt like such an angry loser. I moped around and wasn't very good company, because all I could think about the entire time was the prison. After I got back to Maine, I knew I had to make a move. I just wasn't sure how I was going to pull it off.

BACK AT THE PRISON ABSOLUTELY NOTHING HAD CHANGED. I returned from vacation and, as expected, found myself right on top of the mandate list. My first day back would be a double shift. A new training class had started, and there was lots of gossip and trash talk about the latest set of NOBs, especially the two women in the class. But the real hot gossip was about a promotion that just happened. A certain guard made sergeant, and his father happened to be a senior deputy warden. This newly appointed supervisor was completely unfit to lead other men and, furthermore, manage inmates. The new sergeant's promotion was a thing of utter ridicule throughout every part of the prison. Then again, considering how the place was run, the appointment wasn't a surprise.

Easily one hundred pounds overweight, as lazy as the day was long, and with the communications skills of a dead skunk, this guy was a black eye to the entire department of corrections, in fact, to anyone in any uniform anywhere. The new sergeant was a poster boy for exactly how the department didn't want to be seen. But, apparently the administration was blind to these most obvious facts and the promotion was made.

The new sergeant treated the inmates terribly and the staff even worse and yet, he was promoted. A co-worker, whom I liked a lot and who'd been in the Marines for years prior to working at the prison, told me that these kinds of supervisors are more of a liability than an asset and get "accidentally" shot by their own men while in combat. I stopped dead and asked him was he serious. He in turn, faced me, and said, "Reilly, even if this guy was in shape, would you want someone like him leading you into battle?" My friend was right. Our new supervisor wasn't fit to lead a group of ravenous Boy Scouts through an all-you-can-eat Chinese buffet.

By August, the new slovenly sergeant was having quite an effect on the medium unit. All the good work done during the day by Unit Manager WR, Sergeant T, and Sergeant B was being undermined on second shift by the new, useless sergeant. His management skills were so poor that the guard staff on second shift did whatever they wanted. There was no consistency, leadership, or accountability. The inmates loved the emotional turbulence, thrived on the staff infighting, and soon started acting out. So, it was no surprise when I arrived at work one morning to find the whole Medium Unit in lockdown. There had been a savage beating on second shift. An inmate was almost killed, and there was a big investigation underway. All inmates were locked in their cells until further notice. The captain giving the briefing mentioned half a dozen times that the assaultive inmate was bipolar. I got the impression this was the first time the supervisor had used the word. He must have liked the way the sounds of the syllables felt in his mouth because he kept saying "bipolar" over and over again in almost every sentence. I wasn't the only person to notice this. After about the eighth time he said "bipolar," I looked around and saw numerous other guards rolling their eyes and wishing he would shut up. At the end of the big "bipolar" briefing, the captain asked if anyone had any questions. I couldn't help myself. I raised my hand.

"Yes, Reilly."

"Does bipolar mean you're attracted to members of the opposite sex and those huge white bears that live in the Arctic?"

There was a long pause followed by an uncomfortable silence. All the other staff looked at me. No one, not a single person, thought it was funny.

"No, Reilly, that's not what it bipolar means," said the agitated captain.

Because of the lockdown and the ongoing investigation, that morning, instead of going to the chow hall for breakfast, the meal was going to be served to the inmates a la carte, or should I say, via aluminum cart, which meant the food would be put in brown paper bags and delivered by trustees to each Medium cellblock, A through G. After the deliveries were made, the guards handed out the individual bagged meals to each inmate. The brown bags contained a half-pint carton of milk, a piece of fruit, and a ham-and-cheese sandwich. By prison standards, it was certainly not a bad meal. It was actually real food, not chemical crap that had been made in a factory and then re-heated. It was better than what I had for my own breakfast. After another guard and I handed out all the food, silence settled over the block as the lock-ins began to eat. My co-worker left and I sat at the desk, somewhat enjoying the change of routine. Usually at this time, the circus was well underway, with most of the animals out of their cages.

Bang! Bang! Bang! Someone was pounding on the inside of a cell door. The electronic sensor tripped and let me know the doors' locking system was being stressed. A computerized voice blared at me from the speaker on the control panel: "Unauthorized access! Unauthorized access! Unauthorized access!" The

inmates loved the digital monotone urgency of the computer's pronunciation. Whenever the warning went off, which was about fifty times a day, it always sounded more like "Unauthorized ass-sex! Unauthorized ass-sex! Unauthorized ass-sex!" Every time I heard it, I had a laugh and thought about the audio engineer who designed it and just how horrified he or she would be upon hearing it going off in this environment with all of its evil implications and horror show humor.

Then the screaming started. *What the hell's that?*, I thought. I stood up and looked around. At first, I thought two inmates were fighting inside a cell. That could be bad. Or, it could be a setup for me to open the door, which could end up being much worse.

Bang! Bang! Bang!

I got up out of my chair and walked toward the sound of the banging. As I approached the cell, I heard a deep voice screaming, "CO! Where's my fucking mayonnaise?!"

Through the window of one of the corner cells, I saw inmate GM angrily pounding on the Plexiglas window.

"Hey, you gave me a ham-and-cheese sandwich and no mayonnaise. I can't eat this sandwich without mayonnaise. I need some fucking mayonnaise!"

It was hard to believe what I was hearing. I stood at the door and looked at inmate GM for a moment. He was an older guy, in his late forties, and huge, at least six foot six and close to three hundred pounds. He was doing life for murder and necrophilia. He had killed a couple of women and then kept their corpses in his closet and had been doing the unthinkable to the deceased. When I first started working the block, he came over to the desk, introduced himself, and told me, "Listen, Reilly, I run this unit. It'll be best for you if just sit back and not interfere with the way I do things."

I considered this then responded, "Inmate GM, if you do run this unit, interfering is exactly what I intend to do, and if you talk to me like this again, the first thing I'm going to interfere with is your recreation schedule."

Inmate GM didn't bother me again and certainly didn't run the unit while I was at work.

"Inmate GM, are you hungry?"

He stopped yelling to listen to what I had to say. I always found that if I spoke quietly and calmly, the inmates usually became less agitated, because they wanted to hear what was being said.

"Yeah, of course I'm fucking hungry!"

"Well, look, no one has any mayo, but the sandwich will be fine without it. I'm afraid that's all there is to it. Everyone else is managing just fine."

Inmate GM looked at me like I'd just told him that I'd been on a hot date with his mother. As I walked back to the desk, inmate GM started screaming and cursing so loudly about the lack of mayonnaise that, for a moment, I considered calling the goon squad to have him taken away. After about a minute, he lost steam and quit his yelling and pounding.

Silence returned to the block and I found myself wondering, what locked-down inmates in Russian, Chinese, and African prisons were eating for breakfast this morning and whether they demanding condiments with their meal. Half an hour later, I did a round and felt more like a waiter than a correctional officer, collecting all the trash and leftovers. Inmate GM had thrown his entire sandwich in the trash uneaten. Inmate GM was later beaten to death by another inmate, who was almost certainly being pressured to "pay rent" in the form of sexual favors for the privilege of living on inmate GM's cellblock.

||||||||||

THE LONGER I STAYED AT THE PRISON, THE MORE I FELT A HARDNESS developing in me. The way I interacted with some of the inmates and some of the more difficult staff members was changing. I no longer wanted to build bridges, make friends, and find compromises. The good guys who wanted to work hard, do their job, and try to make a difference were decent company and reliable co-workers. But I thought that some of the other staff members were bad people. They did such a pathetic job that I could get hurt—or worse—as a result of their stupidity and incompetence.

And if some of my incompetent co-workers didn't like the way I was doing things, I now didn't care. It seemed like every day something unprofessional, crazy, or terrible happened, and the more madness I was exposed to, the more nonchalant I became. The prison was definitely changing me. At home I felt myself getting irritated at the children all the time. Sarah would say, "C'mon. They're acting like kids. That's what they're supposed to do."

But that's not how I saw it. If the kids weren't doing what I asked them to do immediately or listened to me the second I opened my mouth, I blew up and started yelling. One evening in September, during dinner, my daughter Lindsey was eating with her fingers, making a mess and goofing around at the table. I asked her several times to use her fork. She continued to eat with her hands. I suddenly found myself on my feet, yanking her out of her chair, and dragging her to the bathroom, standing over her and yelling for her to wash her hands, go back to the table, and eat her food with a fork the way I told her to. I was so angry; I was seconds away from hitting her. Sarah was instantly at the bathroom door. She grabbed a towel, kneeled down in front of Lindsey, and dried her hands. Lindsey was crying, shaking, and dreadfully upset. She was sobbing and saying her arm hurt where I'd grabbed her.

Sarah sent Lindsey back to the kitchen, stood up, and told me, "You can't discipline a child when you're angry. Remember this: The way you treat her now, when she's young, defines the type of man she'll choose as an adult." Sarah then turned and left me standing alone in the bathroom feeling ashamed and sick to my stomach.

ONE MORNING LATER THAT MONTH, AT 5:45 A.M., I WAS IN THE locker room about to change into my uniform. Another guard from the training class ahead of mine laughed and pointed at me. For some reason, he found it hilarious and overtly feminine that I was wearing sandals.

I asked him, "What's wrong with sandals?"

"They're gay, dude, that's what's wrong with them." Oh, boy, here we go again with the gay haters. "Turn the other cheek," whispered a voice in my head. But as that notion entered and quickly left my mind, I said to my macho co-worker, "Hey, c'mon give me a break. Jesus wore sandals." He looked at me, a puzzled expression formed across his Neanderthal face, and before he could respond, I said, "You know who else wore sandals don't you? Yeah, Spartacus! So why don't you fuck off!"

It was the first time I'd ever cursed at a co-worker. The exchange was witnessed by half a dozen other guards who thought the whole thing was hilarious. I hadn't meant it to be humorous. Unfortunately, my relationship with the Neanderthal was never the same after that.

Meanwhile, another member of the winner's circle I had the distinct displeasure of working with had recently been rehired. Some months prior, he'd mouthed off to an inmate and was head-butted right in the face. Immediately after the incident, he tucked his tail between his legs and walked off the job. Imagine everyone's surprise when he reappeared and, believe it or not, got his job back. That's how poorly the place was being run. A guy can't handle himself, gets assaulted, puts other staff in danger, and then leaves. Then, months later, they rehire him. What a joke. The good staff thought it was a slap in the face, and the inmates thought it was absolutely hilarious.

What drove me crazy about this guy was that he was from New York and always pulling the "I'm from New York" tough-guy card. Now, anyone who's been around the block a couple of times knows New York is a great place and there are plenty of tough guys in that town. There are also plenty of tough guys in Texas, Florida, Maine, Mexico, Minnesota, Scotland, and Scandinavia, and just about everywhere else. The thing is, real tough guys don't go around telling everyone how hard they are . . . they don't have to.

I irritated the guy because I didn't buy into the tough-guy act, and I couldn't stand the way he treated the inmates (too friendly when he was outnumbered and way too cocky when he was with other guards). He knew it and I knew it, and for that we disliked each other tremendously.

One evening after being mandated to work a half-shift in the kitchen from 2 to 6 p.m., Officer NYC came to relieve me. He met me in the staff dining hall. He approached as I was putting on my coat and picking up my lunch box. He stopped a few feet short of me, held out his hand, and in front of other staff, sighed and said (using his tough-guy New York voice), "Give me d-keys, den get d-fuck outta my face."

I stopped zipping up my coat, looked at him, and said, "What?!"

"You heard me. Give me d-keys, den get d-fuck outta my face."

I put my lunch box down on the table closest to me and took off my coat. The room became quiet. I walked the couple of steps up to the guy and got within half an inch of his face, my nose almost touching his cheek. I was so close to him, I could feel my own breath bouncing off the side of his face. Then, I said, "Now I'm really in your face. What are you going to do about it?" It was a really dumb move, but I was suddenly overcome by a white-hot anger.

I waited. He didn't move. The room was completely silent. Some of the staff looked away, others stared. I really wanted him to try to hit me. I wanted him to make the first move so that I could defend myself and then attack him. I didn't just want to hit him; I wanted to hurt him, to smash his face in. I wanted to be assaulted so I could rightfully retaliate and really unload on this guy. He didn't do anything. He just stood there looking big, big for nothing and big and stupid. I put the keys and radio down on a table, put my coat back on, picked up my lunch box, and walked to the door absolutely boiling mad. As I waited for the electronically monitored door to open, I called back to the guy and said: "Hey, this place is full of hard men, on both sides of the bars. Just remember, you're not one of them."

The door clicked open and I left, feeling furious and violent and wanting to fight.

The next day, traveling from one area of the prison to another, I was stopped by the only dark-skinned officer on staff. I think he was originally from the Caribbean. I can't remember for sure, but I do, however, remember I liked him a lot. He had a good sense of humor, a great attitude, and was a solid, reliable co-worker. He also, and most importantly, handled the inmates tremendously well. He stopped me in a corridor and started to bust my chops about the incident in the staff dining hall with Officer NYC. He told me to lighten up and not let these sorts of things get to me. Of course, he was right. He said, "Reilly, you gotta be a lover, not a hater." It was good advice. So, I responded by grabbing hold of him and hugging him. Taken aback by my overt display of affection, he tried to push me away. But despite his burly build and superior strength, I held on as tight as I could, rested my head on his shoulder, and sang an entire chorus of "Ebony and Ivory" at the top of my lungs. No inmates were present.

In October, well into my shift, an incident took place in the B-Block laundry room. Each day, in numerical cell succession, inmates have their dirty clothes washed by two laundry trustees. There are always inmates trying to sneak their wash in ahead of their allotted laundry day, and this often causes trouble. For the third time in about an hour, I walked into the washroom and found an inmate hanging out who didn't work there and wasn't due to have his clothes cleaned that day. I can't remember his name, but I do remember that, until that day, I had never had any problem with him and had always found him a little surly but respectful. Finding him out of bounds for the third time annoyed me intently. More than anything, I felt like I was being taken advantage of after giving the guy a break for the first two infractions.

As soon as I saw him, I walked right up to him and said, "That's it. Get out. You're spending the rest of the day locked in your cell."

I pointed to the laundry room door. I was on the edge of being really angry and too close to the inmate at the same time. In a flash, the inmate lunged toward me and tried to head-butt me in the face.

The portable phone in my right hand went flying. I moved to one side as the inmate came at me. I grabbed his shirt with both hands, and pushed him away while keeping hold of him. The two laundry workers bolted for the door. With my elbows locked out, I held on to the inmate, keeping him at arm's length. We staggered back and forth for a second or two and then, as his weight shifted, I kicked his feet out from beneath him. He held onto me, and I held onto him. Together, we fell heavily to the floor. I landed on top of him. As we crashed down to the ground, I managed to press the emergency button on my duty belt. Instantly, I heard the radio crackle, "Man down in B-Block! Man down in B-Block!"

Holding onto each other by our clothes, the inmate and I struggled for control. I buried my head in his chest, pushed down, pinned him to the floor, and then quickly crawled on top of him. I was now sitting on his stomach holding his wrists. His fists were clenched. I couldn't tell if he was holding anything sharp. We stared at each other. He cleared his throat and filled his mouth with snot and saliva. He was about to spit in my face. Quickly transferring both hands to one of his, I managed to get a wrist lock that hurt him enough to enable me to flip him over onto his stomach. I didn't want any of his saliva anywhere near me. I cranked down on his wrist, and he spat out a mouthful of phlegm and began to scream. There was several more loud static radio bursts.

"Man down in B-Block! Man down in B-Block!"

The inmate and I continued to thrash around. I knew the guard in central control couldn't see what was happening because we were on the floor in the laundry room behind a bank of large institutional washers and dryers. We were out of camera view.

After a few more moments of struggle, I felt the inmate running out of gas. I managed to get my handcuffs out of the pouch on my belt, hold on to the guy with one hand for a moment, and snap the cuffs on both wrists with the other. The whole thing had only been going on for about thirty seconds, but it seemed so much longer. Once I had the guy cuffed, I looked up over the washing and drying machines, hoping to see help arriving. There was none. A crowd of inmates suddenly gathered at the door. I remember thinking, *If I don't get a little help, this is going to get ugly.* Standing up over the handcuffed inmate, I started yelling as loud as I could, "Lock in. Everyone lock in."

It seems silly now, but instead of leaving the inmate lying on the floor, I dragged him by the collar of his sweatshirt out of the laundry room and into the middle of the cellblock, yelling over and over again, "Lock in. Lock in."

When I reached the center of the cellblock, the troops arrived. The crowd dispersed and quickly locked in while the assaultive inmate was taken to the hole. The shift supervisor appeared and asked me what happened and if I was OK. I told him what went down and said I was fine.

"You're bleeding, Reilly," he said pointing at my hand. I looked down at blood dripping from my fingers and splattering on the floor next to my boots. Somehow, during the scuffle, while flipping the guy over and cuffing him up, I must have cut myself on the serrated teeth of the handcuffs. The prison's infirmary, grade-A medical facility that it is, said they didn't want to stitch me up so I'd have to go into town to the hospital. I assured them I didn't need stitches but the dark specter of the almighty lawsuit loomed and the shift commander told me I had to go into town and get checked out at the emergency room. He was mildly apologetic and asked, because they were so short-staffed, was there any way I could drive myself. "No problem," I said, and off I went.

On the way to hospital I drove slowly with the car windows down. The air smelled great, sweet, and salty. The tide was either coming in or going out. Before I got to the hospital I stopped at Dunkin' Donuts and got a cup of coffee. I was so glad to be out of the prison. At the emergency room I got a tetanus shot, no stitches, and a hand wrap. It wasn't until later, driving home, that I started to think, *What if that was a situation I couldn't have handled? What if the whole thing blew up and got really out of control? What if I actually got hurt? What if that inmate had a weapon? Would it be a cause worth getting hurt for?* Then, I thought about the night before and my run-in with Officer NYC. What if it got down to fisticuffs and I'd been fired for fighting? What would I tell Sarah and the kids? "Daddy lost his job because he couldn't control himself and got into a punch-up with a macho moron." What kind of example would that set for my kids? I realized that risking anything for an organization whose upper management didn't care about me in the slightest way was simply ludicrous. Feeling the way I did—frustrated, angry, and violent— could only mean one thing: I had to get out.

36

Escape or Go Mad

By November, I was feeling anxious and angry all the time. I wasn't in control of my life. I was on the edge of making bad decisions that would profoundly affect my family's welfare and my own safety. As a younger man, I had often avoided real trouble because I imagined my parents were watching me. I had to now turn this around and act as if my wife and children were watching me. This shift in thinking had to be my new guide. It was also at this turning point I began to look at prisons and their job in the community in a different way. All the statistics tell us that six out of every ten convicts at some point return to prison. Even to my poor math skills, a recidivism rate of sixty percent has to count as a failure.

The more I looked in to it, the more I found that the policymakers who push for reform through liberal treatment and expensive programming and those who lobby for a more punitive, draconian form of justice don't understand or listen to each other because they are both speaking in different languages.

This disconnect stuck in my mind and forced me to ask, is prison too hard or not hard enough? It takes dangerous people off the streets, but does it inflict enough fear and punishment to deter criminals from recommitting crime? Why do people commit and recommit crimes? Are the prison rehab programs working or are they just a smokescreen hiding something else? Why are all these people in prison in the first place and who, if anyone, is profiting from mass incarceration? Are the two sides actively conducting a constructive dialogue? Are they intent on finding a solution, or are they just screaming at each other?

It's my guess that the vast majority of privileged liberal policy-makers have absolutely no notion of how violent, evil men really act. Their motivation is well intentioned, but it comes from a place devoid of real-world experience. I'll bet if all our bleeding-heart, well-meaning friends woke up in the middle of the night to find one or more of our prison's hardened criminals rampaging through their homes, threatening their spouses and children, they wouldn't be looking for peaceful, socially enlightened resolution. They would be calling 911 and begging for a SWAT team with a shoot-to-kill policy to turn up as quickly as humanly possible. NO QUESTIONS ASKED!

Conversely, the other side, the neo-con fearmongers and the Second Amendment xenophobes, just want to hang everyone and blame it all on welfare. Then, brush under the corporate carpet the fact that somewhere along the line, someone suddenly realized perhaps there was really big money to be made and elections that could be won by promising to fight crime by locking up every criminal in the country.

Whether I was wrong or right, these thoughts made me even angrier and more depressed than ever. I felt like I was unknowingly playing a part in something very bad and, like some of the inmates, in the process somehow getting taken advantage of. And perhaps some of the people running some of the prisons were guilty of a much greater crime than the men and women they condemned and incarcerated.

I started having trouble sleeping. I was plagued by terrible dreams. So, when everyone was in bed, I spent hours reading and surfing various government and criminology websites to see what I could find out about the prison system. I came across some staggering statistics. According to the U.S. Bureau of Justice Statistics

(BJS), during the year 2006, federal, state, and local police departments spent about 98 billion dollars. Federal, state, and local governments spent about 46 billion dollars on judicial and legal services nationwide. And federal, state, and local governments spent about 68 billion dollars on corrections. According to the BJS, in 2006 we spent "about" 212 billion dollars on protection, prosecution, and the incarceration of criminals. There was also roughly another billion dollars spent by U.S. Immigration and Customs Enforcement (ICE), responsible for the detention and removal of both criminal and non-criminal undocumented immigrants.

My mind was spinning, so, just for laughs, I wondered what was spent on American school children in that same year. According to the U.S. Department of Education, the total expenditure for elementary and secondary education was 536 billion dollars. Could that be right? In 2006, We the People spent 536 billion on education and a little less than half of that, 213 billion, possibly more, on catching, prosecuting, and locking up bad guys and illegal aliens, many of whom were only guilty of being undocumented. Wow!

Between 1980 and 2006, the number of prisons in the United States doubled from about five hundred to around about one thousand. And the U.S. prison population exploded from half a million to almost two and a half million. What's really amazing is that private prison companies operate more than a quarter of those facilities. These companies include the Corrections Corporation of America (CCA), the GEO Group, Inc., and Cornell Corrections, among others. Between 1970 and 2005, the United States adapted such harsh criminal justice policies that it produced a 700 percent increase in the country's incarceration rate.

The net result of all this is that America locks up a quarter of all the prisoners in the world. To illustrate that figure more dramatically, if all the country's inmates were confined to one city, that city would be the fourth largest in the United States.

Then, when you factor in the people under correctional supervision—juveniles and those on probation and parole—the number jumps to an astonishing 7.2 million, about 3.2 percent of the U.S. population, or one in every thirty-one adults.

The less I slept, the more I researched and read. It started to appear that the U.S. prison system looked less like a tough social issue and more like a big business where inmates were fast becoming a new kind of commodity, a form of income. The old mills and factories were being replaced by the new factories, the prison factories. The only difference: These new factories weren't making anything useful.

The ongoing tragic effects of this dark enterprise are all too apparent. Every year, thousands of petty criminals released from prison return to the free world branded with "felony convictions." With the increasing availability of cheap, user-friendly technology, even blue-collar employers are doing extensive background checks. Employers find that ex-cons are "not what they're looking for." This is creating a whole new socioeconomic subculture, where the poor, uneducated, and disenfranchised, those who live beneath the underdogs, are finding it harder and harder to get ahead. Then when they fail and fall behind, they get fed or refed back into the jaws of a ravenous and rapidly expanding penal $ystem.

Some in academia are calling this new slavery vortex the "the American prison industrial complex." The term "prison industrial complex" refers to all of the businesses and organizations involved in the construction, operation, and promotion of jails, prisons, and juvenile and immigrant detention facilities, and all the services they provide. Such groups include politically powerful private corrections companies and corporations that contract prison labor, construction companies, surveillance and technology companies, and all the associated vendors and the lobbyists that represent them. Prison is no longer just a social conundrum; it's now a multibillion-dollar business.

And so it appears, at least according to my amateur fact-finding and a handful of available government statistics, that locking up poor people and making money from them has become one of our highest national economic priorities. Could this be right? What are we thinking? Why are we building prisons instead of schools? I imagined a conversation between the mayor of a town whose factories have closed down, his council members, representatives of the "prison industrial complex," and a few state politicians. The conversation might go something like this:

"A prison, not in our backyard, I don't think so!" shouts the mayor and all his advisors.

"Well," say the politicians and the powerful prison people, "what if we buy a few thousand acres of land on the edge of town at full market value, build a huge facility, and then employ most of the people who lost their jobs when the factory shut down?"

"Keep talking," says the mayor.

"OK, if you let us build, we'll upgrade the roads. Then you'll get a shopping mall and a Home Depot, Office Depot, TJ Maxx, and probably a strip mall with a six-screen multiplex. Want me to go on?"

"Yeah, go on, go on, tell me more," says the mayor.

"Then, after we build the prison, we'll get you a brand new Super Wal-Mart. Then you guys can buy all the cheap Chinese crap you want, plus all the stuff we should been making in this country but don't anymore. Sound like a deal?"

"Oh, yeah, baby, a Super Wal-Mart! You're the best," says the town's mayor and managers, "We're in. Where do we sign, and when do you guys want to break ground?"

37

The Cooler

December 2006, G-Block

INMATE T WAS GETTING READY TO BE RELEASED. HE WAS KNEELING on the cell floor. With his gray plastic tote directly in front of him, it looked as if he was praying. He was going through his magazines, tossing some up on his cellie's top bunk and the ones he wanted to keep, leaving in his tote. I stood in the doorway and waited for him to finish. As he packed, we talked and laughed about how our relationship had changed. It had had come a long way, from confrontational and tense to smooth and mutually respectful. I asked him how he thought he would do on the outside, how he was going to manage, keep clean, and avoid the temptations of heroin.

"I don't know, Mr. Reilly. Five years is a long time to be out of the scene, not hanging around my friends, doing drugs all the time, robbing, stealing, and doing all kinds of crazy shit just to get high."

"Losers, you mean. Those guys you're talking about are losers, not your friends."

"Aw, come on, man. Why do you have to be like that?"

"OK, you tell me this. In the last five years, how many of your so-called friends have come up here to visit you? How many?"

He stopped what he was doing and looked up at me. "You know something, Mr. Reilly, not one of those assholes came to see me in five years."

"Right, Now do you know what I mean? They're losers, and now it's up to you. Either you decide to make a go of it and try and keep straight, or you go back to your loser friends and end up like most of these guys."

I pointed over my shoulder with my thumb out into the day-room to the other inmates, most of whom were much older men.

"That's how it goes around here. You come into prison in your early twenties and then wake up a couple of weeks later and find out it's your seventieth birthday. And there you have it, your life is over."

At that moment, old inmate C in the next cell called out. "Hey, CO! CO Reilly! Help me, I'm stuck."

The quavering voice was filled with geriatric panic and urgency. I quickly stepped next door into inmate C's handicap cell to find the old boy half on his bunk and half in his wheelchair. The wheelchair was inching slowly toward the cell door. Inmate C was about to fall into the gap. He had obviously forgotten to put the hand brake on, and was about to go down hard. All inmate C needed on top of his long list of existing problems was a broken hip, leg, or both. I moved quickly over to the bunk, got down on one knee, and scooped the old guy up in both my arms and placed him back in the wheelchair. He felt like he weighed about a hundred pounds. Then I kicked the brake of the wheelchair on with my right foot.

He shuffled around until he was sitting up straight, pulled his glasses out from his shirt pocket, put them on and said in a thin, rattling, phlegm-affected voice, "Thanks, boss. That was real nice of ya."

"No problem, Mr. C. That's what I'm here for."

As I turned to leave the cell, inmate T was standing in the door-way, watching and listening to what had just happened. Back in inmate T's cell, I said in low voice, "Do you see what I mean? That's what you're going to turn into if you don't get it together."

Inmate T looked at me, eyes wide, thoughts whizzing through

his head. He nodded slowly. The semi-silence was broken by central control calling me on the radio.

"Officer Reilly, escort Inmate T up to intake-release."

"Ten-four."

After inmate T and I left the block, we walked through the institution side by side, both quiet and both lost in thought. I had a good idea what he was thinking about. How the hell was he going to make it out there, stay clean, find work, get a car, an apartment, buy food and clothes, try to meet a girl, and get something that resembles a routine? He looked terrified. Walking down long, echoing hallways, the guard/inmate relationship evaporated a little with every step closer to intake-release. As we made our way through the facility, I recalled how things had changed between us.

We first met not long after I started. It was part of inmate T's institutional work detail to mop the floor of the cellblock. I remember him doing a lousy job and telling him that what he was doing wasn't good enough. He complained loudly and bitterly to anyone who would listen. He mouthed off about feeling like a slave. He demanded to know if I thought he was Kunta Kinte. In response, I asked him very directly if he really believed I thought of myself as a slaver and a whip cracker. He walked away without responding. A little while later, when he felt the floor was clean enough, he told me he was finished working. I told him he wasn't finished until I said he was and that he was still doing a lousy job and that he was going to have to do it again and again until it was done properly. Inmate T threw down the mop, faced me, and in front of a full audience of maximum-security inmates, yelled, "Why don't you go fuck yourself!"

It was a very tense moment. Inmate T was being taken to task by a new guard, a guy without any reputation or credentials. I was an unknown quantity, someone to be tested and, if possible, taken advantage of, someone who definitely didn't act or look that tough. Inmate T was incredibly angry and on the verge of violence. His hostility radiated toward me like heat waves from a red-hot wood stove. I felt very vulnerable. I glanced over to my left. In the corner of the block, kneeling inside a water pipe closet was one of the maintenance guys. It was a man I had only met once or twice and would say hello to but didn't know by name. What I did know was that he'd been a guard for twenty years and was finishing his time out on the maintenance crew, an easy gig after two decades of being a cast member in the state's longest running, heartbreaking horror show. I could tell he was listening to what was going on but not making any moves to come over. His presence, although a satellite to the confrontation, felt quite comforting. I knew I wasn't alone.

I stood still and asked the inmate in a quiet voice, "Why are you speaking to me this way? I would never speak to you like that. I can't physically make you mop the floor, but if you don't do a decent job, I can cancel your weightlifting, basketball, and GED classes. The decision is yours. If you do the job properly, it will be done in half an hour. If you complain, whine, and insult me, it will take you all day and result in me making some dramatic changes to your living situation."

We looked at each other for a long time, eye to eye. He sighed deeply and said, "Are you going to write me up?"

"No," I replied, "I would like you to start cleaning the floor properly and then when it's done, we'll be all set."

The inmate returned to work, this time mopping diligently, changing the water regularly, moving tables and chairs, cleaning beneath them, and doing what I considered to be a good job. After a while, the old maintenance guy finished his work, got up from his knees, locked the water pipe closet, and then put his carefully numbered tools back into a lock box. He sauntered over to me. As he crossed the dayroom, numerous inmates said hello to him, many of whom he'd probably seen every day for the last twenty years. He walked over to me and said, "You know what you are, don't cha?"

"Er, I don't know. What?"

"You're a cooler, kid, that's what you are."

"What do you mean?" I asked.

"I've been working in this shithole for over twenty years. How you handled that, well, it was real good. Ya know, in a place like this, there are coolers, cowards, power trippers, and agitators. The coolers keep everything on an even keel. The rest of them, well, they just cause hate and discontent. Way to go, kid. You did good, real good."

A day or two after the mopping incident, inmate T decided to become civil and address me as Mr. Reilly. He apologized for what he'd said and thanked me for not writing him up, canceling his classes or having him sent to seg. The great thing about the exchange was that it was witnessed by sixty other maximum-security prisoners, the majority of whom all started to call me *Mr. Reilly, sir,* and *boss,* and thanked me when I was able to help them in some small way.

As I signed inmate T over to the release officer, I wished him the best of luck and told him I hoped to never see him in this place again. He extended his hand and said, "You take care of yourself now, OK."

We reached out for each other's hands and shook a firm, friendly good-bye. We looked each other in the eye, smiled, and nodded. Then, I turned and walked out of the release room. Heading back to the cellblock I was surprised to find that I was having profound feelings of jealousy. I was a prisoner, stuck here, wasting away, dreaming in quiet moments about a dozen different ways to escape, and here's inmate T just walking out of prison, about to get a bus into town and start all over. I couldn't believe how deeply envious I was that inmate T was leaving prison instead of me.

On December 25, 2006, I had to work. I didn't want to but there was no way around it. So, Sarah and I came up with a plan. We

were going to fake Christmas. The kids were only four, six, and eight years old. If we kept them busy in a fun-filled, media-free bubble for the couple of days leading up to the holiday, between going to bed late and getting up late, they would lose track of what day it was. So, we closely monitored the TV and had all our family and friends not call on Christmas Day, but call the day after. It was a big success. And, in 2006, Christmas in the Reilly household arrived on December the 26th.

IN JANUARY AND FEBRUARY OF 2007, MY SEMI-INSOMNIA CONTINUED and all I could do was fume about the information I'd found. I kept going back to it, reading it, re-reading it, and looking at other similar statistics and articles on prisons for profit and wondering if it was really true.

On top of that, what was happening around me seemed to be getting more dangerous and ridiculous by the day and there was so much going on at the prison that it was hard to separate fact from fiction. I heard all sorts of things, like the solitary confinement inmates went on hunger strike. There was a series of horrific suicide attempts. Several staff members were assaulted. The slovenly, rude, lazy, foul-mouthed, unprofessional sergeant, who had recently been promoted because his dad was a senior deputy warden, was now in big trouble for being—surprise, surprise— slovenly, rude, lazy, foul-mouthed and unprofessional, and for assaulting an inmate. Apparently, another officer was in trouble for videotaping a sex romp with an infirmary nurse. This happened the same week he was been involved in a domestic dispute with a girlfriend during which he had allegedly threatened her with a handgun. A guard I had the distinct displeasure of working with regularly was in trouble for writing sexually charged joke letters to inmates. Another guard was in the paper for beating up his wife. Another guard was in trouble for impersonating a police officer and pulling motorists over. Yet another guard was in hot water for having sex with a minor, and another was fired for selling contraband to inmates. On top of all that, about half of all the new classes left before completing a month of work. It went on and on.

After yet another inmate successfully committed suicide in the SMU, an overwrought new officer, who should never have been hired in the first place, walked out of a busy cellblock. He left the entire inmate population out and unsupervised. Every week, good, reliable men whom the prison should have been bending over backward to keep were quitting in disgust, on account of an uncaring, ignorant administration that refused to alter the way the place operated. All the while, the forced overtime kept wearing down the staff that stayed, and an unstoppable flow of drugs poured into the prison because the powers-that-be wouldn't change their ridiculous full-contact visit policy.

One February evening, all three of my kids were sick. They had come down with a vicious stomach virus. At one point, it looked like all three of them were trying to commit fluicide. All three toilets in the house were occupied by children producing pints of diarrhea and vomiting into buckets all at the same time. It was hard to believe there was any more liquid left in their little bodies. As usual, Super-Sarah seemed to be immune. But just before bed, I felt the troublesome, queasy intestinal growling that presaged an attack. By 1 a.m., I was about ten pounds lighter and feeling like a zombie with dysentery. I called work to tell them I wouldn't be there in the morning. I had tons of sick time and didn't call off much. The switchboard put a third-shift captain on the phone. I told him about my issues and the larger family situation and said I was sorry, but I wouldn't be coming to work in the morning. There was a long silence, and then his response was, "No, you're coming in. Get a couple of hours of sleep, then get up and be here by 6."

I told the captain he must be joking, and I wanted to know why he was busting my balls.

He didn't answer the question and just reiterated that I was to report to work by 6 a.m. I responded with a graphic and colorful description of the various high-speed liquids leaving my body at thirty-minute intervals. Seething with anger, I put the phone down and didn't go to work the next day.

Another evening, while working yet another in an endless run of forced overtime, the warden made one of his royal visits to the block I just happened to be working on. This time he actually stopped at my desk and asked me if I was a new member of staff and if this was my usual work assignment. Greatly to the credit of the sergeant escorting the warden, he spoke up and said, "No, warden, this is Officer Reilly. He works first shift over in the Medium Unit. He's one of the good guys. He's been here at MSP for over two years now. He's been mandated to work second shift, but would probably rather be home with his family."

I opened my mouth to speak but before I could say a word, the warden just shrugged nonchalantly and walked away from the desk.

I felt like I was going mad. I was angry all the time. The prison was infecting me. I actually hated some of my co-workers. It felt like I had a bomb about to explode inside my chest. Out grocery shopping one afternoon with my family, I saw a recently released inmate. He saw me, too. He glared at me aggressively and flipped me off. I started shopping around for a shotgun. Did no one see what was happening at work? Was I the only one with my eyes and ears open? Perhaps, the inmate who told me, "If it wasn't for the criminals, you guards wouldn't have jobs," was right. I was a nameless, faceless, expendable, low-grade operative in a slow-moving national disaster, a disaster with no rivals and no foreseeable way of changing course. I started to feel like an inmate, tense and anxious all the time, pent-up and closed in. My heart was in a vise. I felt like I was tied up on a beach while a tidal wave of anger was rising somewhere out there in the near distance, ready to sweep me and my family away. At some point, a co-worker said to me, "Reilly, you look so mad. What's up, man?"

I told him I didn't want to talk about it. My co-worker grinned and said, "This is good, Reilly. This is what you want. You have to learn to love the hate. Once you really start to hate the inmates, the job becomes a lot easier. Everything's a lot simpler then."

What! This sounded like career advice from the Prince of Darkness. I remember thinking; *This is how Nazi Germany started!* I couldn't believe what I was hearing, but I didn't have it in me to reason or argue with the guy. He was already too far gone, completely consumed. So I just turned and walked away.

38

Help Wanted

Monday, March 26, 2007

I SAW IT IN THE HELP WANTED SECTION OF A LOCAL PAPER. THE paper had been left in the desk drawer by a third-shift guard. At the bottom of the page, there was an ad for a local custom boat builder who was hiring casual and semi-skilled labor. Immediately after work, I went down to the boatyard and inquired about the job.

As I walked into the main workshop, I bumped into to a friendly-looking guy who introduced himself as Mac. I introduced myself and showed him the ad from the paper. Mac told me now was a good time to be looking for work. The yard had several big projects on the go and was always on the lookout for good guys.

"You need to talk to Steve," said Mac. He pulled out a radio from a coat pocket and called Steve.

Two minutes later, Steve arrived in a black Chevy pickup truck. Like Mac, Steve was kind and friendly and met me with a warm handshake.

"What experience do you have?"

"A little," I answered. I explained that I knew how to do glass fiber repair work and had spent a little time sailing and fixing fiberglass canoes, but certainly wasn't an expert. But I told Steve, "What I do have is a good attitude and a solid work ethic."

"I'll think it over. Come back tomorrow, and I'll let you know."

I arrived at the boatyard the following day and again met with Steve. After a tour of the place he introduced me to J. B., the head man. He also asked me what experience I had. I told him I had limited experience, but could learn on the job and, if he hired me, I would be an asset to his team. He asked me why I wanted to leave the prison. I told him the truth. It was a poorly managed operation where very bad things happened all the time. I told him I was constantly forced to work mandatory overtime and it was beginning to affect my family life. Working under those conditions was hard for an upbeat family guy with a positive outlook on life.

J. B. paused, looked me up and down, and then said, "Can you start next week?"

"Yes, I can." I replied.

I was going to be earning a little more than I did at the prison, but the health insurance would be a little more expensive. Still, in return I was going to be on a fixed schedule of 7 a.m. to 5:30 p.m., Monday through Thursday, with every Friday, Saturday, and Sunday, and all national holidays off, with pay. We shook hands, and I drove home.

Sarah met me in the driveway. She walked to the car with a questioning look on her face. "That didn't take long; is it a no?"

I shook my head. "No, it's a yes. I start next week."

Four days after my interview, at 5:45 a. m., I opened my locker, took off my regular clothes, and put on the prison guard uniform for the last time. I had been working as a prison guard for five years and seven months. Immediately after roll call, I asked to speak to the shift commander. We went into his office and sat down to talk. I told him that today was my last day and that I was leaving and then I told him why. I don't remember much of our conversation, but I do remember he said he completely understood why I'd want to leave and look for a better job. We both stood up and shook hands. I thanked him for his time and then left.

A little later, I was called to the warden's office. I knocked on the door and a voice called out, "Come in."

I entered and was met by a deputy warden, one of the many, and the warden himself, who sat behind his desk looking down at a piece of paper. I was sure he was reading my name.

"Officer . . . er, Reilly, come in and sit down."

He didn't get up or shake my hand. He just pointed to an empty chair on the other side of the room. I walked over to it, took a seat, and, as I did, the deputy started to tell me how surprised he was to hear the news and wanted to know why I was making such a big and rash decision. He immediately asked me to reconsider and said he'd had his eye on me and as far as he was concerned, I was on the "fast track."

I told him I was flattered by that and then gave a detailed and honest list of reasons why I was leaving. I directed my observations and grievances directly at the warden, who, I'm convinced, had no idea who I was, despite being in my third year. I told him how I felt about the constant forced overtime, the unprofessional staff, and the useless staff training. I talked about how at-risk the guards were, the ludicrous full-contact visit policy, the out-of-control inmate programs, and how, if he looked at who was leaving, he would see that those were the men he should be bending over backward to keep. I probably spoke for less than two minutes. When I was finished, the warden looked me up and down rather contemptuously, and then said, "Do you feel better now?"

"No," I replied.. "I just feel like I've told you the truth."

The warden abruptly stood up, walked over to his office door, and opened it. The meeting was over.

On the way out of the administration area, another deputy warden flanked by two gorilla-like guards asked me, "Well, Reilly, did he talk you into staying?"

"No," I replied. "He did not."

"Well, then, get the fuck out of here."

The deputy warden grunted a foul pig-like laugh and sauntered arrogantly past me. His two idiot henchmen laughed on cue but wouldn't look me in the face. For the rest of the morning, I floated from one assignment to another, said good-bye to a couple of people, and then decided to get changed and leave two hours before the shift was finished.

ALONE IN THE LOCKER ROOM I FELT A PANG OF GUILT AND WONDERED if I was being soft and wimping out. After a few seconds of these thoughts, I knew I wasn't being a quitter. I was jumping off a slave ship and swimming home to save my family and myself. With each piece of uniform I removed—overcoat, boots, duty belt, uniform pants, photo ID, guard's badge, and then lastly my uniform shirt—I felt like a great weight was being lifted from my back. I wasn't quitting; I was doing exactly what my father had taught me to do: I was standing up for myself and voting with my feet.

I was walking out of a system where 50 percent of its inmates didn't belong and the other 50 percent should never be let out. Conversely, 50 percent of the staff didn't get paid or recognized nearly enough for the work they did, and the other 50 percent had no business being in charge of other human beings. On top of that, 100 percent of the people, both employees and prisoners, absolutely hated the place 100 percent of the time. The odds were insurmountable. There was never any way I could find professional fulfillment in a job like that. The decision I was making was a deeply personal one. The job had enabled me to provide modestly for my family, move to a beautiful part of the country, but it had also caused me to doubt the existence of goodness and prompted feelings of hatred toward other men. If I stayed, I'd become incurably sick from swimming in a sea of political, emotional, and psychological sewage, and by the end of it, I'd be ruined and have only myself to blame. It was time to go. As I removed my uniform for the last time, I had an exciting fluttering sensation in my chest.

It was over.

39

Christmas 2010

ABOUT THREE AND A HALF YEARS LATER, AROUND CHRISTMASTIME, while in line at the grocery store, I heard a vaguely familiar voice.

"Reilly, is that you? How are you?"

I turned around to see one of the captains who hired me back in the fall of 2004. I extended my arm, and we shook hands.

"What are you up to, Reilly? I heard you were working for a local boat builder."

"Yeah, that's right. But I'm always looking for something better."

The look on the captain's face went from friendly to formal, and the tone of his voice changed from social to serious. "Listen, Reilly, whatever you do, do not think about coming back to the prison. Things there are worse than ever. We've gone to twelve-hour shifts and everyone hates it. The administration's worse than ever. The morale among the men is worse than ever. The health benefits are worse than ever. And the inmates," he rolled his eyes and let out an exasperated sigh, "are definitely worse than ever. Don't ever come back, Reilly. You're one of the smart ones. You managed to escape."

After the mysterious deaths of two more inmates, the warden was demoted and then quietly "let go." Both deaths are still being investigated by the Maine State Police. To date, no one has been prosecuted, and the old warden's new replacement was recently fired. The slave ship sails on, deeper into the abyss, with no one at the helm, while the press continues to report multiple alleged abuses within the Maine State Prison system.

Appendix

The articles and websites listed below provide additional information on the topics discussed in *Life in Prison Eight Hours at a Time.*

Aizenman, N.C. "New High In U.S. Prison Numbers." *Washington Post,* February 29, 2008. http://www.washingtonpost.com/wp-dyn/content/article/2008/02/28/AR2008022801704.html?sid=ST2008022803016

Burrows, Dan. "Profits for Private Jailers." *Wall Street Journal,* May 27, 2007. http://online.wsj.com/news/articles/SB118022826756215918?mg=reno64-wsj

Carroll, James. "Prison Boom Comes Home to Roost." *Boston Globe,* November 8, 2010, http://www.boston.com/bostonglobe/editorial_opinion/oped/articles/2010/11/08/the_prison_boom_comes_home_to_roost/

Dolan, Scott. "Corrections Officials Investigating Maine State Prison Guards." *Portland Press Herald,* August 1, 2014. http://www.pressherald.com/2014/08/01/tensions-on-guard-staff-lead-to-probe-at-maine-state-prison/

—. "Report Details Accusations Against Maine Prison Guard Charged with Sexually Assaulting Inmate." *Portland Press Herald,*

September 15, 2014. http://www.pressherald.com/2014/09/05/
report-details-accusations-against-maine-prison-guard-charged-
with-sexually-assaulting-inmate/

Fears, Darryl. "New Criminal Record: 7.2 Million." *Washington
Post,* June 12, 2008. http://www.washingtonpost.com/wp-dyn/
content/article/2008/06/11/AR2008061103458.html

Frontline. "Locked Up in America," Airdate: April 22 and 29,
2014. http://www.pbs.org/wgbh/pages/frontline/locked-up-
in-america/

Harding, David. "Maine Prisoner Who Stabbed Fellow Inmate 87
Times Won't Plead Insanity." *New York Daily News,* March 5,
2014. http://www.nydailynews.com/news/national/prisoner-
stabbed-man-87-times-won-plead-insanity-article-1.1711210

Harrison, Judy. "Private prison will create jobs, Milo-area
legislators argue." *Bangor Daily News,* April 29, 2011. http://
bangordailynews.com/?s=maine+state+prison&searchsource=
tophat&sort-by=date-desc&filter_date=April+2011

Johnson, Kevin. "2011 budget gives federal prisons $528M."
USA Today, February 4, 2010. http://usatoday30.usatoday.com/
news/washington/2010-02-03-prison-budget_N.htm

Keber, Lily. "Family Detention." San Diego Immigrant Rights
Consortium, November 22, 2009. http://immigrantsandiego.
org/2010/01/11/hello-world/

Kelly, Dan. "Feds plan to send detained immigrant families to Berks
facility." *Reading Eagle.* August 7, 2009. http://www2.reading
eagle.com/article.aspx?id=151504

Liscano, Miguel. "Hutto Detention Center to Change Direction."
Austin American-Statesman, August 6, 2009. http://www.states
man.com/blogs/content/shared-gen/blogs/austin/williamson/
entries/2009/08/06/hutto_detention_center_to_chan.html/

McLaughlin, Ryan, and Stephen Betts. "Maine State Prison
Inmate Charged with Murder, Allegedly Admits He Killed
Another Prisoner as Retribution." *Bangor Daily News,* September 16, 2014. http://bangordailynews.com/2014/03/04/news/
midcoast/maine-state-prison-inmate-charged-in-connection-
with-death-of-fellow-prisoner/

"Prison Nation." Editorial, *New York Times,* March 10, 2008. http://www.nytimes.com/2008/03/10/opinion/10mon1. html?_r=0

Russell, Eric. "Widow of Inmate Killed at Maine State Prison Awarded $100,000." *Portland Press Herald,* May 8, 2014. http:// www.pressherald.com/2014/05/08/widow_of_sex_offender_ killed_in_maine_state_prison_awarded__100_000_/

Tapley, Lance. "Hunger Strike at Maine's Supermax Prison." *The Phoenix,* October 18, 2006. http://thephoenix.com/ boston/news/25405-hunger-strike-at-maines-supermax-prison/

Williams, Carol J. "Justice Kennedy laments the state of prisons in California, US" Carol J. Williams, *Los Angeles Times,* February 4, 2010. http://articles.latimes.com/2010/feb/04/local/la-me-kennedy4-2010feb04